FROM CRUSADE TO HAZARD

The Denazification of Bremen Germany

Bianka J. Adams

THE SCARECROW PRESS, INC.
Lanham • Toronto • Plymouth, UK

Published by Scarecrow Press, Inc.
A wholly owned subsidiary of The Rowman & Littlefield Publishing Group, Inc.
4501 Forbes Boulevard, Suite 200, Lanham, Maryland 20706
http://www.scarecrowpress.com

Estover Road, Plymouth PL6 7PY, United Kingdom

British Library Cataloguing in Publication Information Available

Library of Congress Cataloging-in-Publication Data

Adams, Bianka J. (Bianka Janssen)
From crusade to hazard : the denazification of Bremen, Germany / Bianka J. Adams.
p. cm.
Includes bibliographical references and index.
ISBN 978-0-8108-5992-0 (pbk. : alk. paper) — ISBN 978-0-8108-7027-7 (ebook)
1. Bremen (Germany)—History—20th century. 2. Denazification—Germany—Bremen. 3. Military government—Germany—Bremen. 4. Bremen (Germany)—Politics and government—20th century. 5. Americans—Germany—Bremen—History—20th century. 6. British—Germany—Bremen—History—20th century. 7. Germany—History—1945–1955. I. Title. DD901.B78A335 2010
943'.520874—dc22 2009021946

∞™ The paper used in this publication meets the minimum requirements of American National Standard for Information Sciences—Permanence of Paper for Printed Library Materials, ANSI/NISO Z39.48-1992. Printed in the United States of America

Wir wissen, daß die deutsche Katastrophe eine selbstverschuldete Katastrophe ist und daß die Quellen allen Übels bei uns selbst gesucht werden müssen. Es liegt in der Konsequenz dieser Dinge, daß wir noch viel hinnehmen müssen, was unser nationales Ehrgefühl verletzt.

— Wilhelm Kaisen in a speech at the opening ceremony for the first elected city council, October 1946 (Wilhelm Kaisen, *Bereitschaft und Zuversicht* [Bremen, Germany: Bremer Schlüssel Verlag Hans Kasten, 1947], 62). [We know that we Germans are to be held guilty for the German catastrophe and that we have to look for the root of all evil in ourselves. From this follows that we will have yet to bear a lot that will injure our national sense of honor.] Translation provided by Adams.

Contents

Acknowledgments

I WOULD LIKE TO THANK THOSE WHO GUIDED and supported me along the way. First and foremost, my gratitude belongs to Dr. Michael O. Wheeler and Robert Gregg of the Advanced Systems and Concepts Office, Defense Threat Reduction Agency, whose backing and understanding made it possible for me to write this book. My deepest appreciation also goes out to DTRA senior historian Dr. Joseph P. Harahan, whose encouragement and continued interest in my progress kept me on the right track. I am also profoundly thankful to Dr. Joan Andorfer for her helpful comments and meticulous attention to detail and to Dr. Robert S. Rush for his ever-probing questions and constructive criticism.

During my research, I was fortunate to be supported by archivists Becky Collier and William Mahoney of the Modern Military Records unit, National Archives and Record Administration, College Park, Maryland. I am likewise indebted to the staff at the State Archives of the city of Bremen and Dr. Andreas Röpke in particular. Furthermore, I am thankful to Mark J. Reardon for his support and guidance in the beginning of the writing process.

I would also like to thank Dr. Martin K. Gordon, series editor at Scarecrow Press, who showed interest in my project. I also appreciate the efforts of my production editor, Kellie Hagan.

Finally, my heartfelt thanks go to my husband, Clark, for his unwavering support and the sacrifices he willingly made.

Introduction

On Christmas 1943, U.S. president Franklin D. Roosevelt proclaimed that the ultimate goal of the war was to uproot and destroy Nazism. Roosevelt's pronouncement was one of the common war aims of the diversified wartime alliance of the United States, United Kingdom, and Soviet Union. Another was to occupy Germany in order to administer a program of decentralization, denazification, demilitarization, and democratization and thus prevent the country from ever threatening the peace again. For that purpose, the German territory would be divided into national occupation zones, one for each of the victorious Allies. Agreement on the location of the Soviet Zone was easily reached. It would naturally be east, in the path of the Red Army. The distribution of the western zones, however, turned into a protracted and, at times, contentious tug of war between the American president and the British prime minister, Winston S. Churchill. Both parties preferred the northwestern zone because of its ports and secure supply lines. Only in the fall of 1944, with British and American troops already advancing onto Germany territory, did Roosevelt yield and agree to accept the southwestern zone if the American forces were guaranteed access to a port on the German coast. Churchill willingly ceded the territory in and around the cities of Bremen and Bremerhaven as an American enclave in the British Zone.

For American and British Military Government planners, the administration of the U.S. enclave of Bremen was an afterthought. They concentrated on larger issues of politics, finance, the economy, and, most importantly, how to deal with the National Socialists. The Americans believed that most Germans were victims of a criminal cast and that the evil Nazi element could be uprooted if only they dug deep enough. The resulting directive therefore ordered that all members of the Nazi Party who had been more than nominal participants had to be removed and excluded from public office and positions of importance in quasi-public and private enterprises. The British did not share the American's assumption about the German people, however, and accepted that they might only be able to correct the most egregious flaws by removing Nazis from public office. The stage for diverging denazification policies and practices in the American and the British zones was set.

For the military government officers who were in many cases veterans of the Allied Military Government in Sicily and the Italian mainland, Germany proved to be the most difficult assignment. The degree of destruction was greater than in previous theaters, and the country was left without a functioning authority. British and American officers soon discovered that the denazification posed a serious impediment to their efforts to rebuild administrative agencies. The Nazis had penetrated German society so thoroughly that it was sometimes impossible to find politically untainted personnel to replace dismissed Nazis. Nevertheless, the Americans held to their ambitious goal of purifying German society in their zone. The British remained committed to their more pragmatic and much less stringent approach.

National zones and the ensuing diverging policies were at the core of problems faced by the military government for the Bremen enclave. It was located entirely within the British Zone, and everything hinged on its geography. While necessary as a port of embarkation for the U.S. forces, the Bremen enclave remained the poor, unloved relation of the main U.S. Zone in the south of Germany, even to the extent that military government directives about food rationing, denazification, amnesties, and political developments generally ignored Bremen's requirements.

The first two years of the occupation in Bremen were tumultuous. Control over civil administration and denazification passed twice between the American and British military governments. The changing administrative control proved to be a challenge to both the American and British military governments. Since neither territorial boundaries nor administrative powers had been clearly defined, they had to invest time and energy to decide these issues while simultaneously trying to establish an efficient military government. Under these circumstances, Bremen's denazification program and its civil administration progressed only in fits and starts.

The occupation in Bremen began in April 1945, when the city surrendered to British forces. True to the Roosevelt-Churchill compromise, the British forces then turned the city over to the U.S. 29th Infantry Division and its attached military government detachments. For the first eight months, Bremen's Military Government operated according to American directives and instructions. At the same time, however, it was quite apparent that the military government had to coordinate almost every action it planned to take with the British neighbors because the city depended on its surrounding region for food, labor, and other services. Consequently, Bremen's denazification program was particularly vulnerable to disagreements about which side was responsible for cases concerning persons who only lived or only worked in Bremen; persons who had lived in Bremen and now resided within the British Zone or vice versa; persons who worked in Bremen for an employer located outside of Bremen; and so on.

Attempting to remedy the situation, the Americans and the British agreed that, beginning in December 1945, the American Military Government in Bremen should enforce British rules. This arrangement lasted throughout 1946. During the year, Bremen's civil and military authorities retired one set of denazification agencies and created an entirely new set. They also changed the structure of the civil administration to conform to British requirements. The problems that had plagued the previous system, however, persisted under the new arrangement. Deliberations about another change began in the fall, and on 1 January 1947, American policies once again applied in Bremen and the enclave became the fourth state in the U.S. Zone. As a result of the experiments, Bremen's denazification program and re-creation of democratic institutions lagged a year behind other states.

The examination of the denazification program in Bremen begins with an exploration of the origins of the U.S. enclave as a last-minute compromise that settled the Anglo-American contest of wills over the distribution of occupation zones in Germany. Detailed accounts of the development of the divergent American and British denazification policies, and the way the Anglo-American Military Government teams applied them in their designated zones, set the scene for an exploration of the peculiarities of the denazification program in Bremen.

The following chapters illustrate that the enclave's situation as an American island in the British Zone produced issues not faced by the other states in the U.S. Zone. One of them was creating three civil administrations according to two sets of rules in a two-year span. While the German personnel that made up these administrations did not change all that much, each iteration delayed elections and demanded involvement by military government officers. Another difficulty was the changing size of the enclave's territory and the related question of who was considered a resident and subject to the American denazification program. Confusion over whose rules applied and the repeated hiring and firing of German employees led to contentious exchanges and, at times, drawn-out fights between the British and American denazification authorities. Naturally, a number of Nazis used this confusion to their own advantage and slipped through the Americans' fingers to have themselves denazified under more lenient British rules just outside the city. Under these circumstances, the enclave's denazification team had to make concessions to try to find a middle way between the American dictum of a radical purge of the population at large and the more pragmatic British goal of simply cleansing the administration.

Oliver J. Frederiksen, *The American Military Occupation of Germany 1945–1953* (Historical Division, Headquarters, U.S. Army, Europe, 1955), 15.

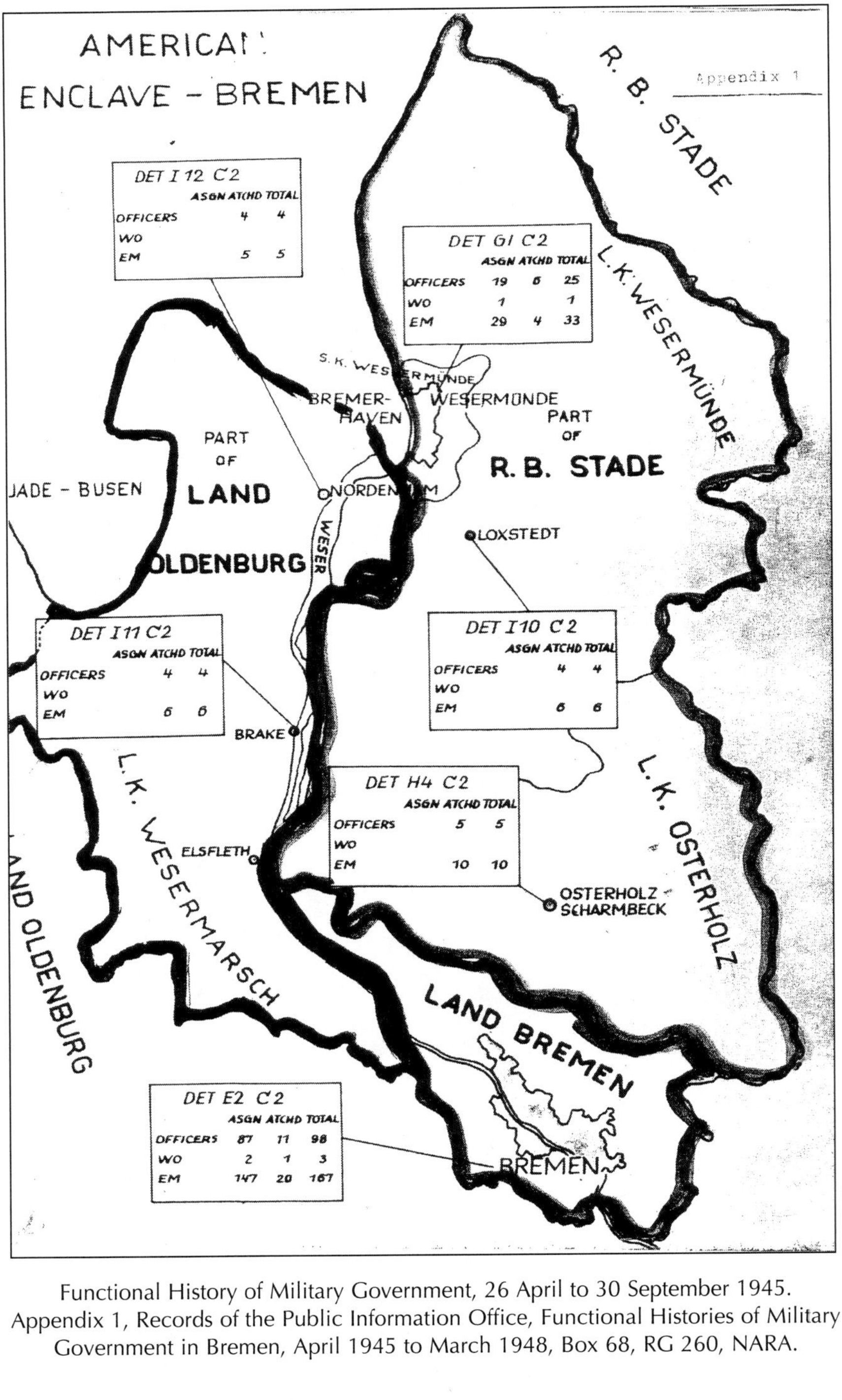

Functional History of Military Government, 26 April to 30 September 1945. Appendix 1, Records of the Public Information Office, Functional Histories of Military Government in Bremen, April 1945 to March 1948, Box 68, RG 260, NARA.

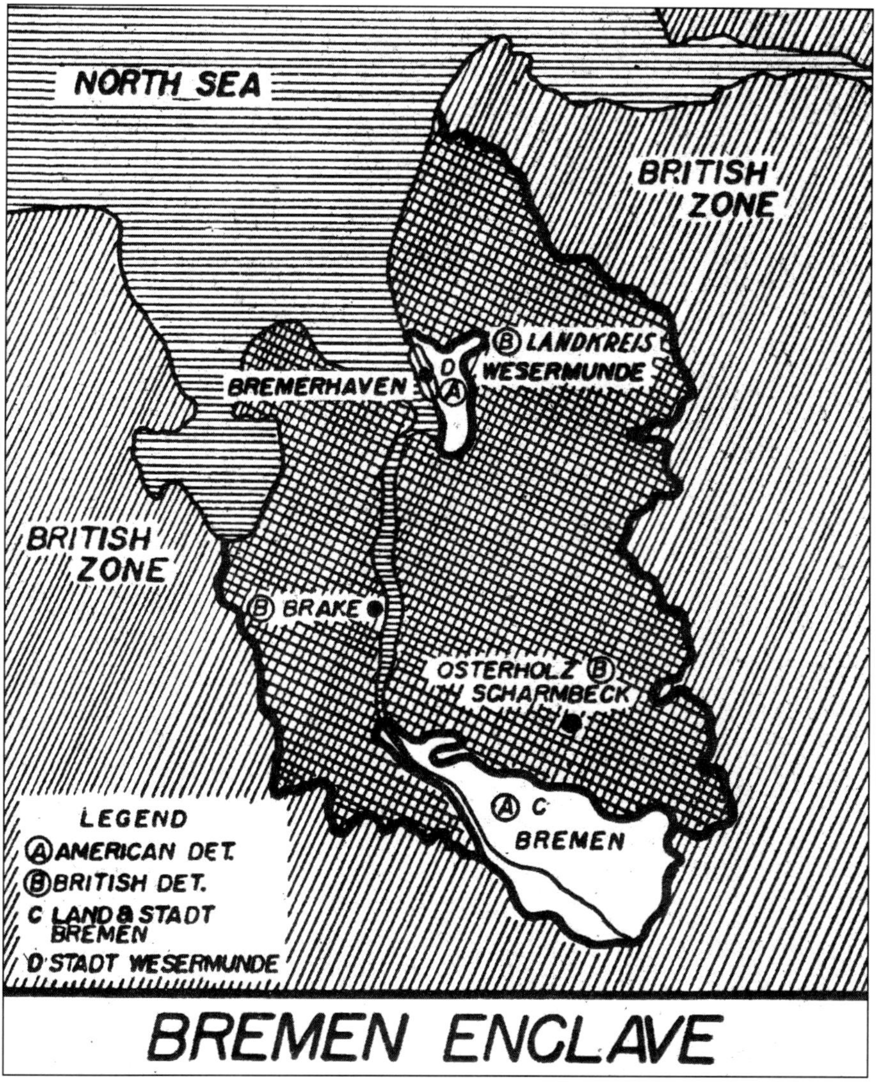

Organization of Military Government Bremen Port Command, 15 January 1946, Records of the Public Safety Division, Records of the Office of Military Government, Bremen, Records of the Denazification Division, Box 224, RG 260, NARA.

1

Inter-Allied Decision Making for Postwar Germany

How should Germany be treated after the war? Should it be occupied? If so, as a whole or in zones? If it was to be divided into zones, which principles would apply? How should the occupying nations deal with the German economy, one that had been the arsenal for two world wars started by Germany? Should all German people be held responsible for the crimes of National Socialism, or should there be a distinction between active supporters and mere followers? These were the basic questions the wartime Allies—the United States, Great Britain, and Soviet Union—had to answer in 1943 before their planning staffs could begin to draw up guidance for the postwar occupation.

The decision-making process proved to be difficult. Beyond the vague agreement that Germany should be occupied, concrete decisions on the shape, duration, and implementation of the occupation were left open even after the first Allied troop occupation in towns along the border with Belgium. Reluctance to commit to definite plans spanned both sides of the Atlantic. In the United States, president Franklin D. Roosevelt hesitated to make decisions that would saddle his country with long-term responsibility for postwar Germany before U.S. forces were able to view conditions in Germany at close range. With an eye toward the next presidential vote in 1944, Roosevelt's political calculations of an interventionist policy that might harm his chances for reelection also played a role. Further contributing to his cautiousness were the military arguments favoring a rapid defeat of Germany in order to turn all resources against Japan. In the United Kingdom, prime minister Winston

Churchill had his own reasons for a cautious approach to making policy decisions for Germany. He faced the dilemma that a weak, divided Germany was in Britain's national security but not in its best economic interest. A quick recovery of the British economy after the war depended on the reconstruction of Germany as a productive and functioning society. Aware that such a monumental undertaking was impossible without the help of the United States, the American government's apparent lack of enthusiasm for greater involvement in the future of Europe concerned Churchill and his cabinet greatly.[1]

Moscow 1943

In this atmosphere of hesitancy and caution, the Conference of Foreign Ministers began its work in Moscow in October 1943. Among the most urgent questions were whether or not Germany should continue to exist as a single state and, if so, what kind of economy it should be allowed to maintain. Reparations were an issue, and a looming question was how to deal with the National Socialists. On German statehood, the foreign ministers decided against dismemberment and instead agreed that Germany should continue to exist in the borders of 1 January 1937. This territory should be divided into occupation zones and an Allied High Commission would administer a program of decentralization, denazification, demilitarization, and democratization. To provide for detailed plans, the conferees set up a European Advisory Commission (EAC) that first met in London in January 1944.[2]

Paralleling diplomatic discussions in Moscow, the Chief of Staff to the Supreme Allied Commander (COSSAC)[3] drew up its own plan about the distribution of occupation zones in the western part of Germany. In this plan, COSSAC linked zonal division to the geographic positioning of Allied forces during planned landings on the coast of Normandy. Accordingly, the British flank in the north would march through the Low Countries into Northwest Germany, occupying that section, and American forces in the South would fight their way through France to take their prospective zone in the Southwest. British government and military leaders agreed with the plan's logic and envisioned three zones: the British in the Northwest, the Soviet in the East, and the American in the Southwest. To supply their landlocked southwestern zone, U.S. forces would use French harbors and depots, adding France to their sphere of influence and responsibility. President Roosevelt, however, objected strenuously to COSSAC's plan and insisted that the United States occupy the Northwest because it needed access to the ports to shorten and secure its lines of communication. He countered that Great Britain should occupy the area from the Rhine south instead.[4]

In the midst of contentious exchanges over who had a better claim to Germany's Northwest, President Roosevelt proclaimed on Christmas 1943 that the ultimate goal of this war was to uproot and destroy "Hitlerism" and "Nazism." Directly addressing the German public, he explained that the United Nations did not seek to enslave them, but they certainly intended to rid them once and for all of Nazism and Prussian militarism.[5] Roosevelt felt that his pronouncement would serve to unite the diversified war alliance behind a war aim on which all parties could agree. Shaken by antagonistic economic and political policies, denazification proved to be the common denominator for the three partners who were held together not by common goals but by a common enemy.[6] Roosevelt's second concern was American public opinion that had to be kept in a favorable mood toward the war effort. Eradicating evil Nazism was a goal Americans held and had provided moral justification for continued fighting.[7]

The Bremen Compromise

In February 1944, the president's and the prime minister's continuing debate over occupation zones reached a new low, when Roosevelt bluntly rejected the idea of occupying Germany's South with supply lines through France: "I am absolutely unwilling to police France and possibly Italy and the Balkans as well. After all, France is your baby and will take a lot of nursing in order to bring it to the point of walking alone. It would be very difficult for me to keep in France my military force or management for any length of time."[8] Unperturbed, Churchill replied that he understood the president's reservations about France but assured him that Great Britain would assume most of the responsibility. He reasoned with Roosevelt to consider the ramifications of his demand for the planning of the Normandy landings, code-named OVERLORD. Reassigning landing areas at this late stage would inevitably result in delays. His main argument, however, was Britain's vital interest in the German Northwest:

> The whole of the German coastline in the North Sea and a large part of their coastline in the Baltic, and therefore all the German naval establishments of any importance and the majority of the naval and shipbuilding yards, would be included in the United States area. The naval disarmament of Germany is a matter of peculiar interest to us and we are better equipped and situated than any other power to ensure that this process is carried out with the maximum thoroughness.[9]

Roosevelt remained unmoved, stressing again that he had no intention to keep any American forces in France, exclaiming, "I just cannot do it!"[10]

The Anglo-American diplomatic deadlock continued into the summer of 1944. By that time, the progress of the war on the Western front in Europe demanded decisions. In June, the Allied forces successfully landed on the French coast and began fighting their way east. The same month, the EAC reached an unofficial agreement that allocated the eastern zone to the Soviet Union but delineated the two Western zones without assigning them.[11] In the U.S. War Department, secretary Henry L. Stimson and his close advisor John J. McCloy, assistant secretary of war, supported the chief of staff to the supreme Allied commander's plan. Acutely aware of the negative consequences a switch of the landing areas for the British and American units could have for the planning and timing of the operation, Stimson tried to reason with Roosevelt. Yet, the president resisted attempts at persuasion even by his closest advisor Harry Hopkins and continued to insist on the Northwest German Zone. Exasperated, Stimson confided to his diary on 31 July: "The most pressing thing is to get the President to decide on which part of Germany will be occupied by the American troops. He is hell-bent to occupy the northern portion. We all think that that is a mistake—that it will only get us into a head-on collision with the British."[12] Churchill's and Roosevelt's next face-to-face meeting was scheduled for the third week of September 1944 in Quebec, Canada. During the conference, British and American planners were anxious to receive definite political guidelines but had to exercise great patience. The president had invited Henry Morgenthau, his secretary of the treasury, to attend the meeting in Quebec because he wanted him to present to the prime minister his plan for Germany to be a second-rate agricultural state. In the weeks leading up the conference, Morgenthau had worked to convince Roosevelt that the destruction of Germany's foremost industrial centers in the Ruhr and Saar areas would free Europe of an oppressive competitor and that Great Britain would have the chance to take over Germany's role as the supplier of Europe's coal. Initially reluctant, Churchill allowed himself to be persuaded by the secretary's argument. On 16 September, he and the president initialed Morgenthau's plan for elimination of the war-making industries in the Ruhr and the Saar and to render Germany an agricultural country.[13]

At the end of the summit, Roosevelt also resigned himself to an occupation zone in the German Southwest, provided that the British granted the American forces the right of access to a port on the German coast. Churchill agreed to his condition and ceded the territory in and around the cities of Bremen and Bremerhaven as an American enclave in the British Zone.[14] Two months later, on 14 November 1944, the EAC's Protocol on Zones of Occupation confirmed the agreement and created the legal basis for the U.S. enclave Bremen:

> For the purpose of facilitating communications between the South-Western Zone and the sea, the Commander-in-Chief of the United States forces in the South-Western Zone will
>
> (a) exercise such control of the ports of Bremen and Bremerhaven and the necessary staging areas in the vicinity thereof as may be agreed hereafter by the United Kingdom and United States military authorities to be necessary to meet his requirements;
> (b) enjoy such transit facilities through the North-Western Zone as may be agreed hereafter by the United Kingdom and United States military authorities to be necessary to meet his requirements.[15]

The other major outcome of the Quebec conference, the Anglo-American leaders' agreement to Morgenthau's pastoralization plan, only survived for a few weeks. As soon as details of the plan became public, the press condemned it, and New York governor Thomas E. Dewey, Roosevelt's challenger in the presidential election campaign, used it to attack the president. His argument was that the severity of the plan would frighten the Germans into prolonging the war. When the plan met an equally chilly reception from cabinet secretaries, the president quickly withdrew his approval. Roosevelt admitted to Secretary Stimson that on further examination he was staggered by this plan and had no idea how he could have initialed this. Churchill explained that he only agreed to the so-called Morgenthau Plan because he gave in to pressure from Roosevelt and Morgenthau.[16]

With the question of zones settled, American and British government officials tackled the thorny issue of who should be in control of the enclave. While the British were prepared to cede control over the port facilities, but not complete administrative control, the Americans maintained that they needed complete control and that the enclave would eventually become part of the U.S. Zone of Occupation. Talks continued through the fall and winter of 1944 into the new year. Just in time for the next meeting of the Big Three at Yalta, Soviet Union, the negotiators reached a compromise that gave the Americans the degree of control they desired in return for making their policies conform to those of the surrounding British Zone. As will be illustrated in later chapters, most of the problems with the administration and denazification of the Bremen enclave stemmed from this compromise.[17]

At the conference, Roosevelt, Churchill, and Joseph Stalin signed an agreement on the zones of occupation. In it, the three leaders also decided to invite France to participate in the occupation and administration through the Allied Control Council for Germany. Since reservations about having to take care of France had weighed heavily on Roosevelt before he decided to accept the southwestern zone, he pointedly remarked that the French should consider his consent to granting them a zone an act of kindness.[18]

With the issue of zones settled, the Big Three turned to the equally pressing matters of how to deal with the National Socialists and militarists and how to make Germany pay for the destruction its politics had caused. The conference's protocol warrants a long citation because it spelled out how the Allies intended to punish the Germans but at the same time held out hope for a peaceful future:

> It is our inflexible purpose to destroy German militarism and Nazism and to ensure that Germany will never again be able to disturb the peace of the world. We are determined to disarm and disband all German armed forces; break up for all time the German General Staff that has repeatedly contrived the resurgence of German militarism; remove or destroy all German military equipment; eliminate or control all German industry that could be used for military production; bring all war criminals to just and swift punishment and exact reparation in kind for the destruction wrought by the Germans; wipe out the Nazi Party, Nazi laws, organizations, and institutions; remove all Nazis and militarist influences from public office and from the cultural and economic life of the German people; and take in harmony such other measures in Germany as may be necessary to the future peace and safety of the world. It is not our purpose to destroy the people of Germany, but only when Nazism and Militarism have been extirpated will there be hope for a decent life for Germans, and a place for them in the comity of nations.[19]

While the protocol was the first statement that announced that the Allies planned to denazify Germany, it left plenty of room for interpretation as to extent and practical measures. Implementation of the program was subject to directives by each occupying power, which resulted in widely diverse implementation of the policy from one zone to another. The same applied to exacting reparations in kind that translated into the dismantling of German industry and infrastructure. Unable to arrive at a fixed amount of reparations, the Allies left the determination to an Allied Reparations Commission, set up for this purpose in Moscow.[20]

Notes

1. Edward N. Petersen, *The American Occupation of Germany: Retreat to Victory* (Detroit, MI: Wayne State University Press, 1978), 21; Donald Cameron Watt, "Großbritannien, die Vereinigten Staaten und Deutschland," in *Die britische Deutschland- und Besatzungspolitik 1945–1949*, ed. Josef Foschepoth and Rolf Steininger, 15–25, 17 (Paderborn, Germany: Ferdinand Schöningh, 1985); Maurice Matloff, *The United*

States Army in World War II. The War Department. Strategic Planning for Coalition Warfare 1943–1944 (Washington, DC: U.S. Army Center of Military History, 1990), 490; Donald Cameron Watt, "Hauptprobleme der Britischen Deutschlandpolitik 1945–1949," in *Die Deutschlandpolitik Grossbritanniens und die Britische Zone 1945–1949*, ed. Claus Scharf and Hans-Jürgen Schröder, 15–28, cf. 16 (Wiesbaden, Germany: Veröffentlichungen des Instituts für Europäische Geschichte Mainz, Beiheft 6, 1979).

2. A detailed account of the conference is in Cordell Hull's *The Memoirs of Cordell Hull. In Two Volumes* (New York: MacMillan, 1948), 2: 1274–91; cf. also Wolfgang Benz, *Von der Besatzungsherrschaft zur Bundesrepublik: Stationen einer Staatsgründung 1946–1949* (Frankfurt am Main, Germany: Fischer Taschenbuch Verlag, 1984), 20; Winston S. Churchill, *The Second World War. Volume V: Closing the Ring* (Boston: Houghton Mifflin, 1951), 298. The three powers were represented by ambassador John G. Winant for the United States, ambassador Sir William Strang for Great Britain, and ambassador F. T. Gousev for the Soviet Union.

3. COSSAC was established in March 1943 and had grown to over a thousand officers and enlisted men by the end of 1943. At this time it began functioning as a supreme headquarters, later called Supreme Headquarters, Allied Expeditionary Force (SHAEF). Harry L. Coles and Albert K. Weinberg, *United States Army in World War II. Special Studies. Civil Affairs: Soldiers Become Governors* (Washington, DC: Office of the Chief of Military History, Department of the Army, 1964), 671.

4. Earl F. Ziemke, *The U.S. Army in the Occupation of Germany 1944–1946*, Army Historical Series (Washington, DC: United States Army Center of Military History, 2003), 116; Tony Sharp, *The Wartime Alliance and the Zonal Division of Germany* (London: Oxford University Press, 1975), 62.

5. R-436, Washington [via U.S. Navy, London], 6 January 1944, 12:15 p.m., Personal and Secret, for the Former Naval Person from the President, in *Churchill and Roosevelt: The Complete Correspondence*, ed. Warren F. Kimball, 3 vols., 2: 652 (Princeton, NJ: Princeton University Press, 1984).

6. Petersen, *The American Occupation of Germany*, 139; cf. Volker Dotterweich, "Die 'Entnazifizierung,'" in *Vorgeschichte der Bundesrepublik Deutschland. Zwischen Kapitulation und Grundgesetz*, ed. Josef Becker, Theo Stammen, and Peter Waldmann, 123–61, 123 (München, Germany: UTB für Wissenschaft, 1979).

7. Lutz Niethammer, *Entnazifizierung in Bayern: Säuberung und Rehabilitierung unter amerikanischer Besatzung* (Frankfurt am Main, Germany: S. Fischer, 1972), 32.

8. R-457, Washington [via U.S. Navy], 7 February 1944, 12:20 p.m., Personal and Secret from the President for the Former Naval Person, in *Churchill and Roosevelt: The Complete Correspondence*, ed. Warren F. Kimball, 3 vols., 2: 709 (Princeton, NJ: Princeton University Press, 1984).

9. C-589, London [via U.S. Army], 23 February 1944, 10162, TOR 1200 2, Prime Minister to President Roosevelt Personal and Most Secret, in *Churchill and Roosevelt: The Complete Correspondence*, ed. Warren F. Kimball, 3 vols., 2: 747 (Princeton, NJ: Princeton University Press, 1984).

10. R-483/1, Letter, Washington [written at Hyde Park, NY], 29 February 1944, in *Churchill and Roosevelt: The Complete Correspondence*, ed. Warren F. Kimball, 3 vols., 2: 766 (Princeton, NJ: Princeton University Press, 1984).

11. Sharp, *The Wartime Alliance*, 79.

12. Henry L. Stimson and McGeorge Bundy, *On Active Service in Peace and War* (New York: Harper, 1948), 568.

13. A detailed account of the Morgenthau Plan and its influence on policy decisions for postwar Germany is in Warren F. Kimball, *Swords of Ploughshares? The Morgenthau Plan for Defeated Nazi Germany, 1943–1946* (Philadelphia: Lippincott, 1976). Stimson describes in great detail his recollections of discussions between himself and Secretary of State Hull and Secretary Morgenthau in the Cabinet Committee, set up in preparation of the Quebec Conference. His account also portrays ensuing activities initiated by him and other members of the administration, in trying to convince Roosevelt of the falsehoods of Morgenthau's plan. Stimson and Bundy, *On Active Service*, 568–77; Final Documents of the Conference, (1) Treatment of Germany, Memorandum Initialed by President Roosevelt and Prime Minister Churchill, Quebec, 15 September 1944, United States of America, Department of State, *Foreign Relations of the United States* [hereafter cited as *FRUS*]. *The Conference at Quebec 1944* (Washington, DC: United States Government Printing Office, 1972), 467.

14. Forrest Pogue, *George C. Marshall: Organizer of Victory 1943–1945* (New York: Viking Press, 1973), 465; for detailed accounts on the entire debate over zones of occupation cf. Ziemke, *The U.S. Army in the Occupation of Germany*, 115–26, as well as Matloff, *The United States Army in World War II*, 490–512.

15. Amending Agreement on Zones of Occupation and Administration of the "Greater Berlin" Area, 14 November 1944. This document amended the preceding "Protocol on Zones of Occupation and Administration of the 'Greater Berlin' Area," passed in EAC on 12 September 1944, describing different zones but only assigning Soviet forces to the eastern zone, leaving the western zones blank. Senate Committee on Foreign Relations, *Documents on Germany, 1944–1959. Background Documents on Germany, 1944–1959, and a Chronology of Political Developments Affecting Berlin, 1945–1956* (Washington, DC: United States Government Printing Office, 1959), 1–4.

16. Stimson and Bundy, *On Active Service*, 581; Winston S. Churchill, *The Second World War. Volume VI: Triumph and Tragedy* (Boston: Houghton Mifflin, 1953), 156; Pogue, *George C. Marshall*, 468; Hull, *The Memoirs of Cordell Hull*, 2: 1619, 1621.

17. Ziemke, *The U.S. Army in the Occupation of Germany*, 125.

18. Sharp, *The Wartime Alliance*, 111. For a full account of the proceedings at the Crimea Conference, cf. *FRUS. Diplomatic Papers. The Conferences at Malta and Yalta 1945* (Washington, DC: United States Government Printing Office, 1955). For the text of the Report of the Crimea Conference, 11 February 1945, see *FRUS. Diplomatic Papers. The Conferences*, 968–75. The EAC reached an agreement on control machinery in Germany on 14 November 1944. This agreement stipulated that the commanders in chief of each of the three Allied nations would assume "supreme authority" in Germany: each in his own zone of occupation and together as members of the "supreme organ of control," the Control Council (Senate Committee on Foreign Relations, *Documents on Germany*, 5–8).

19. Protocol of the Proceedings of the Crimea (Yalta) Conference, 11 February 1945, in Senate Committee on Foreign Relations, *Documents on Germany*, 9; *FRUS. Diplomatic Papers. The Conferences at Malta and Yalta 1945*, 970–71; cf. also Leland

M. Goodrich and Marie J. Carroll, eds., *Documents on American Foreign Relations. Vol. VII: July 1944–June 1945* (Princeton, NJ: Princeton University Press, 1947), The Crimea (Yalta) Conference, 4–11 February 1945, 351.

20. Justus Fürstenau, *Entnazifizierung: Ein Kapitel deutscher Nachkriegsgeschichte* (Neuwied, Germany: Luchterhand, 1969), 21. Karl Dietrich Erdmann points out that the lack of general and binding guidelines for all occupying forces in Germany led to four different approaches toward denazification, each defined according to requirements of the occupying forces. Karl Dietrich Erdmann, *Gebhardt Handbuch der deutschen Geschichte Band 22: Das Ende des Reiches und die Neubildung deutscher Staaten* (München, Germany: Deutscher Taschenbuch Verlag, 1982), 28, 112.

2

Anglo-American Military Government Planning

Operational Planning at SHAEF

IN DECEMBER 1943, CIVIL AFFAIRS planners such as U.S. Army brigadier general Frank McSherry, who had gained his experience in Sicily and Italy, received Chief of Staff to the Supreme Allied Commander's (COSSAC) manual on "Standard Policy and Procedure for Combined Civil Affairs Operations in Northwest Europe" as a planning guide for Germany. The manual summed up the best of Anglo-American civil affairs and military government doctrine and practices. It assigned full control and responsibility for the military government to the military commanders, from General Dwight D. Eisenhower, the supreme Allied commander and military governor, on down.[1]

In April 1944, Combined Chiefs of Staff (CCS) released the Directive for Military Government in Germany prior to Defeat or Surrender (CCS 551) to Eisenhower. As military governor of Germany and Austria, he had supreme legislative, executive, and judicial authority and power in the areas occupied by forces under his command. The CCS also authorized him to delegate those powers to members of his command who might in turn be authorized to subdelegate them.[2] Later in the year, CCS followed up with guides on political issues, financial and economic matters, and relief measures. The political guide instructed Eisenhower on the objectives for his future military administration such that

> the administration shall be firm. It will at the same time be just and humane with respect to the civilian population so far as consistent with strict military

requirements. You will strongly discourage fraternization between Allied troops and the German officials and population. It should be made clear to the local population that military occupation is intended: (1) to aid military operations; (2) to destroy Nazism-Fascism and the Nazi Hierarchy; (3) to maintain and preserve law and order; and (4) to restore normal conditions among the civilian population as soon as possible, insofar as such conditions will not interfere with military operations.[3]

The guide also dealt with issues such as freedom of speech and religion, treatment of prisoners of war found inside German borders, property control, and, most importantly, the extirpation of National Socialism. Measures for achieving this goal ranged from automatic arrest of all leading Nazis, including Adolf Hitler, to censorship and prohibition of any political activity. Besides dissolving the Nazi Party and abolishing all of its laws, courts, and organizations, the guide called for replacement of local government officials. Under the general principle of indirect rule, Eisenhower had leeway to decide if the functioning of the military government was better served by the appointment of officers of the occupation forces or by the use of the services of Germans. Since Allied plans excluded a central government for Germany, indirect rule applied only to local administrations at the Bezirk (district) or Kreis (county) levels.[4]

The financial guide established Allied military marks as the currency for all Allied forces and further provided for tight control over German banking and currency, the reichsmark. The economic and relief guides gave Eisenhower full control to use the German economy in a way that supported the Allied military effort. At the time the CCS drafted the guidelines, the planners assumed that Germany would have enough food and supplies to satisfy requirements for prevention of disease and unrest. Only after Eisenhower pointed out that assumptions about German food production and stores might be too optimistic were plans drawn up for relief supplies for Germany.[5]

While CCS 551 was a preliminary directive for the presurrender or defeat period, the CCS obviously intended it as a long-term policy statement. The tone of the document was moderate but firm, and the mission of the supreme commander was defined as restoration of normal conditions and creation of a peaceful Germany, cleansed of its Nazi elements. For that reason, and because the CCS had not released a follow-up directive at war's end, Eisenhower decided that CCS 551 should continue in force in the postsurrender period.[6]

On 15 June 1944, about two months after the CCS's directive, the German Country Unit, the occupation planning unit of Civil Affairs General Staff Division (G-5) of the Supreme Headquarters, Allied Expeditionary Force issued its "Handbook for Military Government in Germany" to Eisenhower.

This planning staff was organized in divisions paralleling the German ministries they intended to find, seize, and then to operate. The handbook reflected the assumption of a functioning German government. It was the first document to deal with the practical application of occupation policy in Germany. Based in large part on the U.S. Army's brief Field Manual 27-5, Basic Field Manual Military Government (FM 27-5), and the Rules of Land Warfare (FM 27-10), it provided guidance on personnel selection, training, deployment of military government, and military courts; established the exercise of military government as a command responsibility; and determined that the commanding general of a theater of operations would serve as military governor with full legislative, executive, and judicial authority.[7] The handbook had three sections. The first was a general overview that described conditions that occupation forces would probably encounter in Germany. It also explained the organization and workings of the military government. The second section consisted of twelve chapters, each dealing with primary civil affairs–military government functions such as food, finance, education, and denazification. The third section provided sample report forms, other basic information, and the supreme commander's proclamation, ordinances, and laws.[8]

The planners wrote the handbook with a clear intention not to saddle the military governor with responsibility for control or rescue of the German economy. They therefore prescribed a permissive approach toward the German economy, which basically left control mechanisms for the economy in German hands. The theory behind this approach was that the best way to relieve the military government of responsibility for the economy was to let natural economic forces run their course. Similarly, practical considerations allowed the military government officers to make use of certain Nazi organizations after the organizations had been purged. The handbook even permitted retaining functionaries of the Nazi Party in their positions if there were compelling reasons for doing so.[9]

The handbook arrived in Washington when Henry Morgenthau was at his most influential in the Roosevelt cabinet. A proponent of a Carthaginian peace for Germany, he perceived the handbook's proposed treatment of the Germans and their economy as far too lenient and convinced the president to reject it. As a result, the CCS ordered the German Country Unit to redraft the handbook and eliminate all those passages dealing with economic controls the Germans were permitted to retain. The same applied to retention of officials for compelling reasons. After several revisions, the handbook was published in December 1944. In the end, the Country Unit's efforts were of very little consequence for the occupation of Germany since only very junior officers bothered to read the handbook.[10]

American Denazification Policy

Reflecting Morgenthau's powerful influence with the president, a Cabinet Committee set up to make decisions about directives for the occupation included representatives from the Departments of State and War, the agencies traditionally responsible for foreign and defense policy, as well as the Treasury. In this way, Morgenthau ensured his department's role as a major policy-producing agency for Germany. The other two cabinet members, secretary of state Cordell Hull and secretary of war Henry L. Stimson, were mainly interested in stabilizing the European balance of power for which they thought a renewed Germany was essential. Given Morgenthau's passionate advocacy for the harshest possible treatment of the country, disagreements on the committee were inevitable.[11]

The treatment of National Socialists and the extent of a denazification program for the German population would comprise a substantial part of a post-hostilities directive for Germany. Before they could begin to shape a policy to deal with this complex problem, State and War Department officials had to come to grips with the phenomenon of Nazism and how its agents should be punished. They decided on a formula that declared the Nazis a criminal caste that was responsible for all evils committed in the name of the German people. In keeping with this "outlaw theory," the planners avoided assigning collective guilt or punishment but instead called for the extermination of all Nazis. This concept allowed a purified Germany to rebuild itself and eventually reintegrate in the European system of states. Predictably, the Treasury representatives pursued a staunch line of reasoning about the causes for the rise of National Socialism and its proposed cure. Morgenthau believed in the collective guilt of all Germans because he was convinced that Nazism, militarism, and aggression were inherent to the German national character. In his opinion, the country and its citizens deserved only the harshest treatment and occupation forces should restrict their contact with the population to negative functions such as punishments.[12]

By September 1944, the three departments coordinated their efforts and combined their theories into a program for purification of Germany. The State and War Departments succeeded in blocking out the Treasury's harshest demands so that their own theory, a personalized approach toward denazification instead of collective punishments, became official U.S. occupation policy. Accordingly, the U.S. occupation forces' most important task was to expose the organized criminality of Nazism and to rid German public and semipublic institutions of Nazis. This personalized approach was the least common denominator on which the rivaling decision makers were able to agree. In a concession to Morgenthau's demands for draconian measures, all Germans were presumed to be Nazis until they proved their innocence. In theory, this policy automatically disqualified the majority of Germans in the initial phase from participating in or lending support to the denazification program because the Nazis had penetrated every aspect of societal life so completely in their twelve years in power that almost every citizen had to have some connection with the regime. Distinguishing between those who were dyed-in-the-wool Nazis and those who joined the party to keep their jobs was very difficult and required a thorough knowledge of the community. In practice, U.S. military government officers had to rely on the help of local politicians, clergy, and others to restart municipal government, basic services, and the economy. Wherever possible, they chose known anti-Nazis and persons whom the Nazis had removed from office or retired to fill critical positions.[13]

JCS 1067

The following month, the Joint Chiefs of Staff (JCS) released the "Directive to SCAEF [Supreme Commander, Allied Expeditionary Force] Regarding the Military Government of Germany in the Period Immediately Following the Cessation of Organized Resistance," JCS 1067, to Eisenhower. The general had hoped to receive a directive for both the British and American forces under his command, but the CCS refused to approve JCS 1067, considering it too severe. This left the supreme commander in the precarious situation of having to command the three components of his forces according to three different occupation directives. American forces were supposed to follow JCS 1067; British forces would implement a different version of the American policy, while French forces were left without any guidance.[14]

JCS 1067 provided guiding principles for the occupation of Germany and treatment of Nazis. The basic objectives were to emphasize to the Germans that they were occupied, not liberated, and that their country would be disarmed and demilitarized to ensure that it could never again threaten the peace. In its last sentence it took a more conciliatory tone, however, when it held out hope for an eventual reconstruction of German political life on a democratic basis.[15] Guidelines for the denazification program consisted of six parts, five of which were relatively easy to implement: the Nazi Party and all its associations had to be dissolved; all Nazi laws were rendered inoperative; and Nazi property, Nazi archives, and Nazi records had to be taken under control to prevent their destruction by Nazi officials. The sixth part, dealing with the treatment of individual Nazi Party members, was the hardest to implement: "All members of the Nazi party who have been more than nominal participants in its activities, all active supporters of Nazism or militarism and all other persons hostile to Allied purposes will be removed and excluded from public office and from positions of importance in quasi-public and private enterprises."[16] Persons were more than nominal participants if they (1) held an office of any kind, (2) participated in war crimes, (3) believed in Nazism, or (4) had given voluntary support to Nazism. They had to be removed from offices in virtually every agency that provided service for society including civic organizations and German government subsidized corporations, industry, commerce, agriculture, finance, education, and the press. Based on their preference for the "outlaw theory," planners from the Departments of State and War insisted on inclusion of this category in an effort to limit the number of removable persons. Morgenthau's representatives pursued the opposite. Their goal was to affect as many Germans as possible with the insertion of the loosely defined category of all active supporters of Nazism and militarism. Military planners were adamant about adding the third group of removable persons. They claimed that preservation of law and order and prevention of sabotage against occupying forces made this category essential.[17]

Morgenthau and the military planners also agreed on automatic arrests of suspected war criminals and those that posed a security risk. Besides Adolf Hitler and his chief associates, the directive ordered occupation forces to take Nazis and Nazi sympathizers holding important and key positions in government offices, corporations, and the press into custody. The rationale at the time was that "it may generally be assumed in the absence of evidence to the contrary that any persons holding such positions are Nazis or Nazi sympathizers."[18]

The reasoning was as simplistic as it was questionable. It contradicted one of the fundamental principles of the American justice system, which holds that anyone is assumed innocent until proven guilty. Near the end of a most devastating war, however, the military's concern about sabotage by Nazi fanatics and Morgenthau's desire for punishments with long-lasting effects won out.[19]

The British Zone: British Denazification Policy

In the United Kingdom, as in the United States, policy makers' beliefs about the nature of National Socialism and its causes shaped debates and policies. Three different British government agencies were involved in planning for the occupation of Germany. In November 1943, the government set up a Control Commission (Military Section) to plan the military occupation. The secretary of state for war's office took responsibility for economic, political, and other civil affairs matters, while the War Office was in charge of civil affairs in liberated territories. The government expected the Foreign Office to lead a future military government because, at some point, political considerations would outweigh military ones.[20]

In the Foreign Office, Lord Robert Vansittart, who had been permanent deputy understate secretary since 1930, fueled discussion with his staunch views on Germany. In 1941, he published a book on the "national character" of Germans, concluding that National Socialism was not an accident of history or brought on by historical circumstances but rather a natural outgrowth of German mentality. He contended that bellicosity and a Teutonic lust for conquest and domination was an inherent deep-seated flaw in the German national character.[21] Even though Vansittart had some influence with British policy makers, his was by far the most negative attitude toward Germans. Most planners shared a mistrust of Germans that shaped their opinion about the limited usefulness of a denazification program. To them it appeared futile to replace one elite with another equally questionable one. In the Control Commission, the most optimistic outlook prevailed in the Political Division, which advocated close cooperation with antifascists and democratic forces to transform Germans into democrats.[22]

As a result, neither the British Foreign Office nor any other agency advocated draconian policies for Germany. Instead, plans were aimed at establishing security and stability. In the short term, British planners wanted to ensure security for their military government apparatus by preventing the German economy from collapsing. To achieve this, they intended to remove only those Germans hostile to their aims from positions of authority and retain others who were indispensable to running essential agencies. For the long term, the British government assumed the best way to guarantee its own national security was to establish a British-style liberal democratic government in Germany. Hoping that it might revive healthy democratic traditions that had once existed at the local level first, policy makers decided to reeducate Germans and to install popularly elected administrations from the bottom upward.[23]

In October 1944, the War Office released a handbook for *Germany and Austria in the Post-Surrender Period: Policy Directives for Allied Commanders in Chief.* It consisted of a collection of more than forty different directives dealing with issues such as denazification, comprehensive control of society and nonfraternization, control of German administration through indirect rule, and reconstruction of a peace economy.[24] Directive No. 8 dealt with reeducation as an integral part of denazification. As a first step, it ordered military government officers to destroy all educational materials used during the Nazi regime and to substitute it with materials from the Weimar Republic until new materials were available. Then the directive called for categorization of German teachers as "black" (Nazis), "gray" (followers), or "white" (anti-Nazis), which would determine if they could be retained, had to be investigated, or had to be dismissed. The British army used a similar process in prisoner of war camps in Great Britain, where German prisoners were segregated into "black," "gray," and "white" categories.[25]

The War Office handbook was the only policy guidance British Military Government officers received from their government. It provided them with wide and loosely worded directives for the establishment of the military government and first actions. Acutely aware of Britain's weakened position in the world, British planners studiously avoided defining long-term policy goals for the occupation. The combined impact of the end of the Lend-Lease program, a sizable trade deficit, and the anticipation of an enormously costly occupation deepened the crisis of the British economy as it deteriorated from one of the strongest in the world to a position of relative weakness as the world's most indebted country.[26]

Notes

1. Earl F. Ziemke, *The U.S. Army in the Occupation of Germany 1944–1946*, Army Historical Series (Washington, DC: United States Army Center of Military History, 2003), 33, 43–44; see also F. S. V. Donnison, *Civil Affairs and Military Government: North-West Europe 1944–1946* (London: H.M. Stationery Office, 1961), 18–19.
2. Ziemke, *The U.S. Army in the Occupation of Germany*, 59; Donnison, *Civil Affairs and Military Government*, 191; Hajo Holborn, *American Military Government: Its Organization and Policies* (Washington, DC: Infantry Journal Press, 1947), 136.
3. Holborn, *American Military Government*, 137.
4. Holborn, *American Military Government*, 137.
5. Holborn, *American Military Government*, 140–43; Ziemke, *The U.S. Army in the Occupation of Germany*, 59–60.
6. Ziemke, *The U.S. Army in the Occupation of Germany*, 60; Donnison, *Civil Affairs and Military Government*, 195.
7. FM 27-5, Basic Field Manual, Military Government (Washington, DC: United States Government Printing Office, 1940), 1; FM 27-10, Basic Field Manual, Rules of Land Warfare (Washington, DC: United States Government Printing Office, 1940), 73–74.
8. Allied Expeditionary Forces, Supreme Headquarters, Office of the Chief of Staff, *Handbook for Military Government in Germany prior to Defeat or Surrender*, 1944; Occupation Forces in Europe Series, 1945–1946, *Planning for the Occupation of Germany* (Frankfurt am Main, Germany: European Command, Office of the Chief Historian, 1947); Occupation Forces in Europe Series, 1945–1946, *The First Year of the Occupation* (Frankfurt am Main, Germany: European Command, Office of the Chief Historian, 1947), 77–81; Richard W. Stewart, "The United States Army and Training in Military Government and Civil Affairs" (U.S. Army Special Operations Command, Fort Bragg, NC, April 1994, unpublished), 6; Earl F. Ziemke, "Civil Affairs at Thirty," *Military Affairs* 36, no. 4 (December 1972): 131–32; Elmer Plischke, "Denazifying the

Reich," *Review of Politics* 9, no. 2 (April 1947): 155; Ziemke, *The U.S. Army in the Occupation of Germany*, 83–84; Harold Zink, *American Military Government in Germany* (New York: Macmillan, 1947), 130. Zink, one of the authors of the handbook, remarks that Roosevelt rejected it because it treated Germans too lightly. Subsequently, it had to be revised according to Morgenthau's requirements of denazification. Lucius D. Clay, *Decision in Germany* (Garden City, NY: Doubleday, 1950), 8.

9. Donnison, *Civil Affairs and Military Government*, 198, 202–3; Donnison attributes this particular passage to British influence on planning.

10. Donnison, *Civil Affairs and Military Government*, 202–3; Ziemke, *The U.S. Army in the Occupation of Germany*, 90.

11. Paul W. Gulgowski, *The American Military Government of the United States Occupied Zones of Post World War II Germany in Relation to Policies Expressed by its Civilian Governmental Authorities at Home, during the Course of 1944/45 through 1949* (Frankfurt am Main, Germany: Haag + Herchen, 1983), 29; Lutz Niethammer, *Entnazifizierung in Bayern: Säuberung und Rehabilitierung unter amerikanischer Besatzung* (Frankfurt am Main, Germany: S. Fischer, 1972), 34; Volker Dotterweich, "Die 'Entnazifizierung,'" in *Vorgeschichte der Bundesrepublik Deutschland: Zwischen Kapitulation und Grundgesetz*, ed. Josef Becker, Theo Stammen, and Peter Waldmann, 136 (München, Germany: UTB für Wissenschaft, 1979). The last two authors stress the close relationship between the Departments of State and War with, as Dotterweich calls it, "the New York finance oligarchy," which in their opinion explains overriding interest in both departments in the reconstruction of Germany. Before joining President Roosevelt's cabinet in 1940 at the age of seventy-two, Secretary of War Stimson had already had a distinguished career as a lawyer in his private law practice and cabinet officer in two administrations. He had served as secretary of war under president William Howard Taft from 1911 until 1913. During World War I, he served in the army in France and, in 1928, as governor general of the Philippines before president Herbert Hoover appointed him secretary of state in 1929. He therefore had experience with problems of governing subject peoples as well as firsthand experience in war long before his World War II experience as secretary of war.

12. Niethammer, *Entnazifizierung in Bayern*, 34, 47; Dotterweich, "Die 'Entnazifizierung,'" 136–37.

13. Niethammer, *Entnazifizierung in Bayern*, 39–41, 62; Karl Dietrich Erdmann, *Gebhardt Handbuch der deutschen Geschichte Band 22: Das Ende des Reiches* (München, Germany: Deutscher Taschenbuch Verlag, 1982), 113; Dotterweich, "Die 'Entnazifizierung,'" 139; Zink, *American Military Government in Germany*, 135.

14. Ziemke, *The U.S. Army in the Occupation of Germany*, 104. The full text of the Directive to Commander in Chief of United States Forces of Occupation Regarding the Military Government of Germany, 26 April 1945, is printed in United States of America, Department of State, *Foreign Relations of the United States. Diplomatic Papers. 1945. Volume III: European Advisory Commission, Austria, Germany* (Washington, DC: United States Government Printing Office, 1968), 106, 484–503; Barbara Marshall, "British Democratisation Policy in Germany," 191, and Ian Turner, "Denazification in the British Zone," 246, both in *Reconstruction in Post-War Germany: British Occupation Policy and the Western Zones, 1945–55*, ed. Ian Turner (New York: St. Martin's Press,

1989). Turner points out that British policy makers later redrafted JCS 1067 according to their own requirements and issued it on 26 July 1945.

15. Leland M. Goodrich and Marie J. Carroll, eds., *Documents on American Foreign Relations. Vol. VII: July 1944–June 1945* (Princeton, NJ: Princeton University Press, 1947), 195.

16. Goodrich and Carroll, *Documents on American Foreign Relations*, 196–97.

17. Niethammer, *Entnazifizierung in Bayern*, 62.

18. United States of America, Department of State, *Documents on Germany 1944–1985* (Washington, DC: Department of State Publication 9446, 1961), 15–21.

19. Justus Fürstenau, *Entnazifizierung: Ein Kapitel deutscher Nachkriegsgeschichte* (Neuwied, Germany: Luchterhand, 1969), 28; Niethammer, *Entnazifizierung in Bayern*, 64.

20. Jochen Thies, "What Is Going on in Germany? Britische Militärverwaltung in Deutschland 1945/46," in *Die Deutschlandpolitik Grossbritanniens und die Britische Zone 1945–1949*, ed. Claus Scharf and Hans-Jürgen Schröder, 31 (Wiesbaden, Germany: Veröffentlichungen des Instituts für Europäische Geschichte Mainz, Beiheft 6, 1979); Ziemke, *The U.S. Army in the Occupation of Germany*, 92; Donnison, *Civil Affairs and Military Government*, 250–51.

21. Robert Vansittart's book is entitled *Black Record: Germans Past and Present* (London: H. Hamilton, 1941).

22. Turner, "Denazification in the British Zone," 242; David Welch, "Priming the Pump of German Democracy: British 'Re-Education' Policy in Germany after the Second World War," 216, and Ian Turner, "Introduction: The British Occupation and Its Impact on Germany," 4, both in *Reconstruction in Post-War Germany: British Occupation Policy and the Western Zones, 1945–55*, ed. Ian Turner (New York: St. Martin's Press, 1989); Heiner Wember, *Umerziehung im Lager: Internierung und Bestrafung von Nationalsozialisten in der britischen Besatzungszone Deutschlands* (Essen, Germany: Klartext Verlag, 1991), 18.

23. Turner, "Denazification in the British Zone," 239, 244; Turner, "Introduction," 5–6; Marshall, "British Democratisation Policy in Germany," 190–91; Thies, "What Is Going on in Germany?" 30.

24. *Germany and Austria in the Post-Surrender Period: Policy Directives for Allied Commanders in Chief*, handbook, U.S. Army Center of Military History, Fort McNair, DC; Ullrich Schneider, "Nach dem Sieg: Besatzungspolitik und Militärregierung 1945," in *Die britische Deutschland- und Besatzungspolitik 1945–1949*, ed. Josef Foschepoth and Rolf Steininger, 49 (Paderborn, Germany: Ferdinand Schöningh, 1985).

25. Rolf Lutzebäck, *Die Bildungspolitik der Britischen Militärregierung im Spannungsfeld zwischen "education" und "reeducation" in ihrer Besatzungszone, insbesondere in Schleswig-Holstein und Hamburg in den Jahren 1945–1947*, Teil 1 (Frankfurt am Main, Germany: P. Lang, 1991), 54; Welch, "Priming the Pump of German Democracy," 218. For an account of the treatment of German prisoners of war in the United States see Arnold Krammer, *Nazi Prisoners of War in America* (New York: Stein and Day, 1979).

26. Josef Foschepoth, "Großbritannien und die Deutschlandfrage auf den Außenministerkonferenzen 1946/47," in *Die britische Deutschland- und Besatzungspolitik 1945–1949*, ed. Josef Foschepoth and Rolf Steininger, 65 (Paderborn, Germany: Ferdinand Schöningh, 1985); cf. Wember, *Umerziehung im Lager*, 21.

3
Civil Affairs Training

School of Military Government, Charlottesville, Virginia

WITHIN A FEW MONTHS OF THE United States' declaration of war on Germany, Japan, and Italy, preparations for occupation duties in the U.S. War Department Civil Affairs Division began. Responsibility for the recruitment of military and civilian personnel necessary for the military government rested with the Personnel Division (G-1) of the War Department General Staff. For selection criteria, personnel officers referred to the U.S. Army's Field Manual 27-5, which emphasized technical skills such as that found in lawyers, civil engineers, and medical personnel, or administrative experience as judges and former elected officials. Foreign-language skills and knowledge of specific countries and the cultures of their inhabitants were considered desirable but not indispensable.[1] Operating under these guidelines, recruitment of students from within the army was difficult. In the entire force of commissioned officers, there were twenty thousand individuals with the right combination of technical or administrative and language skills, but the School of Military Government received only 15 percent of those it asked for because their units declared them indispensible. Recruitment from civilian life was no easier. The army screened over seventy-five thousand people and found only a very few "who had everything." To maintain the chain of command, these civilian specialists received commissions as reserve officers.[2]

The task of overseeing the training of military government officers fell to Major General Allen W. Gullion who, as Provost Marshal General (PMG), was also responsible for the training of military police officers. General Gullion believed that instead of integrating the new recruits into the Provost Marshal General School for military police officers at Fort Myer in Arlington, Virginia, military government training ought to be conducted in a separate school that was attached to a university such as the University of Virginia in Charlottesville. His idea in all likelihood stemmed from reports that two U.S. Army officers, Major Henry H. Cummings and Lieutenant Charles A. H. Thompson, had written about their experiences in British War Office Intelligence Training Centre–sponsored "politico-military" courses at St. John's College, Cambridge. Instruction in diverse subjects such as occupation law, public health, public works and utilities, fiscal policy, education, public safety, legal matters, communications, public welfare, and general economics required different resources and teachers than a school for military police could offer. Attaching a training center for military government officers to a university would have great advantages because it could provide resident faculty, a library, and other necessary academic resources. Secretary Henry L. Stimson agreed with his assessment.[3]

Such a facility was without precedent in the army training system and thus had no curriculum. For the design of a course of instruction, General Gullion turned to his advisor on civil affairs training, Colonel Jesse Miller, a lawyer in civilian life who had been an officer in the Judge Advocate General Branch in World War I. Miller went to work and created a curriculum that consisted of three parts. For the academic content, he drew heavily on the Cambridge courses. The first part dealt with general principles of a military government, and the second involved the study of the customs, institutions, psychology, and the economies of Germany, Italy, and Japan. The third part was practice oriented and allowed students to develop skills in handling the problems of civil government as they might occur in the field.[4]

The new school under the command of Brigadier General Cornelius W. Wickersham opened on 11 May 1942 with forty-nine student officers attending its first course of sixteen weeks. The curriculum consisted of three major components. The first concentrated on international law, American rules and regulations, and instruction in public administration and politico-military issues. The second prepared the officers for day-to-day affairs, including local and state government, public health and sanitation, and communications. The philosophies, ideologies, and political systems they might encounter in occupied territories were covered as well. Last but not least, the curriculum also trained students for liaison functions. In the third part, students were divided into teams that had to solve a series of practical problems of civil administration. Each team consisted of officers who were engineers, lawyers, public health professionals, communications specialists, and so on. The outcome was to be a plan for the occupation of the area in question, similar to what would occur in an actual theater of war.[5]

In his evaluation of the new school after a little more than one month of operation, General Wickersham concluded that additional training facilities of this kind were needed. He based his conclusions on two premises: the primacy of military government in occupied territories and the possibility of occupying countries such as Germany or Japan that would not allow the Allies to rely on incumbent officials because of their political records. Vacated positions would have to be filled by civil affairs personnel, at least temporarily. Wickersham proposed to supplement the training program in the School of Military Government with other training efforts by civilian agencies in order to ensure sufficient numbers of officers to meet conditions in occupied countries.[6]

Infighting in Washington

While the army contemplated expanding the training program, the "honeymoon" for civil affairs planning and training by the U.S. military ended abruptly in June. Critics in civilian agencies, most prominently Arthur C. Ringland from the War Relief Control Board, demanded a role in civil affairs planning for themselves. The ensuing controversy about military versus civilian planning and implementation involved the highest levels of government, including the president. It overshadowed the planners' work for more than a year.[7]

At the end of August 1942, attacks on General Gullion and the School of Military Government became very pointed. Gullion was accused of being a Fascist because army officers received instruction in fiscal and economic duties. The matter came to Secretary Stimson's attention when Gullion's detractors informed the president of their suspicions. Stimson called it "a typical New Deal attack" from jealous "New Deal cherubs around the throne" who saw the school's curriculum as a threat to their chances of taking charge of these matters themselves.[8]

Despite the "tempest in a teapot," the War Department continued its preparations for a military government without involving civilian agencies. Apparently with the administration's blessing, it announced its own program for a military government on 4 September 1942. The basic principles for all military planning efforts were as follows:

> Any occupation of hostile or Axis-held territory may be divided into two phases: (a) a period of military necessity and (b) an ensuing period when military necessity will no longer exist. During the first phase, it is the obligation of the armed

> forces to establish and maintain military government; during the second phase, civilian authority of some type will probably assume the mission then to be surrendered by the Army. Until the second phase has begun, however, it develops [*sic*] upon the Army to administer the government of any occupied area.[9]

Nearly two months later, the situation changed drastically. President Franklin D. Roosevelt declared that the army had bypassed him in the decision-making process by not informing him about its plans for a military government. He demanded an explanation. He also made it quite plain that the notion of a military government was strange and even somewhat abhorrent because the governing of occupied territories was in most instances a civilian task and required "absolutely first-class men and not second-string men."[10] The Departments of State, the Interior, and the Treasury took the president's comments as an invitation to lay claim to the planning and execution of tasks for which they felt they were much better able to provide the high-quality personnel needed for the job than the army. The president agreed and took steps to prevent military predominance in what he considered a civilian domain. In the meantime, American armies had begun operations in French Northwest Africa. When they entered into their second week, Roosevelt instructed the State Department to assume the leading role in economic, political, and fiscal questions and ordered the Office of Lend-Lease Administration (OLLA) to take responsibility for the supply of food and other essentials in all occupied territories. In response, civilian agencies began immediate and feverish attempts at planning and implementation in competition with each other and the military.[11]

Undaunted by these developments, Secretary Stimson remained steadfast throughout in his conviction that a military government was a natural and inevitable result of military operations in any area where there was not already a fully functioning friendly government. In his opinion, and that of his chief of staff, General George C. Marshall, an orderly civil administration had to be maintained in support of military operations in liberated and occupied territories. Stimson received unexpected support for his position from Secretary of State Cordell Hull. Both secretaries agreed that administration of foreign lands was initially a job for the army. They also accepted that formulation of a political policy was always the responsibility of the State Department.[12]

Meanwhile, twenty-three graduates of the School of Military Government arrived in French Northwest Africa to support the efforts of the State Department. Since collaborating local authorities made establishment of a military government unnecessary, their main duties were to help provide the civilian population with urgently needed supplies. Despite State Department and Lend-Lease representatives' best efforts, however, shortages of basic goods such as cotton, sugar, tea, every kind of fuel, and soap remained acute and began to wear on the patience of the locals. The causes for the civilian agencies' failure to demonstrate successfully why they should be in charge of a military government were straightforward. They lacked the infrastructure to handle transport of the goods they needed. That meant that they had to rely on the army with its monopoly on shipping. The army considered them outsiders who were not part of the chain of command and handled their requests when precious shipping space on cargo ships was left over after combat gear was loaded.[13]

By the beginning of February 1943, it became obvious to political and military leaders that the view that the administration of occupied territories was an inherently civilian task had to undergo revision. The interdependency of military operations and civilian relief efforts to prevent popular unrest was undeniable. The War Department wasted no time and staked its claim to the planning and administration of the military government as an integral part of future military plans of attack. To ensure the maintenance of order and security during the initial period after an invasion, military forces would assume responsibility for food, housing, and health care for the populations. At the end of this indeterminate period, control over the area would return to civil authorities.[14]

The army put the new rules to the test in July with the invasion of Sicily and mainland Italy. The country had suffered greatly and required establishment of a military government. Civil affairs officers gained valuable experience in restoration of law and order, rebuilding communities, and most importantly, in removal and replacement of Fascists in public office. In the fields of justice administration and labor relations, their achievements were even outstanding. Military courts earned a reputation in the general public for being "scrupulously fair" for allowing enemy lawyers in a court-martial by an occupying force. Also, the military government's efforts to organize labor exchanges in liberated towns were of vital importance for the armies. Road maintenance gangs and personnel for bridge repairs made it possible for army engineers to serve the advancing armies more efficiently because they could move their temporary bridging to areas where it was needed most. Yet, even though military government officers proved their usefulness on a daily basis, they faced the same problems with access to transportation, communications, and supplies they had encountered in Northwest Africa. While the leadership in Washington and at headquarters recognized the critical importance of military government officers' mission, tactical commanders focused almost exclusively on combat requirements and allotted scarce resources only when they thought they could spare them.[15]

Anticipating growing demand for military government officers as the frontlines moved closer to Germany and Japan in 1943, the army set up a Civil Affairs Training School (CATS) program in conjunction with more universities in the United States. Civilian specialists destined to service in Europe or the Mediterranean attended Yale, University of Pittsburgh, University of Michigan, Stanford, and Harvard. Personnel intended for the Far Eastern theater went to Northwestern University, Case Western Reserve University, Boston University, and the University of Wisconsin. Once graduated, the recruits continued training at various military camps and in special civilian programs in the United States and England.[16] The PMG's office meanwhile established Specialist and Company Officers' Courses at Fort Custer, Michigan, to train one hundred officers and enlisted personnel per month to perform military occupation police duties. The CATS training program for military government officers ended in late January 1944, when the graduates moved to the theater they were intended to serve.[17]

Graduates of the U.S. Civil Affairs Training Program did not return to their civilian professions or previous army assignments. Instead, the officers moved from the universities they had attended to Camp Reynolds, Pennsylvania, for instruction in pistol firing. From there, they went on to Camp Kilmer, New Jersey, to await transportation to the United Kingdom for specialized training. Their destination was a newly established Civil Affairs Center in Shrivenham. The first group of nearly eight hundred company- and field-grade officers arrived at the center at the end of January 1944. Before training began, the men received their assignments in army group, army, corps, or division staffs. The great majority would serve in 343 planned detachments. The numbers of officers and men assigned to detachments depended on the size of the community they were supposed to administer. U.S. Army planners based their design of the detachments on the assumption that regional and provincial German government offices would stay intact and that military government officers would supervise the German personnel until suitable replacements for them were found. Accordingly, the largest units with nineteen officers and twenty-four enlisted men, so-called A detachments, were assigned to major cities such as Berlin. B detachments for medium-sized municipalities had eleven officers and sixteen enlisted. The bulk of units were smaller C and D detachments with five officers and nine enlisted and four officers and six enlisted men, respectively. They were assigned to rural communities and small towns.[18]

The detachments were part of a European Civil Affairs Division (ECAD), an artificial construct U.S. Army Major General John H. Hilldring, chief of the War Department's Civil Affairs Division, set up at headquarters, European Theater of Operations, U.S. Army, at the end of December 1943. Its main function was to act as a parent organization and to provide all civil affairs units in the European theater with equipment and transportation. The ECAD owed its existence to the hard lessons military government officers had learned in the occupation of Italy where tactical units had often refused their requests for equipment and transportation. As a result, the new division's outstanding feature was its special list of equipment. Civil affairs and military government detachments in Northwest Europe would be able to sustain themselves and have access to the division's nearly two thousand jeeps, weapons carriers, and other vehicles in order to move independently.[19]

By early April 1944, nearly three thousand enlisted men assigned to service with military government detachments in Northwest Europe arrived in England. They were stationed in Manchester where they received billets in an empty hat factory and other dwellings the British Army had requisitioned. For the next two months, they divided their time between attending classes on civil affairs matters and improving and repairing their living quarters. Unlike the officers, 40 percent of whom were civilians commissioned into the army because they possessed skills needed, for most of the men it was their first civil affairs training.[20]

Civil Affairs Staff Centre, Southlands House, Wimbledon Common

In their preparation for occupation duties, the British War Office faced no comparable opposition from within the government. It had a free hand in creating offices and schools for recruitment and training of civil affairs officers.[21] As a colonial power, Great Britain had a long tradition of sending its armed forces to rule its possessions overseas, but the War Office realized at the outset of the war that it would need officers who had a different skill set than colonial officers had to offer. In January 1940, the office expected to send liaison officers to aid European governments during a reconstruction period. For that purpose, it set up eight-week politico-military courses for civil affairs officers at Cambridge University. The curriculum included subjects such as the recent political and economic history of Europe, historical geography, racial theories, systems of government, and modern problems of European countries. After the initial course, Cambridge hosted another three until the end of 1941. The last course included officers from countries under Nazi occupation and two from the United States.[22]

Judged to be too academic in focus, the training courses did not continue in 1942. Instead, the British government set up an interdepartmental agency to coordinate all occupation matters. The Administration of Territories (Europe) Committee began its work in June. In October, it appointed a deputy chief civil affairs officer (DCCAO) in Northwest Europe to recruit, plan, and prepare for relations with civil populations and restoration of civil administrations in countries that Allied forces might occupy. His office soon took steps to establish a Civil Affairs Staff Centre at Southlands House in Wimbledon Common. Chosen for its proximity to London, the DCCAO intended to involve guest speakers from different government offices in the courses to make them more practice oriented than the ones at Cambridge had been. The curriculum was to include some of the academic subjects such as European history and economy but focus mainly on military, regional, and specialized technical and administrative skills.[23]

While curriculum designers worked on the course content, the deputy's staff began recruiting officers and civilians. As in the United States, civilians with specialized skills such as police officers, civil administrators, civil defense workers, and firefighters received commissions into the army. Until 1945, however, their number remained relatively small. The majority of candidates came from the army. Again, similar to the experience across the Atlantic, finding officers with the desired combination of skills for setting up or restoring a civil administration proved difficult. In the beginning, recruiters rejected more than two-thirds of the volunteers. Often among those denied were colonial service officers and Indian civil servants. The recruiters in the deputy's office were concerned that these officers might have developed a "colonial attitude" that would lead them to treat the "natives" under their supervision in an aloof manner and would prevent them from nurturing democratic values and behaviors.[24]

Notwithstanding difficulties with recruitment, the Civil Affairs Staff Centre opened its doors on 25 February 1943 to a class of 150 students. Their course lasted thirteen weeks until the end of May. By that time, the invasion of Sicily was about to begin, and the need to train greater numbers of civil affairs officers as fast as possible became very apparent. To be able to provide the requisite number of officers, the centre shortened the course to five weeks and increased the number of students to three hundred. A year later, course sizes rose by another one hundred, with half of the students receiving training for Northwest Europe and the other half for the Far East. In addition to the training at the Civil Affairs Staff Centre, the British Home Office prepared police officers for military government duties in the Metropolitan Police Training School. Between July 1943 and February 1944, seven groups of eighty-five officers received three weeks of instruction in military requirements and outlook in occupied territories. Upon completion of the course, they returned to normal duty in their police stations until called up for deployment.[25]

Final Preparations

Meanwhile, the War Department appointed Lieutenant General Lucius D. Clay as deputy military governor and commander of the U.S. Group Control

Council, the planning staffs at Supreme Headquarters, Allied Expeditionary Force (SHAEF). Clay, a civil engineer by training, had previously served as the director of materiel, Army Service Forces, and had gained some experience in Normandy Base Camp in October 1944.[26] He arrived at Dwight D. Eisenhower's headquarters at Reims on 7 April 1945 and proceeded at once to shape the future military government for Germany according to his understanding of the upcoming mission. He explained that the army's understanding of the civil affairs mission as assisting combat operations through securing rear areas was insufficient and unsuitable for a long-term occupation, which was political rather than military in nature. He insisted that the success of the occupation depended on the military government's direct access to Eisenhower on a basis parallel to that of U.S. combat forces. To this end, the military government should be removed from the Civil Affairs General Staff Division (G-5) and placed in a separate political structure reporting directly to the supreme commander and the secretary of war. Clay believed that any other approach would make the chain of command too long and give the combat commands primacy over resources that should of necessity go to his own effort. As for his own position, Clay suggested that Eisenhower needed two deputies, one for military matters and another for military government. Since this kind of organization would serve a rapid civilianization of military government personnel and speed up the process of turning over responsibility to the State Department, Eisenhower agreed with Clay.[27]

In the meantime, civil affairs officers had moved behind the advancing troops to secure rear areas in liberated countries and to occupy German towns as they came under Allied control. Originally, these detachments were supposed to be deployed in pinpointed areas to provide for transition from military administration to military government. In practice, though, pinpointing was harder to implement because tactical troops were advancing so rapidly that military government officers were often required to take over areas completely unfamiliar to them. Also, due to rapid advance, they had to draft tactical troops to fulfill military government duties. Areas in need of administration were too extensive for their own personnel resources.[28]

These first experiences in Germany showed that the situation military government detachments encountered was a lot worse than planners had expected. The German authorities the military government officers had hoped to direct had ceased to exist, forcing the occupiers to reestablish government offices on every level. As a result, the ECAD had to revise the structure and organization of its detachments. Except for the Berlin detachment A1A1, which retained its original size and mission, all other detachments were reorganized. The new system contained five different kinds of detachments lettered E through I. The E detachments with twenty-five officers and thirty-five enlisted men were capable of administering the largest administrative units (called Länder) and provinces. The next smaller F detachments, similar in size to the old A detachment, were assigned to smaller districts and larger cities. G, H, and I detachments, ranging in size from nine officers and fifteen enlisted to four officers and six enlisted men, took over towns, counties, and rural areas.[29]

First Experiences: Establishing Order in the U.S. Zone

On 20 April 1945, about two weeks before the official end of the war, General Clay made a startling report to secretary of state James Byrnes:

> Conditions in Germany are getting progressively worse and large sections of all important cities have been obliterated. Of course, we have a long range problem in preventing the restoration of Germany's war potential. However, this is not the short range problem as several years will be required to develop even a sustaining economy to provide a bare minimum standard of living. The coming winter months will be most difficult.
>
> I think that too much of our planning at home has envisaged a Germany in which an existing government has surrendered with a large part of the country intact. In point of fact, it looks as if every foot of ground will have to be occupied. Destruction will be widespread, and government as we know it will be non-existent.[30]

The situation the Allied forces encountered confirmed Clay's worst fears. As they invaded town after town, bitter remnants of the German army fanatically resisted their advance, often leading to the destruction of many smaller settlements that had survived the years of Allied air bombardments without major damage. In most cases, the Nazi magistrates had fled or were in hiding, so that invading military government teams found they had to build up rudimentary governments from the bottom up.[31] Remembering the first days and weeks in Germany, Clay doubted that there had ever been a more complete collapse of government anywhere as there was in Germany.[32]

The first military government detachments arrived in Germany attached to tactical units. These small spearhead detachments signified by the letters H and I posted proclamations, removed remaining Nazis officials, and fulfilled first aid duties in up to six or seven localities per day. Originally, detachments were supposed to deploy to pinpointed areas for which they had trained. In practice, though, the rapid advance of Allied forces in Germany made pinpointing detachments nearly impossible. Military government officers often took over areas completely unfamiliar to them. Another consequence of the rapid Allied advance was that detachments had to draft combat troops to fulfill military government duties because they became responsible for far greater territories than their personnel numbers allowed. Behind them, bigger detachments marked by letters E, F, and G moved into towns and cities as they surrendered.[33]

Germany was in chaos. The economy had come to a standstill, the infrastructure was heavily damaged, and food was scarce. Housing was in a catastrophic state and presented the greatest challenges to military government teams because, in addition to the local German population, at least two million displaced persons originating from all over Europe depended on them for help. Later, refugees and expellees from Eastern German territories placed under Soviet and Polish administration by the Potsdam agreement complicated matters further. To the great relief of the Allies, the German population endured these conditions with remarkable docility and hardly posed a threat to security.[34]

With the end of hostilities in May 1945, a reduction of tactical troops who had served as occupation forces began right away. Many of them were either redeployed to the ongoing war in the Pacific or were eligible for discharge. The rapid reduction in force left the military government with a shortage of personnel for duties such as guarding of military installations, railway transports, and internment camps for war criminals and Nazi activists.[35]

Conditions in the detachment in the Lower Bavarian town of Griesbach near Passau were typical. Established in the end of June, denazification had to take a back seat to the more pressing problem of controlling and feeding some twenty-five thousand Hungarian ex-enemy displaced persons. During July and August, the military government dealt with mostly minor complaints by the Germans and the Hungarians against each other. To prevent violent clashes between the groups, detachment officers investigated charges brought by Germans about Hungarians looting their farms, and dealt with robberies of Hungarians by U.S. soldiers or Germans.[36]

In July 1945, SHAEF was dissolved and American forces withdrew to their designated zone of occupation. For the purpose of administering the occupation, the army had decided on two separate headquarters, one for the combat forces and the other for the military government. Accordingly, the European Theater of Operations, U.S. Army (ETOUSA), headquarters were set up in Frankfurt and the U.S. Group Control Council (USGrCC), the military government headquarters, was located in Berlin. A few months later, on 1 October 1945, USGrCC underwent a metamorphosis into the Office of Military Government of the United States (OMGUS).[37]

At first, both ETOUSA and USGrCC shared joint responsibility for military government planning and practice in Germany. When this practice led to delays in the flow of decisions from top levels to the bottom of the structure, planning for the military government became the sole responsibility of USGrCC. In addition to ensuring a reliable administration of the zone, the army also intended this change to initiate German self-administration to allow a drastic reduction of American personnel.[38]

In August 1945, further organizational decisions followed. ETOUSA divided the U.S. Zone into two military districts, the Eastern District of Bavaria under General George S. Patton and the Western District of Württemberg-Baden and Hesse under General Geoffrey Keyes. The port of Bremen and the sector in Berlin were separate commands under the theater commander. In September 1945, the military government was fully established in counties, cities, and regional administrations that supervised several counties. The next step was the creation of the three states of Bavaria, Württemberg-Baden, and Hesse and their administrations. Berlin and Bremen remained separate organizations. Directors of the military government headed the state offices that were responsible for all forms of government in their respective states.[39]

The largest administrative units military government created in the American Zone were three states or so-called Länder. With the exception of Bavaria, which was an existing traditional state, they were formed in September 1945. In selecting minister presidents, the military government applied relatively simple criteria. The candidates could not have been Nazi Party members and were supposed to have some background and experience. Dr. Reinhold Maier became the first minister president of Württemberg-Baden, and Dr. Karl Geiler was appointed for the same position in Hesse. In Bavaria, the former chairman of the Bavarian People's Party, Fritz Schäffer, was appointed minister president in May 1945. The military government removed him in September, however, because he was not eager to cooperate with its denazification efforts in the Bavarian administration. Dr. Wilhelm Hoegner replaced him.[40]

In the beginning of October, the American Military Government set up the Council of States for the coordination of policies. General Clay explained the rationale: "In view of the delay in establishing the central agencies, however, we have concluded that some German machinery is essential for coordinating the activities of the three Laender in our zone. We plan to create a Council composed of the Minister Presidents of these three Laender to meet monthly for this purpose."[41] The council had a permanent secretariat in Stuttgart that formed working committees to consider matters of common interest, such as resettlement of refugees, food rationing, allocation of transport, and communication facilities. Agreements reached in the council would be applied in each state. During its nearly three years in existence, it issued decrees on difficult matters such as treatment and integration of expellees into society, administration of denazification, rationing food, redressing of Nazi wrongs, land resettlement and reform, and revision of civil procedures as well as criminal code and court procedures.[42]

Along with re-creation of political life and development of democratic institutions, the rapid reduction of American military personnel continued because many troops were eligible for discharge. In Clay's opinion, the draw down also served to hasten the Germans' democratization because the military government could not expect them to take on responsibility without giving it to them. General Eisenhower, now the theater commander, U.S. Forces in the European Theater, agreed and ordered military government detachments to remove themselves from direct control of German civilian administrations by the end of the year. After the elections, but no later than 30 June 1946, local detachments had to be replaced by two-officer liaison and security detachments charged with observing and reporting but not directly intervening in German governmental affairs, except in emergencies.[43]

To revive political life according to democratic principles and to prepare Germans to take over administrative responsibility, the military government began with preparations for democratic elections in municipalities as early as September 1945. Arrangements included the licensing of political parties, registering voters, drawing up election laws, establishing balloting procedures, soliciting candidacies, and other related matters. On 27 August 1945, the military government issued a directive that approved democratic political parties to engage in political activity at the county level. Almost immediately, parties sprang up in all urban centers and in many smaller communities. A general pattern of party foundations emerged very fast. On the left of the political spectrum, Communists and Social Democrats resurrected their local units. At the center and to the right of it, the Christian Democratic Union (CDU) and the Liberal Party established their organizations.[44]

Elections in villages with fewer than twenty thousand inhabitants (*Gemeinden*) were held in January 1946, and larger villages and counties (*Landkreise*) elected their new administrations in April, while city (*Stadt*) dwellers chose their representatives in May. Clay hoped to accomplish more than one objective with elections:

> In my opinion, this program is one of the most important in reestablishing democratic attitudes and methods. It will give the Germans an opportunity to learn democratic procedures on the lower levels before undertaking elections for larger units. At the same time, the elections of such local officials will tend to relieve military government of many duties at that level.[45]

Meanwhile, the military government ordered the three minister presidents to draft their state constitutions. By June 1946, elected constitutional assemblies considered the proposals the first drafts of future constitutions. Their work was finished in October 1946, when they submitted three constitutions for final approval to the military government. Since all three embodied acceptable democratic values and goals, the military government approved them and they were then ratified in referenda. At the same time, the states elected their parliaments so that all three states in the American Zone entered 1947 with popularly elected governments.[46]

The American Denazification Program

In the fall of 1944, the first American Military Government detachment arrived in the city of Aachen. The difficulties it encountered trying to reconstitute and denazify the city's civil administration at the same time foreshadowed the experiences of many other detachments in the months to come. Since most of the American officers did not know how to distinguish between Nazis and non-Nazis, they relied heavily on the advice of local clergy, in this case the bishop, regarding the choice of German administrators. The military government detachment appointed the bishop's choice for mayor, the *Bürgermeister*, and he in turn chose his principal assistant, who chose the next lower officials. Lower courts and the police were reactivated the same way. Unfortunately for the detachment, the bishop's candidate proved to be a Nazi and so were many of the other local administrators with whom the military government worked until this fact was detected and widely publicized by American reporters. The American public was outraged, and this kept pressure on lawmakers to demand very strict treatment of Germans.[47]

After the German surrender in May 1945, the denazification process became more systematic. As soon as American forces arrived in German cities, the denazification process began. They arrested and removed German officials according to "Blacklists" and an "Arrest Categories Handbook" earlier compiled by SHAEF and incorporated into JCS 1067. Those applying to positions with the municipal and other administrations had to fill out a questionnaire (*Fragebogen*)[48] about their activities during the Nazi regime. A special branch that operated under the public safety officer in every larger detachment evaluated the Fragebogen of applicants for vacant positions and communicated its decisions to the sections where the vacant position needed to be filled. Since the Nazi Party's central registry of twelve million cards, which included photographs, fell into American hands, verification of information provided by applicants was relatively easy.[49] As a result, the U.S. Military Government accomplished five of the six elements of the denazification program as defined by JCS 1067—the dissolution of the Nazi Party and all its associations, eradication of Nazi legislation, seizure of Nazi property, seizure of Nazi archives, and seizure of Nazi records—within the first few months of the occupation. The sixth element—the removal and exclusion of individual members or sympathizers of the Nazi Party from positions of responsibility—was the most labor intensive and time consuming to implement and came to represent denazification to the public.[50]

On a day-to-day basis, reconstruction of public administration, public services, economic controls, and rationing had the highest priority for the military government. With only a few officers attached to tactical units, the denazification of municipalities was conducted rather lightly at first.[51] Where they tried it, military government officers had difficulties replacing Nazi affiliated officials and functionaries with administrators not tainted by the regime. In view of the thorough penetration of every single function of government, economy, and society by the Nazis, this task proved to be one of the greatest challenges. During their twelve years in power, the Nazis had subordinated every public, semipublic, and private function in society under the all-pervading hierarchy of the National Socialist German Workers' Party (NSDAP). The economy was organized in mandatory corporate organizations that allowed for complete control of the economic life of the nation and served as an instrument for the goals of the Nazi state. This control extended from supply of raw materials to distribution of food through the "Reich Food Estate." Though not compulsory in the beginning, membership in the NSDAP became increasingly required for advancement in any profession, official or nonofficial. Industrialists, however, were able to circumvent party membership by supplying financial support. This contributed to the difficulty in determining who was a devoted Nazi and who had joined the party for other reasons. Besides destruction of all democratic institutions, the Nazis paid special attention to the judicial sector. Recalcitrant judges were replaced as fast as possible by politically reliable successors, guaranteeing judgments according to the party line.[52]

The Nazis' degree of control over every aspect of public and private life in Germany was particularly strong at the local levels of government. Almost every local bureaucrat had had some ties to the party or its affiliations that, at least in theory, automatically disqualified him in the eyes of American Military Government officers charged with rebuilding and denazifying capable administrations. With the vast number of communities in need of new leadership, the officers realized very quickly that they had to choose between strictly enforced denazification and a functioning local administration. Confronted with this dilemma, they often handled denazification leniently and relied on competent Germans, even if they had been party members, to take over administrative duties. SHAEF condoned the practice and even issued an order on 11 June 1945 that demanded detachments follow policy directives as much as possible without making administration impossible.[53]

The kinds of problems military government detachments had to solve in the Bavarian towns of Dachau, Griesbach, and Augsburg were typical for the early days of the occupation in the U.S. Zone. At Dachau, located just north of Munich, the American officers discovered that the denazification program hindered the efficient operation of public utilities because they were not able to replace highly qualified personnel that had been dismissed because they were party members. When a shortage of technicians threatened to shut down communication lines among detachments, the field officers decided to suspend denazification of essential employees of the telephone company.[54] In Griesbach, located near the Czech border, the military government detachment took similar action. Struggling to reestablish administrative control, but unable to find qualified officials with clean political records, the officers felt compelled to appoint or retain former Nazi Party members. Their motto was "The one eyed is king amongst the blind."[55]

The Augsburg Detachment had different troubles. While the city's magistrate was functioning, the officers encountered resistance when they ordered the local administrators to denazify city government. The city officials refused to comply until August when the detachment appointed Franz Xaver Sennefelder, an old Social Democratic Party of Germany (SPD) man with a concentration camp record, chief of personnel. While the denazification program benefited from Sennefelder's efforts, his party feared that it would be blamed for the hardships caused to families by dismissals of city employees in the next election.[56]

The pragmatic approach taken by field officers in Germany did not escape the American press, which published scathing articles about the practice. One of the authors of these articles was secretary of the treasury Henry Morgenthau. Since he had lost his formerly enjoyed great influence with the executive branch when Harry S. Truman ascended to the presidency, he tried to influence the American public in pursuit of his objectives in Germany. The uproar in the media was so successful that Washington policy makers, under pressure from public opinion, called for a "hard" peace. As a result, military government officers who had given priority to economic and administrative recovery over denazification received orders from Washington to abandon that practice. Many, however, continued to circumvent provisions in JCS 1067 with the tacit approval of their civilian and military superiors in the War Department and in the military government. When secretary Henry L. Stimson visited Germany at the time of the Potsdam Conference, he met with Generals Eisenhower and Clay to talk about occupation policy. Stimson, who had served as U.S. Governor General of the Philippines, did not consider JCS 1067 a realistic policy, and he believed it would not be in effect for a long period of time. To him, it was obvious that Eisenhower and Clay had to do everything to get the country back on its feet and under its own political controls. His advice to the military governor and his deputy about the orders was, "Don't put too much effort in carrying them out the way they're written because you've got a job to do first which is to bring about law and order and the ability of the people in this country to live."[57]

The prominent case of shirking rigorous denazification was that of General Patton, the Military Governor of Bavaria. In August 1945, complaints in the press and from lawmakers prompted General Eisenhower to summon Patton to his headquarters and to order him to obey the terms of JCS 1067 to the letter. The following month, when the army lifted its censorship for interviews with generals, General Patton spoke to reporters about the flaws of the American occupation policy. Criticizing denazification heavily, he compared membership in the Nazi Party with membership in American democratic parties. The ensuing scandal led to not only the general's removal as Military Governor of Bavaria but also the dismissal of his appointee to the post of minister president, Schäffer. An investigation of Schäffer revealed that many members of his cabinet were at best compromised by their past ties to Nazis and, at worst, belonged in the Mandatory Removal category because they had been activists.[58]

On 26 September, four days after Patton's fateful interview, USGrCC released Military Government Law No. 8, making it illegal for those who had not passed the test of the Fragebogen to manage or own private enterprises. The new law changed the whole character of the denazification program. It expanded the program to the entire German economy, stipulating that former nominal party members had to be employed as ordinary laborers. Beyond that, it also differed from ordinary directives that were issued to military government detachments as administrative guidelines because it applied directly to Germans as criminal law. Denazification had become an individualized process with the goal to punish individuals for past crimes.[59]

Publication of Law No. 8 came as a shock to Germans and to military government officers who had to implement the hastily drafted law. While other directives had always defined the kind of enterprises to be denazified, this law made no such distinctions. It affected any former party member who was a skilled employee in a position with any responsibility and relegated him to menial work as an ordinary laborer. It also effectively confiscated every Nazi-owned business. Many Germans were confused as to just what kind of work a Nazi was allowed to do under the heading of "ordinary labor," with the result that small businesses closed one day, opened the next, and closed again the third. Managers of larger businesses thought of different ways to retain their skilled personnel. Since Law No. 8 allowed retention of former Nazis in menial jobs, they changed the job titles of their effected workforce, creating large numbers of highly competent clerks. For those holding key positions, they applied for working permits that the military government granted for "indispensable" workers. Many employees who desperately wanted to keep their jobs tried to conceal their political past by a change of name. German officials soon became suspicious of the great increase in change of surname applications and alerted the Ministry of the Interior. As a result, the ministry issued an ordinance that required close inspection of future applications and the rejection of those by persons with Nazi affiliations.[60]

In Griesbach, where the citizens had developed a habit of using the denazification process as a way to "get even" with personal enemies, the release of Law No. 8 made matters worse for the local detachment. In addition to dealing with denunciations and misinformation, the military government officers faced mounting opposition from the German population who felt that the Americans were throwing many promising democratic citizens into the same pot as the Nazis because they failed to understand local conditions.[61] In the Fuessen, near the Swiss border, local community and church leaders felt the same way about the denazification program and resisted by retaining ex-Nazi officials whom the military government had ordered removed. In this strained atmosphere, Fuessen's population regarded Law No. 8 as yet another bludgeon on the head of a suffering folk. For the local detachment, the law created a host of new problems because it had to try to find ways to run businesses whose owners were ousted. At the end of February 1946, shortly before German authorities assumed responsibility for denazification, the Fuessen Detachment was still suffering from the effects of Law No. 8. Its Property Control Section still had custody of properties for which it could not find new owners.[62]

With Military Government Law No. 8, the American denazification program reached its widest expanse. The attendant problems of control and enforcement also clearly showed the limits of what a military government implanted in Germany was able to accomplish. Military government personnel, and especially the Special Branch, were drowning in files of persons who appealed their cases. The need for German personnel to relieve the workload and slowly take over the whole process became inescapable. In November, General Clay appointed a Denazification Policy Board (DPB) to review the denazification program in the U.S. Zone and to draft a proposal for a new system that placed as much responsibility as possible on German officials for the future. During the time the board was in session, no additional directives were issued. In January 1946, the board finished its review and released its report. It recommended that U.S. occupation policy adopt the rehabilitation of Germans through participation as a new goal. It advocated shifting political and economic power to reliable groups for the creation of a free democratic

German society. The military government adopted the board's findings as its new policy guideline.[63]

In January 1946, the Allied Control Council for Germany adopted Control Council Directive No. 24, an outgrowth of the International Military Tribunal, which had declared all Nazi organizations criminal organizations and by extension made membership in them a criminal offense. The directive specified ninety-nine categories of persons to be removed from office and positions of responsibility. Besides war criminals, military officers, and Nazi Party officeholders of every kind, members of German University Corps and persons who represented the Prussian Junker tradition were also included.[64]

In early spring 1946, when state governments passed the Law for Liberation from National Socialism and Militarism, a new phase in the denazification began. The law introduced five different categories of defendants instead of the earlier two, nominal and active Nazis, and it instituted a system of tribunals that meted out sanctions keyed to offenses, instead of demanding permanent exclusion in every case. The categories were designed to distinguish between those who should be punished for their crimes and those who should be rehabilitated: major offenders, offenders, lesser offenders, followers, and exonerated. The schedule of punishment included up to ten years of prison for major offenders; up to five years for offenders; fines to ten thousand reichsmarks for lesser offenders; and fines to one thousand reichsmarks for followers. The military government had insisted on these punitive measures against lesser offenders and followers, not included in the first draft of the law. Further, Americans demanded that the law conform to Directive No. 24. By forcing a hearing in every case, the military government intended to prevent "blanket acquittals." Instead, the flood of minor cases would later clog the tribunal system and would benefit major offenders and offenders whose trials had to be delayed for months and even years. By the time their cases came to trial, the purgatory zeal of the Americans had given way to strategic interest in the termination of denazification in order to rebuild Germany as an ally against the Soviet Union.[65]

The law went into effect on 5 March 1946, with the U.S. Military Government reserving the right to supervise its execution. Implementation of the law became the responsibility of state-appointed ministers of liberation. Every German above the age of eighteen, about 13.5 million persons in the U.S. Zone, had to submit a registration questionnaire, Meldebogen, which was a shortened version of the Fragebogen, the original questionnaire. Persons found to have a chargeable association with the Nazi regime, eventually 3.5 million or 27 percent, had to appear before tribunals, Spruchkammern, consisting of a chairperson and four other local non-Nazi citizens. Tribunal members were not required to have a law degree. At their hearings, defendants had a chance to plead their case and present evidence such as affidavits from known non-Nazis that attested to their being only nominal members or even having supported antiregime activities. Based on the evidence, the tribunals then placed defendants in one of the five categories and assessed their punishment. Exonerated persons and followers who had paid their fines were considered denazified and rehabilitated.[66]

Besides shifting the burden of the denazification program onto the Germans, the military government intended the law to provide Germans with an opportunity to purify themselves from Nazism. The people it was supposed to liberate, however, met the law with suspicion. As a result, recruitment of locally known non-Nazis for tribunals became extraordinarily difficult because serving meant judging their own friends and the people they had lived with all their lives. To recruit needed personnel, the state governments even had to pass a law requiring citizens to serve on tribunals if so ordered. Due to the large number of people charged, more and more tribunals had to be established, peaking at 545 tribunals requiring in excess of twenty-two thousand personnel members.[67]

Shortcomings in the law's text and additional requirements the Americans attached to it complicated the process even further. The Special Branch, thus far in charge of denazification, was loath to turning over denazification to the Germans. Since it was not in a position to prevent the law from going into effect, it engaged in activities that came close to obstructing the proper German authorities' implementation of the law. Under the guise of supervision, the Special Branch devised a "Delinquency and Error Report" system, contrived to force German denazification tribunals to revise so-called erroneous decisions. This practice caused tribunals to spend more time than necessary on cases of comparatively minor importance, prolonging the denazification process, and playing into the hands of those trying to prevent having their cases reviewed. Another dilatory effect of the Special Branch's actions was that the ministers of liberation hesitated to make unpopular decisions, such as the removals of officials. In all three states within the U.S. Zone, the ministers tended to refer decisions of that nature to the Special Branch.[68]

After three months, it became obvious that the newly created system of Ministries of Liberation and tribunals would not be able to finish denazification in the foreseeable future or even extended future. Clay, denazification's staunchest supporter, realized that the group of chargeable people under the Law for Liberation had to be reduced in order to relieve the system. As early as June 1946, he therefore decided to propose amnesties.

His so-called Youth Amnesty for those born after 1919 was enacted in August 1946, and a couple of months later a Christmas Amnesty for the disabled and those whose income was below a set limit during the Nazi regime followed. Realizing that its large scope harmed the denazification program's effectiveness, Clay defended his amnesties against critics. He argued that these blanket amnesties would greatly expedite the program and would permit concentration on the finding and punishment of the most culpable Nazis.[69]

By 1947, the United States and the Soviet Union had become enemies, and almost at once cordial relations gave way to suspicion and later open hostility. In this changing political climate, goals and objectives of the occupation followed suit. The American public opinion, once the driving force behind more and more stringent denazification laws, now turned against the program as an obstacle to rebuilding Germany and winning the hearts and minds of the country's population in the struggle against communist expansion. As a result, it became difficult for U.S. politicians to support continued funding for the program. Two other factors also contributed considerably to the decision to abandon denazification in favor of speedy economic recovery programs. While negotiating the merger of the American and the British zones into the so-called Bizone, it proved impossible for the two allies to come to an agreement on a Bizonal denazification policy. What little incentive negotiators had for designing a common denazification policy vanished when the Soviets announced in August 1947 that they would begin to rehabilitate all ordinary Nazi Party members with full rights as citizens.[70]

In response, the U.S. Military Government designed legislation to radically reduce the number of persons to be vetted and introduced an expedited tribunal procedure, the Schnellverfahren. Initially, the German authorities tried to slow down the termination of denazification, just as the Special Branch had resisted the loss of control over denazification to German authorities in the spring of 1946. But since the rapid conclusion of denazification became a precondition for accelerated political and economic recovery in the U.S. Zone, the Germans relented and tried more than 540,000 unfinished cases in expedited procedures. A majority of the defendants were in the major offender and offender categories whose trials the tribunals had postponed to deal more quickly with average party members and lesser offenders in order to return them to their jobs. Now that time was running out, many of the heavily implicated former Nazis received lenient sentences to clear the dockets. This last phase of the denazification program was largely responsible for the perception among the German population that the "small fry" were hanged and "big fish" were allowed to escape. The German Bundestag, the parliament of the newly founded Federal Republic of Germany, formally terminated the denazification program in 1950, when the recommended conclusion of denazification was transferred by legislation to the states. The last state to follow this recommendation as late as 11 August 1954 was Bavaria.[71]

The British Zone

Some of the worst conditions in Germany existed in the British Zone because it was heavily populated and lacked an agricultural base. With many areas at first occupied by American, Canadian, or Polish troops, it took the British until the middle of June 1945 to establish military government detachments throughout the zone. Similar to the experiences in the American Zone, arriving military government detachments provided security and had to fulfill relief tasks such as restoring water supply and sewage as fast as possible. The situation the troops from Military Government Detachment 229 encountered in Hanover, located on the River Leine, was characteristic of many larger cities in the British Zone. Due to its strategic position at the intersection of north-south and east-west thoroughfares and near important bridges crossing the Mittellandkanal, the city had been the frequent target of Allied bombing raids. About 60 percent of the town's buildings were destroyed or so heavily damaged that they were uninhabitable. The prewar population of nearly five hundred thousand had decreased to less than half that. Ninety percent of the city had no water supply, and only a quarter of households were supplied with electrical power. Food was also scarce, forcing Germans and around fifty-five thousand displaced persons—most of them freed slave laborers from 270 camps in the area—to roam the streets in search of reserves or stores to loot.[72]

Hanover's detachments officers assumed full control and went looking for officials, who had not been members of the Nazi Party, to head up new administrations. For advice on whom to appoint as *Oberbürgermeister* (first mayor) and chief of police, the detachment officers relied on the local clergy, some wealthier citizens, and prominent members of the anti-Nazi resistance movement who came forward. Among them was the Social Democrat Emil Barth, who had been Hanover's chief of police before the Nazis came to power. His recommendation for the post of mayor was fellow Social Democrat Gustav Bratke, who had been mayor of Misburg, a small town near Hanover. Although concerned that both men were in their late sixties already, the military government appointed Barth to his old position as chief of police and accepted his advice to appoint Bratke as mayor.[73]

The process of establishing a British Military Government Headquarters was also complicated by the fact that other Allied forces first occupied large areas of the British Zone. As a result, the local detachments represented the sole source of governmental power for the first few months of occupation. Only gradually did power shift away from them to regional and later central headquarters. The most common type of military government detachment was the so-called basic brick, consisting of four officers with at least two administrative officers and two public safety officers. In larger communities, detachments had up to seventy officers. Detachments were established at every level of German administration. The lowest level was the Kreis, or town or rural district; the next higher was the *Regierungsbezirk*, roughly equal in size to a British county; and at the highest level were the *Länder* and *Provinzen*, or provinces. During the course of August 1945, the headquarters of the invading British 21st Army Group under the command of Field Marshal Bernard L. Montgomery transformed into the Zonal Military Government. In the following month, it assumed its final shape as Control Commission Group/British Element. Due to massive destruction in larger cities, the British Military Government distributed different elements of its headquarters to five relatively unaffected small towns—Lübbecke, Minden, Bad Oeynhausen, Detmold, and Bünde—about thirty miles west of Hanover and, with the exception of Detmold, located along the Cologne-Berlin Autobahn. As a consequence of the partitioning, different headquarters divisions fought over competencies and slowed down the decision-making process. Another effect of this unique organization was that the Control Commission Group/British Element became isolated from the misery of the majority of the population. Many Germans began to resent the British, who seemed far removed from their world of misery and shabbiness in the sheltered world of the conquerors.[74]

General agreement in the British War and Foreign Office about the advantages of indirect rule to the contrary, the British Military Government administered Germany directly on every level. Accordingly, the number of personnel at the end of 1945 had reached twenty-six thousand soldiers. The enormous size of their apparatus allowed the British to accomplish many major tasks such as sufficient repairs to German infrastructure for almost normal transport of goods and people. They also cared for and repatriated about two million displaced persons and provided for nearly three million German soldiers who had surrendered to British troops. The political weekly *The Economist* opined that this impressive record was not lost on the occupied in whose opinion, in the beginning of 1946, the British Zone of Occupation was the best administered of all four zones. After the first six months of full-scale occupation, however, many experienced and well-trained veterans left Germany to resume their civilian careers in Great Britain. Their replacements were mainly young, untrained officers and civilians easily spared at home and attracted by a good salary. Only in the middle of 1946, when the British military had problems recruiting personnel for military government duty, did the British begin transferring administrative tasks to Germans.[75]

The Anglo-American Allies approached the Potsdam objective to democratize and decentralize the German governmental system in very different ways. While the Americans had chosen a learning-by-doing method to democratization, the British Military Government had less faith in the ability of Germans to learn democracy. In practice, the British modeled their reform program on their own brand of democracy "from the bottom upwards." Once introduced, British personnel supervised the German bureaucracies at every level and much more tightly than Americans considered necessary. On the zonal level, the British Military Government revived some central German administrative structures, so-called central offices, to provide a base for practical measures such as distribution of building materials and rationing of food. Any local administrative structures were strictly decentralized and depoliticized. They consisted of democratically elected local councils with a mayor as a representative figurehead. The council would form a number of smaller subcommittees that provided effective control of the different sections of the administration. As in Britain, a town clerk who was accountable to the council headed these subcommittees that were run by nonpolitical civil servants.[76]

The principle of selecting nonpolitical representatives also applied to the next larger administrative unit, the so-called Nominated Representative Council. Initially formed to draft a city's constitutions and statutes, the British soon decided that Nominated Representative Councils should be considered city governments. When they insisted that the councils' membership should be on nonpolitical, representing "estates" or particular social categories, however, they encountered resistance from Germans. Those willing to serve were adamant about their right to party affiliation because to them to be nonpolitical could only mean two things: either that one had been a Nazi or that one did not have the moral courage to stand up for one's beliefs and was therefore a potential Nazi. As a result, most members of Nominated Representative Councils considered themselves as belonging to and representing a political party rather than an estate.[77]

The British Military Government lacked political guidance and therefore would have preferred to hold off on the re-creation of German parties.[78] Developments in the neighboring zones, however, determined the pace. The Soviet Military Administration had ordered licensing of parties in June, and the Americans ordered licensing in the beginning of August, following the end of the Potsdam Conference. These considerations as well as fear of Nazi underground activities moved the British in September 1945 to allow officially licensed political parties.[79]

In their treatment of emerging political parties, the British painstakingly avoided the impression of favoring one party over another so that all emerging parties would have a fair chance. As in the U.S. Zone, Social Democrats and Communists were the first to re-create their pre-1933 party organizations. To level the playing field somewhat, the British Military Government banned their youth and sport organizations, which had been their main recruitment tools. Other parties in the British Zone were the conservative Christian Democratic Party (which had roots in the old Catholic Center Party but was essentially a new party) and the liberal Free Democratic Party. In giving all political parties an equal chance to develop under the same conditions, the British wanted to ensure that none of them would be perceived as the party of the Allies.[80]

Creating states, the Länder, presented the British Military Government with a special set of problems. Most of the territory that made up the British Zone belonged to Prussia, the state of which the Allies blamed Germany's imperialistic and militaristic past. The process of carving completely new Länder from Prussian counties and districts began in the middle of 1946. Until the old state was officially dissolved in November, Prussian provinces and newly created Länder coexisted in the British Zone. The new Länder were Schleswig-Holstein in the Northeast; Hanover—in December 1946 renamed Lower Saxony—bordered by the Soviet Zone in the East and the Netherlands in the West; and North Rhine-Westphalia, which included the Ruhr valley industrial area and the ancient city-state of Hamburg. The first British-appointed minister presidents were Theodor Hans Steltzer (CDU) for Schleswig-Holstein; Hinrich Wilhelm Kopf (SPD) for Lower Saxony; Rudolf Amelunxen (no party affiliation) for North Rhine-Westphalia; and Rudolf Petersen (no party affiliation) as first mayor of Hamburg. They were responsible for forming state governments that were responsible to the British Military Government–appointed members of the new Länder legislatures.

In April 1947, the states held their first postwar elections. The newly elected lawmakers immediately went to work on drafting state constitutions according to strict British guidelines that prescribed the nonpolitical nature of civil service, the introduction of the British-style voting system, and the creation of parliamentary committees to carry out legislative work. Any reference to a German nation-state had to be excluded so that future international arrangements would not be prejudiced.[81]

Though nominally the same as in the American Zone, states in the British Zone of Occupation lacked much of the independence granted to American Länder. The Central Offices that acted as ministries in the absence of national administrative organs severely limited their decision-making powers. The same held true for the Zonal Advisory Council. Similarities between it and the Council of States in the American Zone existed in name only since the British Military Government rejected any attempt by the Advisory Council to obtain legislative and executive power.[82]

On 1 January 1947, the American and British zones merged into the so-called Bizone. The fusion had a twofold effect on British occupation policy and implementation. On the one hand, Great Britain obtained from the United States a long-term commitment, which she had sought since the end of hostilities, to stay engaged on the European continent. On the other, Britain lost the ability to conduct an independent occupation policy. In jointly created agencies, such as the Joint Export-Import Agency and the Joint Foreign Exchange Agency, the size of each country's financial contribution to occupation costs determined voting shares. In the beginning, Great Britain was able to pay about 50 percent of the costs, but soon she had to reduce her input due to an untenable fiscal situation. Since Germany had not been able to pay for up to 70 percent of its food supplies and other imports, the British paid for them with gold and dollar reserves from American loans.

As a consequence, the United States largely determined the shape of the future Germany. British plans for the nationalization of heavy industries in the Ruhr valley and the introduction of central agencies for administration of the zones gave way to American-style federalism and economics. Another factor that shaped policies in the two years before the formation of the Federal Republic was concern that Germany as a whole might be drawn into an alliance with the Soviet Union.[83]

Nevertheless, British occupation policy and practice had a lasting impact on the new German state. Even though nationalization of heavy industry never materialized, a system of codetermination that allowed employees a voice in management decisions in the coal and steel industry prevailed. According to the system, every larger business had to establish works councils with eleven delegates, five each for employees and management and an impartial "eleventh man." A firm's management had to consult these councils on decisions directly related to working conditions. This way, potential conflicts could be defused before they erupted, sparing Germany antagonizing labor-management struggles plaguing other industrialized societies. Another lasting contribution was emergence of a party system centered on two major moderate political parties and stable alternating governments formed by these parties.[84]

British Denazification Practices: Keeping It Simple

Initially, until SHAEF was dissolved in July 1945, denazification in the British Zone was implemented in a similar fashion in the Anglo-American Zones of Occupation. Upon entering Germany, occupation forces arrested blacklisted persons, eliminated Nazi legislation, disbanded the Nazi Party and all its organizations, and vetted existing town administrations by requiring mayors to submit lists of town officials that indicated their former party affiliations. To eliminate the roots that allowed Nazism to grow, the troops also seized all means of mass communication, education, and entertainment, including broadcasting, press, films, theater, and schools. Placed under strictest control, the Anglo-American Allies used them as tools in a process to reeducate the German population. While committed to the goal of eliminating Nazi influence in Germany, the British preferred a more cautious approach to denazification. Early on, the British Military Government decided that a systematic purge of anyone who in some way had been associated with the Nazi Party or any other Nazi organization was impossible. Over time, as American ambition spurred by domestic criticism intensified and expanded the circle of persons affected by the program, the British grew more reluctant to follow suit in their zone.[85]

The denazification program posed a dilemma for the British element of the Control Commission: they were persuaded that, implemented systematically, the program had the potential to lead to administrative and economic collapse. The British Zone was more densely populated and, at the same time, harder hit by destruction than the other zones, convincing its military government that the need to keep the revived German administration working and to provide the population with food, water, and some protection from disease outweighed the need to purge German society of Nazism. If famine, epidemics, or anarchy were to break out, the British calculated that it would hurt them and their forces as much as the Germans. In the event, world opinion and self-protection would force them to restore order and undertake far greater relief operations than would have been necessary otherwise. Furthermore, they believed it was precisely the development of such conditions that could result in a resurgence of Nazism or the emergence of Communism.[86]

Accordingly, the British Military Government handled denazification of private industry rather lightly and in some cases neglected it altogether. While the British were prepared to accept some encroachment on economic efficiency in the first year of occupation, they did so only for certain parts of the economy. Industries that were vital for the survival of the population, notably agriculture, were exempt. When denazification led to the removal of many of the Ruhr coal industry's managerial and technical personnel, severely diminishing its efficiency, this industry was exempted as well. Where denazification continued, functional officers explored loopholes in the legislation or simply ignored instructions to retain skilled German personnel.[87]

As a result, the British Military Government directed denazification efforts mainly toward removal and exclusion of persons with Nazi affiliations from positions within local government and administrative organizations. At the core, the British denazification program aimed at maintaining security in its zone through removal of persons hostile to British occupation goals. Left without comprehensive guidelines, since it had refused to adopt the American directive JCS 1067, the British Military Government relied on instructions designed for the purge of financial institutions. The method it adopted for vetting public officeholders and applicants for positions in the public sector was the questionnaire, as it was used in the American Zone. At headquarters, public safety officers of a Special Branch checked questionnaires against captured party records. Each questionnaire was classified in one of four categories: M, removal or nonappointment mandatory; D, removal or nonappointment within discretion of the military government; NEG, no objection to appointment or retention; R, retention or appointment recommended. Thus, denazification practice evolved before the existence of legislation regulating its extent and implementation.[88]

German Denazification Panels

At the end of 1945, the vast number of cases to be categorized so completely overwhelmed Special Branch personnel that the need to involve Germans in the process became unavoidable. As a first step, the military government issued instructions to province and district governments to set up German Advisory Committees to assist in assessing cases in the discretionary removal category. In January 1946, it followed up with Zonal Policy Instruction (ZPI) 3, formally handing responsibility for denazification to German authorities. Under the new policy, German Denazification Panels, German review boards, and British review boards sorted out cases with the goal of hastening the denazification process as much as possible. The release of Control Council Directive No. 24 that same month did not change that course. The British Foreign Office greeted the quadripartite denazification legislation with derision, describing it as an expression of "sheerest madness" that was hard to beat as an example of "systematic and meticulous imbecility." It therefore decided to ignore the letters of the directive and instructed the military government to use common sense in applying this piece of legislation.[89]

In August 1946, the military government further reduced the denazification program's demands on personnel with the release of ZPI 38 on Disposal and Categorization of War Criminals, Nazis, and militarists. Intended as a tool to legitimize the release of thousands of prisoners in internment camps, the instruction cleared the way for the inmates' categorization, downgrading, and subsequent discharge. When details about ZPI 38 became public, many Germans reacted with consternation. Fearing an uproar if they went ahead with the categorization of prisoners, the British postponed it until October, when the Control Council issued Directive No. 38, which adopted the five categories of the Law for Liberation in the American Zone for all of Germany.[90]

An integral part of British denazification efforts was the so-called reeducation. The objective of reeducation was not simply to restore schools with democratically minded teachers and textbooks but also to reeducate all Germans to eliminate the roots that allowed Nazism to grow. In order to facilitate this broad-based education effort, occupation forces seized all means of mass communication, education, and entertainment, including broadcasting, press, films, theater, and schools, upon entering Germany. The military government placed them under strictest control and used them as tools in the reeducation process.[91]

The extent of the task led many within the military government to assume that a long, colonial-style occupation was to be expected. An officer in the Control Commission summarized the view pervading the Foreign Office and Control Commission on the reformability of Germans: "Military Government officials resembled civilised and agreeable officers in a rather forward-looking Bedouin country—tending to treat Germans in the beginning very much as intelligent natives."[92] Despite their obvious disdain for acts committed by Germans, the British Military Government chose not to impose reform of the school system on Germans. Instead, the Education Branch preferred to establish mutual trust and an exchange of ideas, not to force reeducation down German throats. Länder governments assumed direct responsibility for education in the beginning of 1947, which left the Education Branch with the power to supervise and veto if necessary. The approach chosen by the British Military Government in tackling an education system built on unquestioned obedience to authority, so-called Kathedergehorsam, eventually led to the re-creation of the German education system, as it existed prior to the takeover by the National Socialists.[93]

In the beginning of 1947, when the United States and Great Britain decided to merge the economic administration of their zones to form the Bizone, negotiations about a more coordinated denazification policy failed. Neither ally had great interest in continuing the denazification program. In August, when the Soviet Military Administration announced they had completed denazification in their zone, the British Military Government took it as an opportunity to transfer responsibility for denazification to the Länder governments, reserving only categorization of individuals in the two highest categories for themselves. Subsequent legislation aimed at a speedy conclusion of denazification.[94]

The year 1947 was a turning point for denazification in Germany. In the international realm, relations between the Western Allies and the Soviet Union had undergone a transformation from caution, to suspicion, to open hostility, relegating policies not designed to win over partners for the respective sides insignificant. Denazification, as all occupation powers had experienced, had proved to be a controversial policy within the military government as well as among Germans. Although it certainly produced ardent supporters in both camps, it became a burden as time progressed. In the end, the new Federal Republic of Germany had to finish denazification.

Notes

1. FM 27-5, Basic Field Manual, Military Government (Washington, DC: United States Government Printing Office, 1940), 2.

2. Statement of Col. Jesse I. Miller, Director of the Military Government Division, Provost Marshal General's Office, Friday, 21 January 1944, Hearings before the Committee on Military Affairs, House of Representatives, Seventy-Eighth Congress, Second Session, Part 2, 21 and 25 January 1944 (Washington, DC: United States Government Printing Office, 1944), 5–6, 17.

3. Richard W. Stewart, "The United States Army and Training in Military Government and Civil Affairs" (U.S. Army Special Operations Command, Fort Bragg, NC, April 1994, unpublished), 6; Earl F. Ziemke, "Civil Affairs at Thirty," *Military Affairs* 36, no. 4 (December 1972): 131–32; Robert K. Wright, *Military Police*, Army Lineage Series (Washington, DC: U.S. Army Center of Military History, 1992), 10–11.

4. Ziemke, "Civil Affairs at Thirty," 131.

5. Outline of Curriculum, First Course (May–August 1942) submitted by Commandant, School of Military Government to the Adjutant General, 13 May 1942, in *United States Army in World War II. Special Studies. Civil Affairs: Soldiers Become Governors*, ed. Harry L. Coles and Albert K. Weinberg, 11–12 (Washington, DC: Office of the Chief of Military History, Department of the Army, 1964); Statement of Col. Jesse I. Miller, Tuesday, 25 January 1944, 13–14.

6. Memorandum, Wickersham, Commandant, School of Military Government, for Provost Marshal General, 17 June 1942, in *United States Army in World War II. Special Studies. Civil Affairs: Soldiers Become Governors*, ed. Harry L. Coles and Albert K. Weinberg, 12–13 (Washington, DC: Office of the Chief of Military History, Department of the Army, 1964).

7. Memorandum, Arthur C. Ringland, War Relief Control Board, 20 June 1942, forwarded to President Franklin D. Roosevelt, in *United States Army in World War II. Special Studies. Civil Affairs: Soldiers Become Governors*, ed. Harry L. Coles and Albert K. Weinberg, 14 (Washington, DC: Office of the Chief of Military History, Department of the Army, 1964).

8. Henry L. Stimson and McGeorge Bundy, *On Active Service in Peace and War* (New York: Harper, 1948), 553–54.

9. Synopsis of War Department Program for Military Government, 4 September 1942, in *United States Army in World War II. Special Studies. Civil Affairs: Soldiers Become Governors*, ed. Harry L. Coles and Albert K. Weinberg, 19 (Washington, DC: Office of the Chief of Military History, Department of the Army, 1964).

10. Memorandum, Roosevelt for the Secretary of War, 29 October 1942, in *United States Army in World War II. Special Studies. Civil Affairs: Soldiers Become Governors*, ed. Harry L. Coles and Albert K. Weinberg, 22 (Washington, DC: Office of the Chief of Military History, Department of the Army, 1964).

11. Letter, Roosevelt to Hull, 18 November 1942; Paraphrase of a Message, War Department to Eisenhower, 24 November 1942, both in *United States Army in World War II. Special Studies. Civil Affairs: Soldiers Become Governors*, ed. Harry L. Coles and

Albert K. Weinberg, 37–38 (Washington, DC: Office of the Chief of Military History, Department of the Army, 1964).

12. Stimson and Bundy, *On Active Service*, 554.

13. George F. Howe, *United States Army in World War II. The Mediterranean Theater of Operations. North-West Africa: Seizing the Initiative in the West* (Washington, DC: U.S. Army Center of Military History, 1991 [1957]), 58.

14. War Department Statement of Policy, 1 February 1943, in *United States Army in World War II. Special Studies. Civil Affairs: Soldiers Become Governors*, ed. Harry L. Coles and Albert K. Weinberg, 64 (Washington, DC: Office of the Chief of Military History, Department of the Army, 1964).

15. Charles Reginald Schiller Harris, *Allied Administration of Italy 1943–1945* (London: H. M. Stationery Office, 1957), 369–72.

16. Occupation Forces in Europe Series, 1945–1946, *Planning for the Occupation of Germany* (Frankfurt am Main, Germany: European Command, Office of the Chief Historian, 1947); Occupation Forces in Europe Series, 1945–1946, *The First Year of the Occupation* (Frankfurt am Main, Germany: European Command, Office of the Chief Historian, 1947), 77–81; Stewart, "The United States Army," 6; Ziemke, "Civil Affairs at Thirty," 131–32.

17. Stewart, "The United States Army," 12.

18. Earl F. Ziemke, *The U.S. Army in the Occupation of Germany 1944–1946*, Army Historical Series (Washington, DC: United States Army Center of Military History, 2003), 62–64.

19. Ziemke, *The U.S. Army in the Occupation of Germany*, 68–71.

20. Ziemke, *The U.S. Army in the Occupation of Germany*, 72–74.

21. The British and Canadian military establishments distinguished between "civil affairs" and "military government" based on where soldiers performed these functions. "Civil affairs" was military government in one's own or friendly territory and "military government" was civil affairs conducted in enemy territory.

22. F. S. V. Donnison, *Civil Affairs and Military Government: Central Organization and Planning* (London: H. M. Stationery Office, 1966), 295–96.

23. Donnison, *Civil Affairs and Military Government*, 297–301. When it created the DCCAO, the committee envisioned that a chief civil affairs officer would replace him as soon as the occupation began.

24. Donnison, *Civil Affairs and Military Government*, 291–93.

25. Donnison, *Civil Affairs and Military Government*, 293–305.

26. Ziemke, *The U.S. Army in the Occupation of Germany*, 222–24; Lucius D. Clay, *Decision in Germany* (Garden City, NY: Doubleday, 1950), 2.

27. Occupation Forces in Europe Series, 1945–1946, *Civil Affairs* (Frankfurt am Main, Germany: European Command, Office of the Chief Historian, 1947); Hans Jürgen Schraut, "U.S. Forces in Germany, 1945–1955," in *U.S. Military Forces in Europe: The Early Years, 1945–1970*, ed. Simon W. Duke and Wolfgang Krieger, 154–61 (Boulder, CO: Westview Press, 1993); Jean Edward Smith, *Lucius D. Clay: An American Life* (New York: H. Holt, 1990), 223–25.

28. Oliver J. Frederiksen, *The American Military Occupation of Germany 1945–1953* (Historical Division, Headquarters, U.S. Army, Europe, 1955), 6.

29. Ziemke, *The U.S. Army in the Occupation of Germany*, 76–77.

30. Conditions in Germany, From Clay to Byrnes, 20 April 1945, in *The Papers of Lucius D. Clay: Germany 1945–1949*, ed. Jean Edward Smith, 2 vols., 1: 6 (Bloomington: Indiana University Press, 1974).

31. Wolfgang Friedmann, *The Allied Military Government of Germany* (London: Stevens and Sons, 1947), 14–16; cf. Lothar Kettenacker, "Großbritannien und die zukünftige Kontrolle Deutschlands," in *Die britische Deutschland- und Besatzungspolitik 1945–1949*, ed. Josef Foschepoth and Rolf Steininger, 44 (Paderborn, Germany: Ferdinand Schöningh, 1985). For a detailed account of the damage Allied bombardment caused in Germany, see Jörg Friedrich, *Der Brand: Deutschland im Bombenkrieg 1940–1945* (München, Germany: Propyläen Verlag, 2002).

32. General Lucius Clay, USA (Ret.), Third Interview by Colonel R. Joe Rogers, 24 January 1973, p. 25, Senior Officers Debriefing Program, U.S. Army Military History Research Collection, Carlisle Barracks, Pennsylvania.

33. Earl F. Ziemke, "Improvising Stability and Change in Postwar Germany," in *Americans as Proconsuls: United States Military Government in Germany and Japan, 1944–1952*, ed. Robert Wolfe, 56–57 (Carbondale: Southern Illinois University Press, 1984); Frederiksen, *The American Military Occupation of Germany 1945–1953*, 6.

34. Dirk Berg-Schlosser, "Die Konstituierung des Wirtschaftssystems," in *Vorgeschichte der Bundesrepublik Deutschland: Zwischen Kapitulation und Grundgesetz*, ed. Josef Becker, Theo Stammen, and Peter Waldmann, 94–95 (München, Germany: UTB für Wissenschaft, 1979); Ziemke, "Improvising Stability and Change in Postwar Germany," 56; Anne Deighton, "Cold-War Diplomacy: British Policy towards Germany's Role in Europe, 1945–9," in *Reconstruction in Post-War Germany: British Occupation Policy and the Western Zones, 1945–55*, ed. Ian Turner, 21 (New York: St. Martin's Press, 1989).

35. Ziemke, *The U.S. Army in the Occupation of Germany*, 320; Clay, *Decision in Germany*, 65.

36. Detachment Historical Reports, Griesbach D-378, Records of the Office of Military Government for Bavaria, Records of the Intelligence Division (OMGB-ID), Box 200, Records of United States Occupation Headquarters, World War II, Records of the Office of Military Government for Germany (U.S.), Record Group (RG) 260, National Archives and Record Administration (NARA), College Park, Maryland.

37. Occupation Forces in Europe Series, 1945–1946, *Planning for the Occupation of Germany*, 98, 102, 113, 114; Harold Zink, *American Military Government in Germany* (New York: Macmillan, 1947), 141.

38. Elmer Plischke, "Denazifying the Reich," *Review of Politics* 9, no. 2 (April 1947): 153–73, 155; Lutz Niethammer, *Entnazifizierung in Bayern: Säuberung und Rehabilitierung unter amerikanischer Besatzung* (Frankfurt am Main, Germany: S. Fischer, 1972), 146, 149.

39. Clay, *Decision in Germany*, 52–55, 85.

40. Wolfgang Benz, *Potsdam 1945: Besatzungsherrschft und Neuaufbau in Vier-Zonen-Deutschland* (München, Germany: Deutscher Taschenbuch Verlag, 1994), 127, cf. 47; Conditions in Germany, From Clay to McCloy, 5 October 1945, in *The Papers of Lucius D. Clay: Germany 1945–1949*, ed. Jean Edward Smith, 2 vols., 1: 94 (Bloomington: Indiana University Press, 1974). Clay mentioned in his letter to McCloy that Schäffer

thought the American "program for removing Nazis went too far" and that he had appointed a government that only represented the right wing of the political spectrum.

41. Conditions in Germany, From Clay to McCloy, 1: 92.

42. Clay, *Decision in Germany*, 86, 98–102.

43. Ziemke, "Improvising Stability and Change in Postwar Germany," 64–65.

44. From Clay to Walter H. Mallory, 27 November 1945, Enclosure No. 2, p. 2, Records of the Office of Military Government for Germany (U.S.) Adjutant General 1945–1946, Box 53, RG 260, NARA; cf. Clay, *Decision in Germany*, 92–93.

45. Conditions in Germany, From Clay to McCloy, 3 September 1945, 1: 67.

46. Clay, *Decision in Germany*, 88–91; cf. Benz, *Potsdam 1945*, 136. The military government retained supervisory powers over the new state governments.

47. Joseph Starr, *U.S. Military Government in Germany: Operations from March to Mid-July 1945* (Karlsruhe, Germany: European Command, Historical Division, 1950), 39–40. This was general procedure for constituting a municipal government (Zink, *American Military Government in Germany*, 133–35). This practice was still common in detachments that were established after Aachen and was also employed by British forces (Niethammer, *Entnazifizierung in Bayern*, 65).

48. In 1943, the army had developed a similar instrument to screen and purge Fascists from public office in Italy (Gary A. Trogdon, "A Decade of Catching Spies: The United States Army's Counter Intelligence Corps, 1943–1953" [Unpublished Ph.D. diss., University of Nebraska, 2001], 48–49). The original Fragebogen consisted of twenty-three questions dealing mainly with vital statistics. However, experience gained in the first months of denazification showed that "some party members were able to evade this screening process due to the inadequacy of the questions in the old type fragebogen" (Functional History of Military Government [FHMG], 26 April–30 September 1945, p. 15, Records of the Public Information Office, Box 68). The new type of Fragebogen, the so-called tapeworm, consisted of 131 questions of which more than half dealt with political activities and memberships of any kind (FHMG, October 1945–June 1946, p. 3, Records of the Denazification Division, Functional Histories of Military Government in Bremen, April 1945–March 1948, Box 168, RG 260, NARA). Cf. Robert F. Knox, Major CE, Deputy, to All Branches, DET. G1C2, ECAD, 20 August 1945, Records of the Denazification Division, Box 159, RG 260, NARA.

49. Ziemke, *The U.S. Army in the Occupation of Germany*, 380.

50. Elmer Plischke, "Denazification in Germany: A Policy Analysis," in *Americans as Proconsuls: United States Military Government in Germany and Japan, 1944–1952*, ed. Robert Wolfe, 209–11 (Carbondale: Southern Illinois University Press, 1984).

Other aspects also related to the denazification of Germany were arrest and punishment of war criminals and Nazi leaders. Trials of these criminals before courts-martial, military government courts, and the Nuremberg Military Tribunal will only be mentioned as they pertain to removal and exclusion of Nazis from positions of responsibility.

51. Niethammer, *Entnazifizierung in Bayern*, 147.

52. Starr, *U.S. Military Government in Germany*, 132; Ziemke, "Improvising Stability and Change in Postwar Germany," 57; Lothar Kettenacker, "Großbritannien und die zukünftige Kontrolle Deutschlands," in *Die britische Deutschland- und Besatzungspolitik 1945–1949*, ed. Josef Foschepoth and Rolf Steininger, 46 (Paderborn,

Germany: Ferdinand Schöningh, 1985); Friedmann, *The Allied Military Government of Germany*, 4–17.

53. Ziemke, *The U.S. Army in the Occupation of Germany*, 381–82. According to Walter Dorn's recollections, the same did not hold true for development of the German economy. He maintained that, although some American businessmen and their staffs believed that denazification was the main impediment for economic recovery, the real cause for delay was general confusion and lack of resources as a consequence of the war. Lutz Niethammer, ed., *Walter L. Dorn: Inspektionsreisen durch die U.S.-Zone. Notizen, Denkschriften und Erinnerungen* (Stuttgart, Germany: R. Oldenbourg Verlag, 1973), 121; Justus Fürstenau, *Entnazifizierung: Ein Kapitel deutscher Nachkriegsgeschichte* (Neuwied, Germany: Luchterhand, 1969), 36; see also Volker Dotterweich, "Die 'Entnazifizierung,'" in *Vorgeschichte der Bundesrepublik Deutschland. Zwischen Kapitulation und Grundgesetz*, ed. Josef Becker, Theo Stammen, and Peter Waldmann, 143 (München, Germany: UTB für Wissenschaft, 1979); John Gimbel, *The American Occupation of Germany: Politics and the Military, 1945–1949* (Stanford, CA: Stanford University Press, 1968), 101.

54. Detachments Historical Reports, Dachau E-367, 4 August 1945 and 24 August 1945, OMGB—Intelligence Division (ID), Box 213, RG 260, NARA.

55. Detachments Historical Reports, Dachau E-367, 1 April 1946.

56. Records of Predecessor Offices, Field Research Detachment—Augsburg, Denazification and Demilitarization, 3 April 1946, OMGB-ID, Box 145, RG 260, NARA. Franz Xaver Sennefelder (1886–1960) joined the SPD in 1908 and served as a member of Augsburg's magistrate from 1924 to 1933. In 1933, the Nazi regime arrested him nine times and sent him to Dachau Concentration Camp twice "Sozialistische Mitteilungen: News for German Socialist in England," Nr. 77/78–1945, August/September, p. 22, Newsletter herausgegeben vom Exilvorstand der Sozialdemokratischen Partei Deutschlands (SOPADE) 1939–1948, Ungekürzte Online Ausgabe, Herausgegeben von der Friedrich Ebert Stiftung, at http://library.fes.de/fulltext/sozmit/som-von-aussen.htm (accessed 15 May 2008).

57. General Lucius Clay, USA (Ret.), Third Interview by Colonel R. Joe Rogers, 24 January 1973, 5; Paul W. Gulgowski, *The American Military Government of the United States Occupied Zones of Post World War II Germany in Relation to Policies Expressed by its Civilian Governmental Authorities at Home, during the Course of 1944/45 through 1949* (Frankfurt am Main, Germany: Haag + Herchen, 1983), 33; Zink, *American Military Government in Germany*, 140; Gimbel, *The American Occupation of Germany*, 1–3. Gimbel points out that the attempt to establish a "minimum economy" in 1945 was labeled "soft" peace.

58. Gulgowski, *The American Military Government*, 223; Niethammer, *Entnazifizierung in Bayern*, 234. Niethammer suspects that Patton's statement about the need for Nazi Party membership in the Third Reich was intended as a comparison with the spoils system in nineteenth-century America. Wolfgang Benz, *Von der Besatzungsherrschaft zur Bundesrepublik: Stationen einer Staatsgründung 1946–1949* (Frankfurt am Main, Germany: Fischer Taschenbuch Verlag, 1984), 26; Tom Bower, *The Pledge Betrayed: America and Britain and the Denazification of Postwar Germany* (Garden City, NY: Doubleday, 1982), 135.

59. Clay, *Decision in Germany*, 68; Niethammer, *Entnazifizierung in Bayern*, 157, 241; Gimbel, *The American Occupation of Germany*, 39, 101.

60. Ziemke, *The U.S. Army in the Occupation of Germany*, 387; Niethammer, *Entnazifizierung in Bayern*, 246; Land Bayern, 11–18 October 1945, Weekly Report No. 24, 18 October to 25 October 1945, in *Entnazifizierung in Bayern: Säuberung und Rehabilitierung unter amerikanischer Besatzung*, ed. Lutz Niethammer (Frankfurt am Main, Germany: S. Fischer, 1972).

61. Detachment Historical Reports, Griesbach D-378, OMGB-ID, Box 200, RG 260, NARA.

62. Detachment Historical Reports, Fuessen G-299, September 1945, October 1945, 28 February 1946, OMGB-ID, Box 225, RG 260, NARA.

63. Niethammer, *Entnazifizierung in Bayern*, 273; Niethammer notes that some of the staunchest opponents to denazification were appointed to serve on the DPB; cf. Gimbel, *The American Occupation of Germany*, 102–3.

64. Directive No. 24, Removal from Office and from Positions of Responsibility of Nazis and of Persons Hostile to Allied Purposes, 12 January 1946, Control Council, Office of Military Government for Bremen, Records of the Denazification Division, Box 157, RG 260, NARA; Ziemke, *The U.S. Army in the Occupation of Germany*, 430.

65. Ziemke, *The U.S. Army in the Occupation of Germany*, 430.

66. Clay, *Decision in Germany*, 69–70. Clay was heavily criticized for his decision to turn denazification over to the Germans, but he was convinced that Germans "were far better able . . . to determine the real Nazi." Ziemke, *The U.S. Army in the Occupation of Germany*, 431.

67. Ziemke, *The U.S. Army in the Occupation of Germany*, 439; Dotterweich, "Die 'Entnazifizierung,'" 145; Clay, *Decision in Germany*, 259.

68. Edward N. Petersen, *The American Occupation of Germany: Retreat to Victory* (Detroit, MI: Wayne State University Press, 1978), 149–50; cf. Niethammer, *Walter L. Dorn* , 90–92, 100.

69. Clay, *Decision in Germany*, 260; Denazification, From Clay Personal to Echols, 3 June 1946, 1: 168; Denazification, From Clay Personal to Echols, 15 December 1946, 285.

70. Dotterweich, "Die 'Entnazifizierung,'" 147; Petersen, *The American Occupation of Germany*, 151; cf. Friedmann, *The Allied Military Government of Germany*, 125.

71. Dotterweich, "Die 'Entnazifizierung,'" 148.

72. Barbara Marshall, "The Democratization of Local Politics in the British Zone of Germany: Hanover 1945–47," *Journal of Contemporary History* 21, no. 3 (July 1986): 416–17.

73. Emil Barth was a printer and journalist who had been Hanover's chief of police until the Nazis removed him in 1933 ("Sozialistische Mitteilungen," 22). Gustav Bratke had also worked as a printer and bookbinder and journalist before he became mayor of Misburg. In 1933, the Nazis wasted no time to drive him out of office and to arrest him on false charges of embezzlement. Biographical information online at Stadtarchiv Hannover, at http://internet.hannover-stadt.de/stadtarchiv/ges/person/bratke/bratke.html (accessed 27 May 2008); Marshall, "The Democratization of Local Politics," 419.

74. Rolf Lutzebäck, *Die Bildungspolitik der Britischen Militärregierung im Spannungsfeld zwischen "education" und "reeducation" in ihrer Besatzungszone, insbesondere*

in Schleswig-Holstein und Hamburg in den Jahren 1945–1947, Teil 1 (Frankfurt am Main, Germany: P. Lang, 1991), 66; Donnison, *Civil Affairs and Military Government*, 225–30, 242–44; cf. Friedmann, *The Allied Military Government of Germany*, 44–46, 57–58; Benz, *Potsdam 1945*, 74; Jochen Thies, "What Is Going on in Germany?" Britische Militärverwaltung in Deutschland 1945/46," in *Die Deutschlandpolitik Grossbritanniens und die Britische Zone 1945–1949*, ed. Claus Scharf and Hans-Jürgen Schröder, 37 (Wiesbaden, Germany: Veröffentlichungen des Instituts für Europäische Geschichte Mainz, Beiheft 6, 1979).

75. Benz, *Potsdam 1945*, 80; Thies, "What Is Going on in Germany?" 38; Ullrich Schneider, "Nach dem Sieg: Besatzungspolitik und Militärregierung 1945," in *Die britische Deutschland- und Besatzungspolitik 1945–1949*, ed. Josef Foschepoth and Rolf Steininger, 56 (Paderborn, Germany: Ferdinand Schöningh, 1985); Friedmann, *The Allied Military Government of Germany*, 36, 46.

76. Donald Cameron Watt, "Großbritannien, die Vereinigten Staaten und Deutschland," in *Die britische Deutschland- und Besatzungspolitik 1945–1949*, ed. Josef Foschepoth and Rolf Steininger, 19–20 (Paderborn, Germany: Ferdinand Schöningh, 1985); Friedmann, *The Allied Military Government of Germany*, 38; Barbara Marshall, "British Democratisation Policy in Germany," in *Reconstruction in Post-War Germany: British Occupation Policy and the Western Zones, 1945–55*, ed. Ian Turner, 195–96 (New York: St. Martin's Press, 1989); Marshall, "The Democratization of Local Politics," 424.

77. Schneider, "Nach dem Sieg," 54; Marshall, "British Democratisation Policy in Germany," 198.

78. During hostilities, occupation of Germany had been the responsibility of the War Office. After Germany's surrender, the War Office and Foreign Office struggled over responsibility for the military government in Germany. In view of enormous domestic social problems, the new Labour government showed little interest in the issue of governing Germany. Responsibility for military government in Germany was therefore assigned to a new department with a separate minister, the Chancellor of the Duchy of Lancaster (cf. Berg-Schlosser, "Die Konstituierung des Wirtschaftssystems," 104; Donnison, *Civil Affairs and Military Government*, 276).

79. Marshall, "British Democratisation Policy in Germany," 208; Benz, *Potsdam 1945*, 140.

80. Marshall, "British Democratisation Policy in Germany," 210–12.

81. Marshall, "British Democratisation Policy in Germany, 199–201; cf. Benz, *Potsdam 1945*, 121–22.

82. Benz, *Potsdam 1945*, 131–32.

83. Berg-Schlosser, "Die Konstituierung des Wirtschaftssystems," 106; Watt, "Großbritannien," 20–23; Marshall, "British Democratisation Policy in Germany," 202; Hans-Peter Schwarz, *Vom Reich zur Bundesrepublik: Deutschland im Widerstreit der außenpolitischen Konzeptionen in den Jahren der Besatzungsherrschaft 1945–1949* (Stuttgart, Germany: Klett-Cotta, 1980), 172–73.

84. Berg-Schlosser, "Die Konstituierung des Wirtschaftssystems," 105; Ian Turner, "Introduction: The British Occupation and Its Impact on Germany," in *Reconstruction in Post-War Germany: British Occupation Policy and the Western Zones, 1945–55*, ed. Ian Turner, 11 (New York: St. Martin's Press, 1989).

85. Donnison, *Civil Affairs and Military Government*, 360, 367, 372; cf. Ian Turner, "Denazification in the British Zone," in *Reconstruction in Post-War Germany: British Occupation Policy and the Western Zones, 1945–55*, ed. Ian Turner, 244–45, 248 (New York: St. Martin's Press, 1989); Friedmann, *The Allied Military Government of Germany*, 114; Benz, *Von der Besatzungsherrschaft zur Bundesrepublik*, 15–16; Benz, *Potsdam 1945*, 173.

86. Donnison, *Civil Affairs and Military Government*, 365–66.

87. Turner, "Denazification in the British Zone," 257–59.

88. Donnison, *Civil Affairs and Military Government*, 364; Turner, "Denazification in the British Zone," 248; cf. Schneider, "Nach dem Sieg," 60.

89. Zone Policy Instruction No. 3 of 17 January 1946, p. 1, Main Headquarters, Control Commission For Germany (British Element), De-Nazification Measures in the British Zone, Records of the Office of Military Government for Bremen, Records of the Denazification Division, Box 159, RG 260, NARA; Allied Control Authority, Control Council Directive No. 24 (removal from office and from positions of responsibility of Nazis and of persons hostile to allied purposes), 12 January 1946, pp. 98–113, Germany (territory Allied occupation, 1945–1955, U.S. Zone); Office of Military Government, Civil Administration Division, Denazification: Cumulative Review, Report, 1 April 1947–30 April 1948 (n.p., Lithographed by the Adjutant General, OMGUS, 1948), at http://digital.library.wisc.edu/1711.dl/History.Denazi (accessed 23 May 2008); Turner, "Denazification in the British Zone," 252.

90. HQ/06101/SecG, 12 August 1946, Zonal Executive Offices Control Commission for Germany (British Element), Zone Policy Instruction No. 38, Disposal and Categorization of War Criminals, Nazis, and Militarists, Records of the Office of Military Government for Bremen, Records of the Denazification Division, Box 170; Allied Control Authority, Control Council Directive No. 38 (the arrest and punishment of war criminals, Nazis, and Militarists and the internment, control, and surveillance of potentially dangerous Germans), 12 October 1946, pp. 114–36, Germany (territory Allied occupation, 1945–1955, U.S. Zone); Office of Military Government, Civil Administration Division, Denazification: Cumulative Review; Turner, "Denazification in the British Zone," 255.

91. Donnison, *Civil Affairs and Military Government*, 372.

92. David Welch, "Priming the Pump of German Democracy: British 'Re-Education' Policy in Germany after the Second World War," in *Reconstruction in Post-War Germany: British Occupation Policy and the Western Zones, 1945–55*, ed. Ian Turner, 221–22 (New York: St. Martin's Press, 1989).

93. Welch, "Priming the Pump of German Democracy," 224.

94. Military Government, Germany, British Zone of Control, Ordinance No. 110 (transfer to the Land Governments of Responsibility for Denazification), 1 October 1947, pp. 150–55, Germany (territory Allied occupation, 1945–1955, U.S. Zone); Office of Military Government, Civil Administration Division, Denazification: Cumulative Review; Turner, "Denazification in the British Zone," 262–65.

4

Denazifying Bremen

1945: The American Denazification

PURGING A CONQUERED NATION'S society of its harmful political elements is not an easy mission for the victors even under the best of circumstances. This complicated task was exacerbated in Bremen by the changing administrative control between the United States and Great Britain. Because it was located entirely within the British Occupation Zone, the Americans and the British attempted to pass off responsibility for Bremen to each other during the first two years of military government. The administration and denazification of the U.S. enclave in Bremen was clearly an afterthought for military government planners in the United States and the United Kingdom. Required as a port for the U.S. Zone of Occupation in the south of Germany, the American enclave in Bremen had to contend with the fact that it owed its existence to necessity.

Although British forces initially occupied the city, the U.S. 29th Infantry Division established a military government in April 1945. For the first eight months, Bremen's Military Government operated according to American directives and instructions; during a second phase, beginning in December 1945 and lasting throughout 1946, the same military government enforced British rules. A third phase began on 1 January 1947, when American policies once again applied and the enclave became the fourth state in the U.S. Zone of Occupation. Under the circumstances, Bremen became a field for experimentation by both the United Kingdom and the United States, with each using different approaches to denazifying the city's population and re-creating its civil administration. As a result of the changes in approach, Bremen's denazification program and re-creation of democratic institutions lagged a year behind other states in the U.S. Zone.

The three distinct chronological phases in the administrative development of the enclave also had a profound impact on denazification. In sequence, the Americans, then the British, and finally the Americans again, determined the legislation for the implementation of denazification. Considering the different philosophies of an American dictum of a radical purge of the population and the less ambitious British goal of cleansing the administration, the U.S. denazification teams in Bremen had the difficult task of finding solutions to problems inherent in finding, removing, and replacing employees as well as those arising from the contentious relationship between the two powers. The unique, insular geographical setting of the Bremen enclave exacerbated the work of the Special Branch and later the Denazification Division. The changing territorial boundaries, unclear administrative relationships, and disputed venues for individual cases inevitably led to disillusionment among the American and German denazification personnel. The implementation of denazification in the Bremen enclave, though similar to that of the American Zone, was unique because of strong British influence, especially during the second year of the occupation.

A Short History of Bremen

In September 1944, president Franklin D. Roosevelt and prime minister Winston Churchill reached a compromise that designated the port city of Bremen, and areas immediately adjacent, as an American enclave in the eventual British occupational area that would serve as a supply port for the U.S. occupational area in the south of Germany. The North German port city of Bremen had a long history of struggle for independence within the larger political community, stretching back to the time of Charlemagne in the eighth century. First established as a bishopric, it grew steadily as a trading center due in large part to its harbor at the mouth of the river Weser. In 1358, it joined the Hanseatic League, a powerful free trade federation of northern European cities, and soon its merchants became wealthy enough to challenge the bishop for control of the city. Their efforts to gain independence from the church and the right to govern themselves continued for another three centuries. By the end of the Thirty Years' War in 1648, they had gained the status of a free city, answerable only to the emperor of the Holy Roman Empire. Bremen retained its independence until 1871, when it became a Free Hanseatic City with a standing equivalent to that of a federal state within the newly founded German Reich. Twenty years earlier, in the wake of the revolution of 1848, Bremen gave property-owning male citizens the right to vote for the city council called Bürgerschaft, which in turn elected a government, or Senat, with a mayor, or *Bürgermeister*, as its president.[1]

Bremen was the last state with a democratically elected government in Hitler's Germany. In the elections in November 1930, the National Socialist German Workers' Party (NSDAP) in Bremen had gained 32 of the 120 seats in the Bürgerschaft. In the next two years, the party tried to overthrow the Senat in three unsuccessful votes of no confidence. Finally, Bremen's Nazis had to enlist Berlin's help because they knew that their chances to take the Senat by democratic means were as slight as winning the elections. Bremen's Senat only ceded its independence to the Nazi government in March 1933. Although it remained nominally independent, from then on a Nazi-appointed governor ruled the city.[2]

During the Third Reich, Bremen was one of the centers of the German armaments industry. Situated on both banks of the Weser River close to where it empties into the North Sea, Bremen was Germany's second-largest port after Hamburg and one of its most important industrial cities. Its shipyards, aircraft, and automobile factories were essential to the war economy. The Deschimag-Weser AG and Atlas yards in the northwestern part of the city along the Weser River, and the Bremer Vulkan yards in the suburb of Vegesack, produced more than one-third of Nazi Germany's submarine fleet. The Focke-Wulf aircraft works, with its three plants in and around Bremen, supplied the German Luftwaffe with various types of bombers, fighters, and reconnaissance planes. The Borgward automobile factories in Bremen's eastern suburbs of Hastedt and Sebaldsbrück produced tanks, trucks, tractors, and torpedoes for the Wehrmacht. Other war industries in Bremen included the Lloyd-Dynamo electrical engines plant in Hemelingen, the Norddeutsche Hütte steel factory, the Deschimag subsidiary Weser Flugzeugbau aircraft works, and the Vacuum Öl and Korff Öl refineries.

As a center of Nazi war production, Bremen became one of the prime targets for Allied bombardments. From 1940 on, the city sustained extensive damage to its residential housing, infrastructure, and industries in 173 Allied air raids. To protect its citizenry, Bremen's authorities built more than 130 bomb shelters, most of them aboveground, multileveled bunkers that could accommodate nearly two hundred thousand people or about half of the city's prewar population of 445,000. By April 1945, nearly 60 percent of Bremen's houses were reduced to rubble and up to 90 percent of its harbor infrastructure was destroyed. Among Bremen's war dead were four thousand residents who perished in Allied bombing raids.[3]

Surrender and First Steps

With Bremen designated as a U.S. enclave on British territory, the Supreme Headquarters, Allied Expeditionary Force directed the British 21st Army Group under the command of Field Marshal Bernard L. Montgomery to secure the area and later turn it over to U.S. forces. The U.S. Ninth Army was responsible for organizing the enclave's occupation force, designated as Task Force Bremen. The task force commander was also the Enclave Military District commander. In addition to the task force of one infantry division with supporting troops, the Ninth Army set up an Air Task Force Bremen of one bomber group. The navy provided Naval Task Force 126 for the port area and the harbors. The 378th Infantry of the U.S. 95th Division under the command of Major General Harry L. Twaddle made up the bulk of the task force. It was supported by, among others, tank and tank destroyer battalions; ordnance disposal squads, depot companies, and maintenance companies; medical collecting, ambulance, and clearing companies; an evacuation hospital and a medical depot; quartermaster truck, railhead, and service companies; a United Nations Relief and Rehabilitation Administration (UNRRA) detachment; and Lieutenant Colonel Bion C. Welker's U.S. Military Government Detachment E2C2. Welker's group was the first of a total of six that moved into the counties of Osterholz, Wesermünde, and Wesermarsch by the end of June. In addition, army engineer troops were assigned to the enclave to perform all general engineering work, rehabilitate roads, and construct semipermanent bridges across the Weser, Hunte, and Hamm rivers.[4]

At the end of March 1945, the 21st Army Group advanced very rapidly through Holland and Northwest Germany. With the Canadian First Army on the left and the British Second Army on the right, Montgomery's forces reached the vicinity south of Bremen on 1 April. Here the field marshal ordered his army group to split up, leaving Lieutenant General Miles C. Dempsey's Second Army with the task of taking Bremen. The Second Army's XII and VIII corps received orders to outflank the city, while Lieutenant General Brian Horrocks's XXX Corps led the assault. With four divisions, the British 3rd and 52nd (Lowland) Divisions and the 51st (Highland) and 43rd (Wessex) Divisions, the XXX Corps began attacking Bremen's southern suburbs on 11 April.

Meanwhile, in Bremen, Paul Wegener, Nazi Party *Gauleiter* (a regional leader of the Nazi Party) of Gau Weser-Ems and governor of the city, and Max Schümann, Bremen's Nazi Party Kreisleiter (district leader) decided to carry out their Führer's order and defend the city to the end. Mayor Richard Duckwitz and his powerless administration wanted to surrender the city without a fight, but Wegener ordered them to support Schümann's efforts to set up the Volkssturm (German militia composed of men who were either too young, too old, or physically unfit for regular military service) and construct roadblocks. Bremen's military defense was in the hands of garrison commander Generalmajor Werner Siber and veteran combat commander Generalleutnant Fritz Becker. Their forces of nearly 4,800 were a disparate mixture of soldiers, policemen, and civilians from Wehrmacht units, Waffen SS, flak (antiaircraft defense), and Volkssturm. To hinder the Allies' advance on the city, Generalmajor Siber ordered the flooding of a seven-mile strip of land south of Bremen stretching from the village of Dreye to the Bremen-Delmenhorst railway.[5]

The bitter fighting in and around Bremen ended on 26 April when the city's garrison surrendered. By that time, the British prisoner of war cage held more than 2,700 German soldiers. In Bremen's rubble-strewn streets, German civilians joined thousands of released slave laborers and displaced persons mostly from Russia, Poland, and Ukraine in looting food and liquor stores, clothing warehouses, factories, and freight trains. Fighting, rape, and murder, particularly among the Russians and Poles, forced British combat troops to intervene. They succeeded in restoring order quickly.[6] When U.S. occupation troops arrived, they found the public safety situation in Bremen stable. To ensure continued safety and stability, they ordered 50 of approximately 250 police officers, who were present in the city, to report for temporary day patrol duty. The other police officers were moved to a local prisoner of war cage until their files could be vetted. Except for some instances of looting by displaced persons, public order and security prevailed in Bremen. Seven two-man Provost Marshal patrol teams equipped with radios and armored cars provided security during the day, and two operated at night. The Germans were under stand-still orders that prohibited them from leaving their homes. That rule was relaxed the following day when women were allowed to leave their houses between ten and eleven o'clock in the morning and again between three and four o'clock in the afternoon.[7]

Reconstituting Civil Administrations

The British forces also took the first steps toward re-creating a functioning civil administration in Bremen. They removed the Nazi-appointed governor and replaced him with the "conspicuously cooperative" police president, Generalmajor Johannes Schroers, who became Reigning Lord Mayor.[8] Lieutenant Colonel Welker's military government detachment administered critical services in heavily damaged urban areas of Bremen and Wesermünde before turning its attention to civil administration. Only four days later, on 30 April 1945, Welker ordered Schroers's removal and internment because he had been a leading member of the elite Nazi Schutzstaffel (SS). Erich Vagts, the chair of the ultraconservative German National People's Party (DNVP) and former Senator for Health, became Schroers's successor. Vagts had been a member of Bremen's Bürgerschaft since 1928 and had held his *senatorial* post from March until September 1933. He impressed Welker with his "senatorial stature" and seeming administrative experience. During his mandatory Counterintelligence Corps (CIC) interview, he also convinced the investigators of his own political reliability and that of his key cabinet officials or *Senatoren*: "Insofar as positions are vacant and the dismissed people are to be replaced, my first consideration will always be their technical and administrative qualifications. As far as their political qualifications are concerned, my first concern will be that they have not had any connections with the Nazis."[9] A few days later, Dr. Walter Dorn, deputy military governor general Lucius D. Clay's advisor on the denazification program, arrived in Bremen to assist Welker with the establishment of a city government. Dorn, who was a professor at New York's Columbia University in civilian life, immediately called Welker's choice of mayor into question. While Vagts had not been a member of the NSDAP because the Nazis turned down his application for membership, deeming him politically unreliable, he had collaborated with the Nazi regime. In 1935, the Nazis even appointed him Bremen's representative with the Reich government, a post he held until 1945.[10] Dorn's objections notwithstanding, Welker continued to support Vagts and even endowed him with more extensive powers than his position of mayor would normally have entailed.[11]

In the first week of May, an advanced team, under the command of Major Raymond M. Davis, formed Detachment G1C2 in Wesermünde.[12] The unit found the Wesermünde city administration functioning under the leadership of Dr. Walter Delius, who was arrested by the CIC and interned. After initially replacing Delius with an unsuitable candidate, Davis appointed Dr. Helmuth Koch mayor. Like Vagts, Koch was a member of the DNVP. He began his civil service career in 1922 and had advanced to the position of office director when the Nazis removed him in 1937. Gerhard Van Heukelum, the leader of the Social Democratic Party of Germany (SPD) before 1933 and editor of its newspaper, became Koch's deputy. Both received orders to establish a new city administration.[13]

While the military government detachment concentrated on reconstituting a civil administration, elements of the 95th began to move into Bremen. On 7 May, however, the division received orders from 12th Army Group to leave the enclave and redeploy to the Pacific Theater of Operations instead. The 29th U.S. Infantry Division, the Blue and Grey, under the command of Major General Charles H. Gerhardt began relieving the units of the 95th immediately. In the middle of May, the British Second Army turned the Enclave Military

District over to the 29th. General Gerhardt was now the commanding officer of Task Force Bremen and of the Enclave Military District. At the same time, U.S. Army Major General Harry B. Vaughan assumed command of Bremen Port Command (BPC), which was in charge of rebuilding and operating the city's port and its facilities.[14]

The district included the state of Bremen and the counties Osterholz, Wesermarsch, and Wesermünde. The biggest cities were Bremen, population 289,000 (prewar 445,000); Wesermünde, population 72,000 (prewar 110,000); Nordenham, population 24,000 (prewar 20,000); and Brake, population 14,000 (prewar 10,000). The district also encompassed 173 villages with populations ranging from five to six thousand. Much of the area was rural, with a considerable part of the land under cultivation. Farmers used the remainder of the land as pasture for large herds of dairy and beef cattle. The division did not foresee food shortage for the winter months.[15]

Bremen and Wesermünde had sustained heavy damage from air bombardments. The resulting housing shortages explained the shift of populations from the cities into the rural areas. In the cities people lived in overcrowded and inadequate shelters. Those who could not find any other housing occupied barns or built shacks out of salvage material they found in the rubble. The division expected they would experience "considerable discomfort" in their unheated dwellings during the wintertime. While public health and medical care were adequate in most areas of the enclave, the military government was concerned about the heavy damage to the sewage system in Bremen. The city's water and power supply was interrupted. The city used to receive most of its water from a water main leading from the Harz Mountains to Bremen. This line had been interrupted in October 1944. In the meantime, two supply lines leading over the Kaiser Wilhelm and Adolf Hitler (later renamed Franklin Roosevelt) bridges supplied the city. These were destroyed by Nazi troops when the Allies approached. As a result, Bremen's citizens were without electricity and had to rely on wells. Repairs to the power plant and restoration of the water supply resumed at the beginning of May. The rural villages for the most part did not have sewage systems, received most of their drinking water from wells, and had poor sanitation. This did not present a problem, however, because they had never had indoor plumbing and were resistant to possible pollutants in their water.[16]

The 29th Division divided the territory into four sectors, one for each regiment and one for the Division Artillery. The 116th Infantry was assigned the area around Bremerhaven and Wesermünde and the 115th Bremen-Vegesack. The 175th occupied the area between the 115th and 116th, east of the Weser River. Division Artillery controlled the territory west of the river. The companies and batteries quartered in requisitioned German houses. The division headquarters moved after a short stay in Bremen to Flak Kaserne, a large, undamaged antiaircraft school in Grohn, ten miles northwest of Bremen. The Blue and Grey troops guarded the headquarters building and key installations, patrolled by motor. In each battalion one company or battery was an alert mobile reserve, ready to move quickly on call to any area within the enclave if the need for military force should arise. The 29th also established a perimeter guard around the enclave to control entry and exit from the area. Division Artillery set up watch posts and patrols along the Jadebusen and the North Sea coast to prevent the entry or departure of vessels at any point other than Bremerhaven, which was controlled by Naval Task Force 126.[17]

The Purge Begins

As was the case in the other occupation zones in Germany, the denazification program began in Bremen with the arrival of Allied troops on 27 April 1945. At the time, the military government estimated that the city employed approximately six thousand civil servants and four thousand other employees. It also counted another two thousand employees who were on the payroll but had not yet returned from service in the Wehrmacht. The actual number of civil servants was about 3,900 and other salaried employees around 4,900.[18] Lieutenant Colonel Welker decided on a procedure that assigned responsibility for the implementation of denazification to the officers in charge of local government and administrative functions. Vagts, as head of Bremen's civil administration, transmitted the military government's order to the heads of the different departments. They had to register all officials and pensioners who had joined the Nazi Party before 1 April 1933 and remove objectionable officials. The Labor Office then registered all removed personnel. Vagts demanded that these measures be implemented regardless of whether or not the person had already filled out a Fragebogen (or questionnaire), the military government's primary instrument for vetting personnel. The detachment's functional officers located and met with their German counterparts and supervised removal of Nazis and militarists from their sections.[19] Detachment G1C2 followed the same procedure in Wesermünde.[20]

The first Fragebogen consisted of twenty-three questions that dealt mainly with vital statistics. Within a few months, however, this old-type questionnaire proved wholly inadequate because it allowed some party members to evade the screening process.[21] In response, the military government issued a new type of Fragebogen at the end of August. It consisted of 131 questions, with more than half devoted to political activities and memberships of any kind. Introduction of the "tapeworm," as the Germans quickly dubbed the new questionnaire because of its length, meant that all previously screened persons had to be rescreened.[22] From June until August, the 29th Infantry Division's Counterintelligence Branch (CIB) processed the Fragebogen of approximately 22,000 persons and dismissed or barred more than 2,400 of them from employment. The Special Branch of the Public Safety Branch acted as the office of record for the Fragebogen of civil servants. The 29th CIB also vetted persons applying to the military government to replace dismissed officials during this period.[23]

On 4 July, the 29th Division received orders from Seventh Army, which had taken over from Ninth Army in the middle of June, to conduct local raids throughout the area from time to time. The division's G-3 operations officer requested modification of the directive for Bremen's circumstances. He instructed the liaison officer at Seventh Army to explain that implementation of that order presented particular problems for Bremen. Not only were there two other elements, the navy and BPC, in the enclave, but also the 29th had additional CIC forces attached to screen the area. The operations officer was concerned that these raids would interrupt work on naval and BPC priority projects. He further elaborated that the demand for labor in Bremen was so great and the availability so small that every able citizen was screened to determine if he could work as a laborer. The ones that CIC found to be suspicious were interned immediately. The G-3 also mentioned that the 29th Division's Reconnaissance Troop had already conducted raids similar to those required by the Seventh Army in areas that CIC had not screened completely. In reply, the Seventh Army G-3 objected to making modifications because the screening of personnel would not find hidden weapons caches or transmitters. Consequently, troops from the 29th carried out spot checks without detecting any violations.[24]

On 21 July, the forces of the 29th participated in a U.S. Zone–wide forty-eight-hour check and search operation code-named TALLYHO. Their objectives were to check the credentials of all civilian or military persons in the enclave, to search all premises and individuals for prohibited articles, such as firearms and stolen U.S. government property, and to search for evidence of black marketeering. Staged in secret, the operation began at 4:30 in the morning. Three hours later, the 116th Infantry reported that they had picked up one girl with a fifty-gallon gas canister that she claimed to have received from the Red Cross. At the end of the operation, the 29th Division had checked 364,192 persons and made 1,212 arrests. Confiscated contraband included ninety-four gallons of gas, two military vehicle tires, British and American GI clothing, GI foodstuff, some small arms, some Nazi propaganda material, and eleven radio transmitters.[25]

When Major John W. Boyd and First Lieutenant Jesse S. Morse, the first especially trained denazification officers, arrived in Bremen during the last week of July, Special Branch assumed responsibility for the vetting and evaluating of the Fragebogen, searching records, and investigating persons. At that time, the CIB established and maintained a Bremen Document Center that served as a repository for filed Fragebogen, Nazi Party records, and information collected by CIC.[26] To support Special Branch's expanded mission, Major Boyd began almost immediately to select politically untainted Germans for a training program in the Office of Strategic Services School in Bad Orb. At the school, Germans trained to become evaluators, record-searchers, and investigators. The first five people completed their course on 21 August 1945. Forty-eight-year-old master tool and die maker Heinrich Kröplin was a typical example of the "reliable" Germans Major Boyd selected. A World War I veteran who had served in the German navy, Kröplin became a member of the SPD in 1918. In 1924, he also joined the *Reichsbanner Schwarz-Rot-Gold* (Reich Flag Black-Red-Gold), a paramilitary group closely linked to the SPD, set up to defend the Weimar Republic against radical right-wing organizations seeking to destroy it. His first altercation with the law occurred that same year and resulted in a fine for harassment during a strike. When the Nazis came to power, he lost his job and his party. In 1934, the Gestapo arrested him for trying to organize an illegal political group, and the following year he was sentenced to twelve months' imprisonment for attempted high treason. Kröplin attended one of the last courses in Bad Orb and graduated as an evaluator on 3 October 1945. All in all, the school trained thirty-eight citizens of Bremen.[27]

Kaisen Succeeds Vagts

When Dorn was unable to convince Welker to dismiss Vagts as mayor, he extended his stay and began contacting politicians who had served in the Bremen legislature before the Nazis took control of the city. The two most important were Social Democrat Wilhelm Kaisen and Conservative Theodor Spitta; they had both participated in anti-Nazi political activities during the Hitler years.[28] Kaisen had led the SPD caucus in the 1920s in Bremen's Bürgerschaft (state parliament). Earning his living as editor of his party's newspaper, he had served as Senator for Welfare from 1928 until 1933. When the Nazis came to power, he was forced to resign his office and to withdraw from public life. Kaisen survived the Nazi dictatorship as a subsistence farmer in Borgfeld, a suburb of Bremen.[29] Spitta, a member of the moderately conservative German Democratic Party (DP), was a lawyer who specialized in constitutional law. First elected to a seat in the Bürgerschaft in 1905, he served on several law and order committees. In 1919, he became a state *senator* and a year later the deputy mayor of Bremen. A year later, he helped write Bremen's new constitution. Forced to retire in 1933, he survived the Third Reich on his state pension.[30] Dorn successfully "invited and urged" both politicians to assume responsibility in the new city government. He also convinced two independent candidates, three Liberals, three Social Democrats, and two Communists, who were the leaders of the antifascist movement in Bremen, to join the newly appointed Senate on 6 June 1945.[31]

Over the course of July 1945, the CIC investigated alleged shielding of Nazis by Vagts. When the background investigations proved the Nazi Party affiliations of five individuals, Dorn replaced them with his own choices.[32] In the process, Vagts became a liability to Welker. On 1 August 1945, the detachment commander finally agreed to replace him with Kaisen. At the same time, he appointed Spitta as deputy mayor. In a Senate session two days later, Kaisen explained the circumstances leading to Vagts's dismissal and announced that the title of Reigning Lord Mayor, a creation of the Nazis, had been abolished and that he would instead hold the traditional title of mayor and president of the Senate. Kaisen went on to govern Bremen in this capacity for the next twenty years.[33]

The Denazification Machinery Grows . . .

In August the number of dismissed city employees in Bremen had grown to 1,873, of whom about 328 were civil servants. In Wesermünde, 866 officials and employees had been dismissed. Of these, 269 worked for the city administration and 295 for state and Reich agencies.[34] With the numbers continuing to increase rapidly, Kaisen, Bremen's newly appointed mayor, pleaded with the military government to give them a chance to appeal their cases. To provide an institutional framework, he suggested the establishment of German appeal boards (*Berufungsausschuß*) and American review boards.[35] The military government concurred and instructed him to establish the boards.[36] By the middle of October, one main committee and eight subcommittees began their work. The Senate had worked out an elaborate appeal procedure, designed to channel appeals from applicants through the senatorial personnel office, to the appropriate subcommittee and finally the main committee. The final decision about an appeal remained the prerogative of the newly established Military Government Review Board.[37] Officials in Wesermünde had to wait until the end of November 1945 for an opportunity to appeal their dismissals. In the meantime, they directed their applications for reinstatement to the headquarters of the local G1C2 detachment, swamping it in the process.[38] On 17 December 1945, Mayor Koch directed the establishment of five review boards that were equivalent to Bremen's appeal boards.[39]

The German appeal and review boards served two purposes. Beyond providing citizens who felt they had been treated unfairly with an opportunity to make their case, they also became a mechanism for Bremen's authorities to reinstate them. While not intended as such, the military government did not force an end to the practice. It recognized the great difficulty in finding suitable replacements for positions in the administration, courts, and schools because of the need for highly trained experts and professionals. In other areas, such as fire departments, prisons, and also public health services, replacements requiring less formal training and education were easier to find.[40]

Military Government Law No. 8

The introduction of Military Government Law No. 8 on 25 September extended the denazification program to the enclave's entire economy. Employees with any Nazi affiliations were prohibited from holding positions of responsibility. They could only be employed as common laborers. For medical doctors or other specialists with skills that were nearly impossible to replace, managers could apply to the military government for a temporary and revocable retention authorization. To prove they had complied with the law, employers had to prepare and submit to the local Labor Office personnel rosters of employees other than those employed in ordinary labor that were retained or removed, together with a statement about their Nazi affiliation. The first roster was due on 20 October. Initially, similar reports were due on the tenth day of subsequent months, but the practice was soon discontinued. If employers failed to comply, they became criminally liable. Anticipating that a large percentage of those removed from their jobs would want to appeal their cases, the law contained provisions for the establishment of review boards (*Prüfungsausschuß*). Again, the final decision in all cases rested with a Military Government Review Board of three officers. Authorities in Bremen and Wesermünde began establishing the new boards at the same time. In Bremen the main committee had forty-five members—sixteen representing employers, another sixteen employees, six representing the legal professions, and seven medical doctors.[41]

Initially, German anxiety that the strict application of Law No. 8 would paralyze the economic life proved unfounded.[42] More worrisome for the enclave was the lack of coordination in American and British denazification procedures. Differences became even more pronounced because of the close proximity of the two approaches. In a number of instances, officials who had been dismissed according to American standards were actually promoted in Hamburg and Oldenburg to such positions as headmasters. Persons dismissed from managerial positions in Bremen were allowed to assume similar positions in British occupied territory.[43] Other problems of coordination between the Allies resulted from the peculiar geography of the Bremen enclave. Since regional authorities had overlapping administrative boundaries, question of venue arose repeatedly. Compounding an already complicated situation were semipublic institutions such as the Northwest German Power Corporation that had its headquarters and part of its jurisdiction outside the enclave. When a number of engineers and other employees were dismissed in Bremen, the British Military Government summoned those not domiciled at Bremen to Stade, near Hamburg. There, the former employees were "fragebogened by the British according to their standards," and all were reinstated.[44]

The difficulties associated with the denazification of Northwest German Power Corporation employees were symptomatic of the problems the enclave's administrative organs faced on a daily basis. Wesermünde's detachment bore the brunt of it. Originally consisting of three separate administrative entities, Wesermünde was a postwar artificial construct of the Allies with unclear administrative channels and venues:

> Stadtkreis [city] Wesermünde includes the borough of Bremerhaven (not to be confused with the port of Bremerhaven). The borough of Bremerhaven formerly belonged to the Land [state] Bremen, but was incorporated into the community of Wesermünde under the Nazi government; it is now being called Wesermünde-Mitte. The other boroughs constituting the community of Wesermünde are Geestemünde and Lehe, the latter previously belonging to Hannover.[45]

The boroughs formerly belonging to Hanover were cut off from their traditional administrative channels and lacked new ones to replace them. German administrators were confused about who was in charge of vital areas such as rationing, payment of labor, and economic control.[46] To complicate the situation further, the acting superior president of the Province of Hanover, who operated under British supervision, maintained that all communities outside the port area remained "Hanover communal unions" in the Province of Hanover. He interpreted this to mean that only his office could issue orders to agencies located in Wesermünde. He even went so far as to refuse to acknowledge the Americans' right to govern Bremen as an enclave in the British Zone. In his opinion, American interests in Bremen should be confined to usage of the port, which did not necessitate control over administrative issues.[47] These circumstances rendered city agencies in Wesermünde virtually without any higher echelons.[48] The need for a reorganization of administrative control in the enclave was very apparent. As a result, the Allied Control Council in Berlin established a combined U.S.-UK committee on 30 July 1945 and charged it with determining and recommending the proper structure for the administrative control of the Bremen enclave.[49]

By the end of October, the general outlines of the committee's proposal to turn the administration of the enclave over to British control had become public knowledge. Many people in the enclave looked forward to the takeover with great hopes, not least because of the wide notoriety of cases of employees who were dismissed by the Americans in Bremen one day and hired by the British outside of Bremen the next. As a result, Special Branch noted it received fewer questionnaires than in previous months and that the number of appeals had also dropped. The officers attributed the change to the reluctance on the part of many businessmen to file their Fragebogen or to appeal their cases based on the assumption that the British denazification was less harsh.[50] The officers also hinted that the appeal and review board procedures were somewhat affected by the anticipation of a change of policy due to the British taking over the enclave. While the boards still evaluated questionnaires, they seemed to withhold decisions, pending future policies.[51] By the end of 1945, the military government summed up its observations about the German boards. It stated that the boards initially commenced their work very conscientiously but then tended to relax into the practice of allowing appeals in a most liberal manner. The effect had been that the military government had to review and decide a large majority of the cases. The military government concluded there was no doubt that the German boards reacted to great uncertainty surrounding the fate of Law No. 8 under British policy and the general opinion that the law itself is too stringent.[52]

Handover to British Rule

On 10 December 1945, General Clay and British deputy military governor Sir Brian Robertson signed an "Agreement of Military Government Responsibility in the Bremen Enclave," to take effect at the beginning of 1946. It redrew the borders of the enclave and placed it under British administration. During the negotiations, the committee discovered that, strictly speaking, Bremerhaven was just a small, uninhabited dock area and the city of Wesermünde had only served as a staging area for the port. With the approval of the council, the committee decided to include the city of Wesermünde as part of the territory remaining under U.S. control.[53]

> (a) The administration of military government in the Enclave less Bremen and Bremerhaven will be turned over to the British Zone Commander.
>
> (b) The United States Military Government teams at Bremen and Bremerhaven, as well as British military government teams to be stationed in the Enclave, will follow the policy instructions issued by the British military government authorities, subject to the condition that if the team receives instructions from the British which interfere with the carrying out of the effective operation of the BPC, or interfere with area security, all military government teams may and, upon the request of the U.S. Sub-District Commander, will suspend action on such instructions.[54]

Within the enclave, the agreement assigned responsibility for security and the military government to the commanding general, BPC. Consequently, BPC established a G-5 section to be able to deal with civil affairs. This process was finished in early January 1946, when the new section assumed control over the Bremen and Wesermünde detachments.[55] This arrangement only lasted until 15 April 1946, when BPC was dissolved and Colonel Welker became commander of a newly created Office of Military Government for Bremen Enclave (U.S.).[56]

Initially, the officers of the Bremen Detachment looked forward to a "new era" that promised changes in the administrative setup of the enclave. Their hope was that the new arrangement with the British would remedy the three difficulties created by the original boundaries and the distribution of responsibility in the enclave:

1. Lack of unified command for the Enclave.
2. Lack of awareness by some higher echelons that the Enclave existed.
3. Necessity of constant coordination with British forces and German civilian agencies.[57]

The first of these points, in particular, led to a slew of interrelated problems for the military government in the enclave. Since general officers commanded both BPC as well as the 29th Infantry Division, the military government was already at a disadvantage because it was under the command of a lieutenant colonel. More importantly, BPC had priority on practically everything, including material, labor, and housing, because it provided the reason for the existence of the enclave. Next in line for distribution of resources was the 29th Division, which had to ensure "comfort and welfare" for its fifteen thousand officers and men. The military government received the goods and services it needed from what remained after the other commands had taken their share. This circumstance complicated the implementation of the military government's mission significantly because housing shortages and lack of materials slowed down the rebuilding of industry for civilian production. To prevent this kind of competition and to ensure the military government's control over resources in the U.S. Zone, General Clay had insisted on separating military government from tactical commands.[58]

General Clay's order to increase food rations for Germans in December 1945 was an illustration of the lack of awareness at the deputy military governor's headquarters of the situation in Bremen. Since his directive lacked assignment of provisions for the enclave, exasperated E2C2 detachment officers became frustrated over the time and energy they would have to expend in negotiations with the British Military Government and German civilian authorities. Bremen was not included in food exchanges and other arrangements for the U.S. Zone, reducing the enclave to a "beggar" for food, labor, power, fuel—practically everything—in the British Zone.[59]

1946: The British Denazification

"The New Era": British Rule and Police-Style Occupation

At the end of 1945, rumors about American plans to surrender Bremen entirely to British control persisted throughout the city. The citizens of Bremen characterized the last months before the changeover of military government from American to British rule as a "period of pressures."[60] On 2 January 1946, the enclave experienced the full impact of its new circumstances. A conference between American and British Military Government representatives scheduled for that day was cancelled. Instead, the British merely informed their American counterparts that decisions affecting the reorganization of the former Reich administrations in Bremen had "already been arrived at" and that the conference would not serve a useful purpose. The new British order altered the old system of controls for the State Economics Office (*Landeswirtschaftsamt*, now renamed *Wirtschaftsamt*), the Finance Office (*Oberfinanzpräsidium*, now *Finanzamt*), and the State Labor Office (*Landesarbeitsamt*, now *Hauptarbeitsamt*).[61] In effect, the changes imposed by the British restricted the venue of these offices and in many cases placed them under control of the Hanover provincial government. This led to considerable confusion, not only among German administrators, but also among American Military Government personnel. An example of this was an order to transfer all revenues collected by Bremen's Finance Office to Hanover's Finance Office, which would then return funds for occupation costs to Bremen. An American finance officer expressed his section's strong skepticism about this new procedure:

> If the British are willing to agree that they will pay all expenses of the port operation, meeting promptly without question all demands for funds from Bremen Port Command, then they are more than welcome to the funds collected here. Otherwise it is obvious that to conduct an efficient port operation adequate funds must be available, without the necessity of persuading someone in Hannover or any other place that money should be provided for that expense.[62]

As a consequence, Bremen's Finance Section ignored Berlin's orders to comply with the new regulation. By September 1946, it still had not transferred revenues to Hanover.[63]

While Bremen's Military Government grappled with adjustments to British rules, the soldiers of the 29th Division prepared to return to the United States. The redeployment of combat forces from the European Theater, which had begun immediately after cessation of hostilities, accelerated during the fall after Japan's surrender and reached its peak in the spring of 1946 with twenty to thirty thousand leaving per week. Troop levels fell quickly from a high of over 1.6 million when the Germans surrendered to approximately 1.1 million at the end of the year. Meanwhile, the security situation remained stable throughout. As in the U.S. Zone, except for cases of pilferage and other crimes, Bremen's population "conducted itself admirably," leading the U.S. War Department to consider even lower troop levels for the occupation. To make up for the loss of occupation forces, the army began to establish a district constabulary in November 1945. The training included disciplinary matters and physical conditioning, weapons qualifications, riot control, street and house fighting, and specialized instruction in military government ordinances, laws, and directives. The constabulary also received instruction in the examination of documents, sabotage devices, raids, searches, and arrests. In the process, the 311th Infantry, a reinforced regimental combat team of the 78th Infantry Division, replaced the 29th Division in February, and one of its companies reorganized as a Cavalry Reconnaissance Troop (Mechanized) to serve as the District Constabulary. When the 29th Infantry relieved the 311th in June, the District Constabulary was discontinued.[64]

British-Style Denazification

Processing appeals under Law No. 8 and other denazification directives continued in the first half of 1946. American and British military government officers had agreed on this procedure in a series of preparatory conferences in December 1945. Dated 14 December 1945, the terms of the agreement specified that persons who had been denazified, to mean dismissed, under American standards, including Law No. 8, prior to 10 December, would be considered unemployable by the British throughout the entire Hanover region; that British standards were to apply on all Fragebogen submitted for vetting after 10 December; that persons subject to Law No. 8 at any time before 10 December would be dealt with according to its terms, whether their rosters had been filed or not; and, finally, that Law No. 8 should not apply to persons commencing business or assuming supervisory positions after 10 December.[65]

Persons dismissed from their positions in trade and industry and civil administration continued to file appeals in increasing numbers. In the period from November 1945 until March 1946, the German review and appeal boards received more than 7,600 appeals, of which 3,500 had been filed in

British tanks and infantry cleaning up resistance in Bremen on 25 April 1945. Office of War Information, RG 208, NARA.

In Bremen, the military government group for the city of Bremen discussing plans for the care, housing, and feeding of the people of the city. From left to right are Major Joseph Shanel, Lieutenant Colonel Douglas Meservey, Lieutenant Colonel Bion C. Welker, Major M. S. Haguwood, and Lieutenant Paul Roche. 26 April 1945. U.S. Army Signal Corps, RG 111, NARA.

Twin spires of the cathedral in Bremen, Germany, were painted green as camouflage against aerial bombardment. 1 May 1945. U.S. Army Signal Corps, RG 111, NARA.

Repair docks in the port of Bremen, Germany, are undamaged. 1 May 1945. U.S. Army Signal Corps, RG 111, NARA.

Aerial view of Bremen, Germany, on 9 July 1945. U.S. Army Signal Corps, RG 111, NARA.

Only the foundations of buildings were left after the Allies rained ten-ton bombs on this section of Bremen. 9 July 1945. U.S. Army Signal Corps, RG 111, NARA.

The Adolf Hitler Brücke in Bremen after Allied bombardment. 9 July 1945. U.S. Army Signal Corps, RG 111, NARA.

Major General Charles H. Gerhardt, commanding general 29th Infantry Division, taken in Bremen, Germany, in June 1945. U.S. Army Signal Corps, RG 111, NARA.

Soldiers of the 29th Infantry Division stand guard on the docks of Bremerhaven. The date is 4 June 1945. U.S. Army Signal Corps, RG 111, NARA.

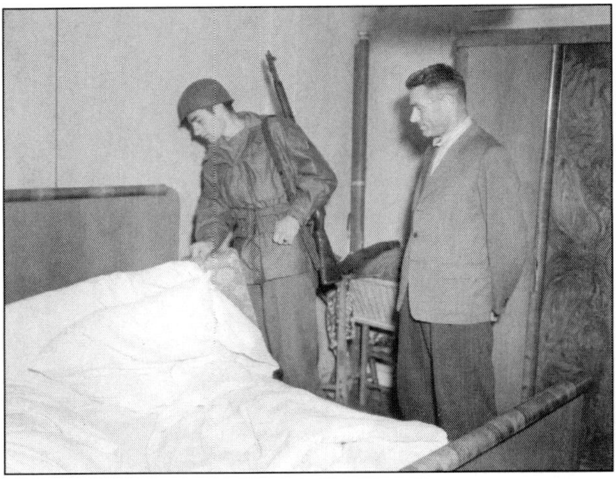

Operation "TALLYHO." All German civilians living in the Bremen area were told to evacuate their homes by U.S. soldiers who knocked on their doors at three o'clock in the morning on 21 July 1945. The soldiers made a comprehensive search of all homes and checked identity papers. The troops were also looking for firearms, knives, displaced persons, AWOL GIs, and stocks of GI food and clothing being used for black market purposes. Here a soldier searches a mattress for hidden weapons while the owner watches. U.S. Army Signal Corps, RG 111, NARA.

Nazi, arrested for refusing to allow Americans to search his home, is escorted to a jeep during a surprise "TALLYHO" operation. This particular phase of the inspection for unauthorized items in possession of German civilians is in Bremen, Germany. 21 November 1945. U.S. Army Signal Corps, RG 111, NARA.

Operation "TALLYHO." In the Bremen phase of the surprise search for unauthorized items, Sergeant Koski of Cleveland, Ohio, and Private Ernest T. Roberts of Seminole, Oklahoma, ex. right, check identity papers of Germans. 21 November 1945. U.S. Army Signal Corps, RG 111, NARA.

Private Roberts checks a bookcase for banned publications during "TALLYHO." 21 November 1945. U.S. Army Signal Corps, RG 111, NARA.

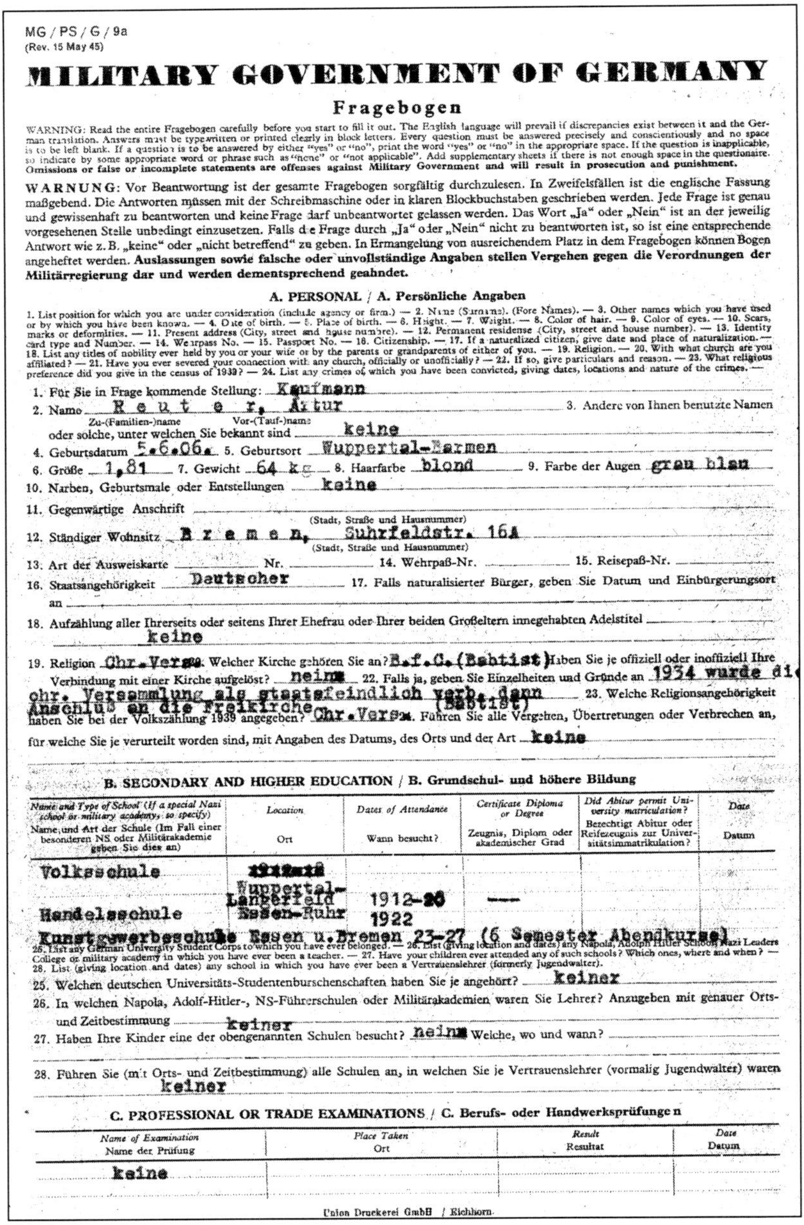

MG / PS / G / 9a
(Rev. 15 May 45)

MILITARY GOVERNMENT OF GERMANY

Fragebogen

WARNING: Read the entire Fragebogen carefully before you start to fill it out. The English language will prevail if discrepancies exist between it and the German translation. Answers must be typewritten or printed clearly in block letters. Every question must be answered precisely and conscientiously and no space is to be left blank. If a question is to be answered by either "yes" or "no", print the word "yes" or "no" in the appropriate space. If the question is inapplicable, so indicate by some appropriate word or phrase such as "none" or "not applicable". Add supplementary sheets if there is not enough space in the questionaire. **Omissions or false or incomplete statements are offenses against Military Government and will result in prosecution and punishment.**

WARNUNG: Vor Beantwortung ist der gesamte Fragebogen sorgfältig durchzulesen. In Zweifelsfällen ist die englische Fassung maßgebend. Die Antworten müssen mit der Schreibmaschine oder in klaren Blockbuchstaben geschrieben werden. Jede Frage ist genau und gewissenhaft zu beantworten und keine Frage darf unbeantwortet gelassen werden. Das Wort „Ja" oder „Nein" ist an der jeweilig vorgesehenen Stelle unbedingt einzusetzen. Falls die Frage durch „Ja" oder „Nein" nicht zu beantworten ist, so ist eine entsprechende Antwort wie z. B. „keine" oder „nicht betreffend" zu geben. In Ermangelung von ausreichendem Platz in dem Fragebogen können Bogen angeheftet werden. **Auslassungen sowie falsche oder unvollständige Angaben stellen Vergehen gegen die Verordnungen der Militärregierung dar und werden dementsprechend geahndet.**

A. PERSONAL / A. Persönliche Angaben

1. List position for which you are under consideration (include agency or firm.) — 2. Name (Surname). (Fore Names). — 3. Other names which you have used or by which you have been known. — 4. Date of birth. — 5. Place of birth. — 6. Height. — 7. Weight. — 8. Color of hair. — 9. Color of eyes. — 10. Scars, marks or deformities. — 11. Present address (City, street and house numbre). — 12. Permanent residense (City, street and house number). — 13. Identity card type and Number. — 14. Wearpass No. — 15. Passport No. — 16. Citizenship. — 17. If a naturalized citizen, give date and place of naturalization. — 18. List any titles of nobility ever held by you or your wife or by the parents or grandparents of either of you. — 19. Religion. — 20. With what church are you affiliated? — 21. Have you ever severed your connection with any church, officially or unofficially? — 22. If so, give particulars and reason. — 23. What religious preference did you give in the census of 1939? — 24. List any crimes of which you have been convicted, giving dates, locations and nature of the crimes. —

1. Für Sie in Frage kommende Stellung: Kaufmann
2. Name Reuter, Artur (Zu-(Familien-)name, Vor-(Tauf-)name) 3. Andere von Ihnen benutzte Namen oder solche, unter welchen Sie bekannt sind keine
4. Geburtsdatum 5.6.06. 5. Geburtsort Wuppertal-Barmen
6. Größe 1,81 7. Gewicht 64 kg 8. Haarfarbe blond 9. Farbe der Augen grau blau
10. Narben, Geburtsmale oder Entstellungen keine
11. Gegenwärtige Anschrift (Stadt, Straße und Hausnummer)
12. Ständiger Wohnsitz Bremen, Suhrfeldstr. 16A (Stadt, Straße und Hausnummer)
13. Art der Ausweiskarte Nr. 14. Wehrpaß-Nr. 15. Reisepaß-Nr.
16. Staatsangehörigkeit Deutscher 17. Falls naturalisierter Bürger, geben Sie Datum und Einbürgerungsort an
18. Aufzählung aller Ihrerseits oder seitens Ihrer Ehefrau oder Ihrer beiden Großeltern innegehabten Adelstitel keine
19. Religion Chr. Vers. 20. Welcher Kirche gehören Sie an? B.f.C. (Babtist) 21. Haben Sie je offiziell oder inoffiziell Ihre Verbindung mit einer Kirche aufgelöst? nein 22. Falls ja, geben Sie Einzelheiten und Gründe an 1934 wurde die chr. Versammlung als staatsfeindlich verb. dann Anschluß an die Freikirche (Babtist) 23. Welche Religionsangehörigkeit haben Sie bei der Volkszählung 1939 angegeben? Chr. Vers. 24. Führen Sie alle Vergehen, Übertretungen oder Verbrechen an, für welche Sie je verurteilt worden sind, mit Angaben des Datums, des Orts und der Art keine

B. SECONDARY AND HIGHER EDUCATION / B. Grundschul- und höhere Bildung

Name and Type of School (If a special Nazi school or military academy, so specify) Name und Art der Schule (Im Fall einer besonderen NS oder Militärakademie geben Sie dies an)	*Location* Ort	*Dates of Attendance* Wann besucht?	*Certificate Diploma or Degree* Zeugnis, Diplom oder akademischer Grad	*Did Abitur permit University matriculation?* Berechtigt Abitur oder Reifezeugnis zur Universitätsimmatrikulation?	*Date* Datum
Volksschule	Wuppertal-Langerfeld	1912-20	—		
Handelsschule	Essen-Ruhr	1922			
Kunstgewerbeschule Essen u. Bremen 23-27 (6 Semester Abendkurse)					

25. List any German University Student Corps to which you have ever belonged. — 26. List (giving location and dates) any Napola, Adolph Hitler School, Nazi Leaders College or military academy in which you have ever been a teacher. — 27. Have your children ever attended any of such schools? Which ones, where and when? — 28. List (giving location and dates) any school in which you have ever been a Vertrauenslehrer (formerly Jugendwalter).

25. Welchen deutschen Universitäts-Studentenburschenschaften haben Sie je angehört? keiner
26. In welchen Napola, Adolf-Hitler-, NS-Führerschulen oder Militärakademien waren Sie Lehrer? Anzugeben mit genauer Orts- und Zeitbestimmung keiner
27. Haben Ihre Kinder eine der obengenannten Schulen besucht? nein Welche, wo und wann?
28. Führen Sie (mit Orts- und Zeitbestimmung) alle Schulen an, in welchen Sie je Vertrauenslehrer (vormalig Jugendwalter) waren keiner

C. PROFESSIONAL OR TRADE EXAMINATIONS / C. Berufs- oder Handwerksprüfungen

Name of Examination Name der Prüfung	*Place Taken* Ort	*Result* Resultat	*Date* Datum
keine			

Union Druckerei GmbH / Eichhorn

The German population soon nicknamed the Military Government questionnaire the *Bandwurm* (tapeworm) because of its length and the way it continued when turned over. The bottom of the first page lined up with the top of the flip side. Only the first two pages are shown. Fragebogen Artur Reuter, 31 Aug 1945, Records of the Office of Military Government, Bremen, Records of the Denazification Division, Box 157, RG 260, NARA.

D. CHRONOLOGICALRECORD OF FULL TIME EMPLOYMENT AND MILITARY SERVICE

29. Give a chronological history of your employment and military service beginning with 1st of January 1931, accounting for all promotions or demotions, transfers, periods of unemployment, attendance at educational institutions (other than those covered in Section B) or training schools and full-time service with para military organizations. (Part time employment is to be recorded in Section F.) Use a separate line for each change in your position or rank or to indicate periods of unemployment or attendance at training schools or transfers from one military or para military organization to another.

D. Chronologische Aufzählung jeglicher Hauptanstellungen und des Militärdienstes

29. Geben Sie in zeitlicher Folge eine Aufzählung Ihrer Beschäftigung und Ihres Militärdienstes seit dem 1. Januar 1931 an, mit Begründungen für alle Beförderungen oder Degradierungen, Versetzungen, Arbeitslosigkeit, Besuch von Bildungsanstalten (außer solchen, die bereits in B angeführt sind) oder Ausbildungsschulen, und Volldienst in militärähnlichen Organisationen (Nebenbeschäftigungen sind in Abschnitt F anzugeben). Benutzen Sie eine gesonderte Zeile für jeden Wechsel in Stellung oder Rang, oder zur Angabe von Arbeitslosigkeits-Zeitabschnitten, oder für den Besuch von Ausbildungsschulen oder für Versetzungen von einer militärischen oder militärähnlichen Organisation zu einer anderen.

From Von	*To* Bis	*Employer and Address or Military Unit* Arbeitgeber und Anschrift oder Militäranschrift	*Name and Title of Immediate Superior or C. O.* Name und Titel des Dienstvorgesetzten od. vorgesetzter Offz.	*Position or Rank* Stellung oder Dienstgrad	*Duties and Responsibilities* Art der Tätigkeit und Verantwortungsbereich	*Reasons for change of Status or Cessation of Service* Grund für Änderung oder Beendigung des Dienstverhältnisses
1931	40	Fa. A Klingeberg, Bremen	Inh. Scheffler	Abt. Leiter		Einberufung
1940	- März40	Landesschützenlehrg. Greifswald -P	Obl. Meyer	Flieger	Ausbildung	
1940 März	42 Jan.	Lds. Schützenzug 52/XI Bremen	Hptm.Michaelsen	Gefr.	Schreiber	
1942	42 März	Ausb. Abt. Ütersen Holstein	unbek.	Gefr.	Uffz. Lehrgang	
1942	42 Sept	Flugh.Ber.12/XI Delmenhorst	Oberst Angelroth	Uffz. Anw. Uffz.	Schreiber	
1942	42 Okt.	Erg.Fl.Horst Afrika, Foggia	Kdtr. unbek.	Uffz.	Kammer	
1942 Okt.	44	O.B.Süd und Lftfl.Kdo.2 Taormina/Sizilien Frascati/Rom	Obstltn. Dietrich	Uffz.	Zeichner u. Schreiber	
1944 Febr.	44 Sept.	Fl.Ers. Btl.17 Freiburg	Oberst Weise Kdt. von Flgpl.Leipheim	Uffz.	allg. Pers.	
1944 Sept	45 April	SS Wachkomp. Augsburg	Hptm. Hennelotter	Uschaf.	Wachposten	
		1945 März-April Revier-Lazarett-Revier-Aufenthalt in Dachau				
45 April	Ende	Kampfkdt. Scharnitz Tir.	unbek.	Uffz.	Meldefahrer	

30. Were you deferred from Military Service? — 31. If so, explain circumstances completely. — 32. Have you ever been a member of the General Staff Corps? — 33. When? — 34. Have you ever been a Nazi Military Leadership Officer? — 35. When and in what unit? — 36. Did you serve as part of the Military Government or Wehrkreis administration in any country occupied by Germany including Austria and Sudetenland? — 37. If so, give particulars of offices held, duties performed, location and period of service. — 38. Do you have any military orders or other military honors? — 39. If so, state what was awarded you the date, reasons and occasion for its bestowal.

30. Waren Sie vom Militärdienst zurückgestellt? nein 31. Falls ja, geben Sie die genauen Umstände an ______ 32. Waren Sie Generalstäbler? ______

33. Wann? ______ 34. Waren Sie NS-Führungsoffizier? nein 35. Wann und in welchem Truppenverband? ______

36. Haben Sie in der Militärregierung oder Wehrkreisverwaltung irgendeines der von Deutschland besetzten Länder, einschließlich Österreich und Sudetenland, gedient? nein 37. Falls ja, geben Sie Einzelheiten über Ihre Ämter und Pflichten, sowie Ort und Zeitdauer des Dienstes ______

38. Sind Sie berechtigt, militärische Orden oder andere militärische Ehrenauszeichnungen zu tragen? nein 39. Falls ja, geben Sie an, was Ihnen verliehen wurde, das Datum, den Grund und Anlaß für die Verleihung ______

Page 2 of the *Bandwurm*.

Much of the German civilian population in Bremen is still kept busy clearing the streets of bombing rubble. 15 January 1946. U.S. Army Signal Corps, RG 111, NARA.

The main market in Bremen, Germany, where crowds of Germans begin to gather at dawn for their rations and remain until meats and vegetables are entirely gone. 29 June 1946. U.S. Army Signal Corps, RG 111, NARA.

A German housewife in Bremen, Germany, is buying her weekly ration of meat, for which she must furnish her own wrapping paper. Meat lines are not as common in Bremen, as those for fruits and vegetables, because most of the housewives have no meat points. 29 June 1946. U.S. Army Signal Corps, RG 111, NARA.

At the butter and bread stand in Bremen, Germany, housewives pay close attention to the amount of butter on the scales and also to the smaller amounts of cheese. Each person receives seven pounds of bread a week and 150 grams of butter per month. 29 June 1946. U.S. Army Signal Corps, RG 111, NARA.

A German housewife in Bremen, Germany, prepares a typical German meal after waiting in line all day for her rations. 29 June 1946. U.S. Army Signal Corps, RG 111, NARA.

The new Senate for the city of Bremen, Germany. It was reconstituted after the election of 12 October 1947. In the front row, in uniform, is Captain Charles R. Jeffs, deputy director of OMG Bremen. To his left are Bürgermeister Wilhelm Kaisen, president of the Senate, and Thomas F. Dunn, director of OMG Bremen. He is the man wearing glasses. U.S. Army Signal Corps, RG 111, NARA.

Bremen's *Schullandheime.* Annual FHMG in Land Bremen, January to December 1948, Appendix 21, Records of the Public Information Office, Functional Histories of Military Government in Bremen. Apr. 1945 to Mar. 1948, Box 76, RG 260, NARA.

the last days before the 28 February deadline for appeals under Law No. 8. In order to deal with the increase, Bremen's administration organized additional review boards in January 1946 to deal with cases of civil service employees and firms with more than 250 employees or capital of more than one million reichsmarks. The new boards tried to handle as many of their cases as possible based exclusively on the written records. Their method for avoiding time-consuming hearings was to allow appellants to submit exonerating evidence such as affidavits of politically untainted persons in support of their appeals.[66] To increase the speed and efficiency of processing cases, the boards published appellants' names in the *Weser-Kurier*, the local German newspaper, requesting the public to contact them with information on the people under review.[67] While two-thirds of the responses were positive, the military government investigated the denunciations and shared the results with the boards. Publicizing the names in the newspaper proved so useful in assisting the boards' decision making that they not only continued the practice but later also used radio broadcasts for this purpose.[68]

At the end of March, Bremen's appeal boards had ruled on more than 2,200 cases of dismissed civil servants and nearly 1,200 other city employees. Their decisions generally favored the appellants. Only 521 civil servants lost their jobs. At the same time, the number of salaried employees rose by 382, which, taken together, amounted to a loss of 1.6 percent of the city's labor force. The boards in Wesermünde heard 790 cases of which they found 404, or 51 percent, worthy of employment.[69]

While the old boards worked on the appeals submitted under American rules, in the middle of January 1946 the British Military Government issued Zone Policy Instruction No. 3 (ZPI 3) containing new denazification regulations designed to hand partial responsibility for the program to the German people.[70] It took nearly half a year, however, before the new policy went into effect in Bremen because the city had to set up the new administrative structures necessary for its implementation.

In their own zone, the British preferred a different, more directive approach to Germany's democratization than the Americans. Instead of allowing the citizens to vote in the first free elections of municipal governments, similar to those held in the U.S. Zone beginning in January, the British Military Government preferred appointed administrations, so-called Nominated Representative Councils. Bremen's Office of Military Government (OMG) appointed such a council, which retained the traditional name *Bürgerschaft*, in April. The sixty-member legislature allotted twenty-seven seats to the SPD, twenty-one to the DP, nine to the Communist Party, and three to independent candidates.[71] In the same month, the military government also appointed forty members to establish a Nominated Representative Council for the city of

Wesermünde. In it, all political parties as well as spokespersons for labor, professions, trade, and industry were represented. The Wesermünde council held its first session on 16 April and appointed two commissions, the first charged with appointing city officials and preparing a new city constitution. The city council completed these tasks in June, and on 1 July the military government approved the new city constitution.[72]

With the administrative bodies in place, British and American Military Government officers embarked on a series of conferences to establish a Standing Operating Procedure for the denazification of the civil government and trade and industry in the enclave.[73] According to the procedure, all business owners, agency or office directors, supervisors, and persons in positions that gave them access to information control or dissemination had to fill out a *Fragebogen* and a supplement with questions about the reasons for submittal—application for employment; continued employment; or application for a telephone membership in Nazi intelligence-gathering organizations—and about past dismissals under any Allied Military Government rules. If a military unit employed a person, the supervising officer would submit both documents to Special Branch for vetting. The denazification of all personnel not working for the military became the responsibility of a *Bürgerschaft*-appointed German Denazification Panel. To assist in collecting, examining, assessing, and recommending courses of action, the panel would in turn appoint German Denazification Committees. The committees would submit the *Fragebogen* to the panel. This method gave the panel an opportunity to examine the Fragebogen and make its own recommendation on a panel Action Sheet, which it attached to each Fragebogen, before forwarding it to the Special Branch for decision. This procedure had the advantage that persons who would, in accordance with directives, be in the "Mandatory Removal" category because they had held offices in the NSDAP or its affiliated organizations, but who were known to be no more than nominal Nazis, could be classified as "Nominal Nazis" and retained. On the other hand, a person who would not fall under a "Mandatory Removal" category but had proven by his actions to be more than a nominal Nazi could be recommended for dismissal on the Action Sheet.[74] Based on the documents, the Special Branch would then determine whether a person belonged in the mandatory or discretionary removal category; could be retained; or even deserved preferential treatment due to evidence of anti-Nazi activities.[75] To deal with the expected appeals, the *Bürgerschaft* established German review boards with a German lawyer as chair and four additional members. Similar to the committees, the boards had the right to make recommendations and submit them to the Military Government Review Board Branch for final decisions.[76]

On 1 June 1946, the Bürgerschaft appointed Friedrich Aevermann (SPD), Willi Ewert (SPD), August Hitzfeld (no party affiliation), Carl Katz (SPD), Adolf Peters (Communist Party of Germany [KPD]), Hermann Prüser (KPD), Heinrich Possitt (SPD), Oskar Schulze (SPD), and Walter Stoever (no party affiliation) as members of the German Denazification Panel. Among the nine were two representatives of employee associations, two self-employed, one business owner, one dockworker, and three civil servants. Aevermann became the panel's chairman. A veteran of World War I, he was a teacher by training who lost his position when the Nazis came to power. In 1945, the U.S. Military Government appointed him Bremen's school superintendent.[77]

By 31 August 1946, the number of German Denazification Committees had grown to sixty-one, and the Special Branch was satisfied with their work.[78] The number of German review boards also grew due to the volume of appeals. In setting up the boards, Bremen's *Bürgerschaft* developed a habit of having members of a professional group review the cases of their peers so that dentists would judge other dentists, and lawyers would judge other lawyers. When it became apparent, however, that some of the boards tended to be too lenient in their judgment of professional colleagues, the Military Government Review Board issued special instructions on the composition of future boards. These had to be formed from "professionally mixed groups."[79] The military government also received reports of bribery and corruption in the panel office. A CIC investigation revealed that a German official allowed two employees to misuse information submitted to the office for their own criminal purposes. The two were arrested and sentenced in the military government court.[80]

Changes in Military Government and First Elections

The military government in Bremen also underwent organizational changes. On 20 September 1946, Lieutenant Colonel Gordon Browning succeeded Welker, who had stayed on in civilian capacity after his retirement from active service. When Browning, a former governor of Tennessee, returned to the United States in December, Thomas F. Dunn became his successor. Dunn transferred from the War Shipping Administration on 11 December 1946, to assume his position as director of the military government in Bremen. In January 1947, Captain Charles R. Jeffs, U.S. Navy, filled the theretofore vacant position of deputy director.[81]

Along with the changes in leadership in fall 1946, the Special Branch absorbed the personnel and functions of the Investigation Section, the Public Safety Branch, and the review board in an effort to save manpower and to avoid duplication of effort. In the process, the Special Branch established a new German Denazification Section in charge of supervising the German

Denazification Panel, committees, and review boards. Henry J. Oberlander, the former chief of the review board, became its first chief in Bremen. Walter V. Burrows, formerly the administrative assistant to the review board, transferred to lead Wesermünde's German Denazification Section. Captain Jesse S. Morse remained chief of the Special Branch, Bremen enclave.[82]

Bremen's municipal government changed as well. On 13 October, the city held its first free election since 1933. It proceeded according to the British modified individual candidate system that gave every eligible citizen—former Nazi Party members excluded—two votes. The first vote elected candidates in sixteen electoral districts directly for sixty of the council's eighty seats. The second determined the political parties' proportional share of the remaining twenty seats. The parties usually chose their candidates from reserve lists that their leadership had assembled earlier. The result was a landslide victory for the SPD with a fifty-one-seat majority. The following month, the Bürgerschaft decided on the distribution of functional committees or departments. Ten would be permanent, and three others, among them a Committee on Denazification, were designated as special. At the end of November, the council formally elected members of the senate to head the various committees. Kaisen remained head of the administration as president of the Senate and became Senator for Police and Interior Administration.[83]

In his acceptance speech, Kaisen elaborated on the program for his administration. His foremost concern was the recovery of the economy that, according to him, was dependent on massive infusions of materiel and investments from foreign countries. He also pointed out that Bremen had delivered more than its share of reparations and urged the Allies to stop the dismantling of factories "if every hope of finding a way out of our misery is not to be killed."[84] As an essential part of rebuilding Bremen into a democratic society, Kaisen mentioned denazification. Commenting on the noticeable difference in interest that the victors and vanquished had in the program, he quipped that, according to the military government, denazification could be finished in Bremen inside of six months while "German branches speak of six years."[85]

Rethinking the "New Era"

Ever since the beginning of the "new era," there was evidence that the American Military Government officers habitually acted on either American or British directives depending on the situation. Compounding the confusion was Bremen's unclear status especially when compared to that of the newly created states in the U.S. Zone. Kaisen commented to the Bürgerschaft that Bremen's position was certainly "very peculiar." In June 1946, when the British made no secret of their desire to make Bremen part of a proposed state of Lower

Saxony, the Anglo-American military governments began high-level discussions to determine the city's future.[86]

In the Bremen Detachment, opinions about British intentions varied widely. One view, expounded by Harold H. Crabill, director of the Civil Administration Division, argued that the United States had an obligation to defend Bremen's right to self-determination because of the American belief in freedom. Major Boyd, Internal Affairs and Communications Division, supported his opinion and added that safety in the enclave would be better served if Bremen were to return to American control entirely.[87] A different view, voiced by Robert W. Johnson, chief legal officer, argued that the creation of a state in the enclave would be inconsistent with agreements reached with France and the Soviet Union. In his view, Bremen had never ceased to be part of the Northwestern or British Zone:

> An incorporation of the Enclave into the American Zone as an integral part thereof would require not only UK and US consent, but French and USSR as well. And since it is geographically, administratively, sociologically and economically a part of the Northwestern Zone, its severance therefrom might well cause difficulties far greater than those already caused to Germany by the four present Zonal divisions.[88]

At the OMG (U.S.) headquarters, General Clay ordered Henry Parkman, director of the Civil Administration Division, to prepare a study on the enclave's future. Parkman soon left for Bremen to conduct interviews with members of the city's civil and military government leadership.[89] Welker and Kaisen agreed that Bremen had to remain under American control as a free city-state with direct representation on the Council of States of the U.S. Zone and on the soon-to-be-established Bizonal agencies. Parkman noted that Welker was "emphatic" in his opinion that Bremen should not be turned over to the British because he believed the British would build up Hamburg to the detriment of Bremen.[90] Parkman further reported that Kaisen shared Welker's assessment of British motives. The mayor pointed out to Parkman that "living under [a] split dual military government" had proved to be impossible. He strongly recommended that Bremen should be fully under the U.S. Military Government and should ultimately return to its status as an independent city-state with a direct relationship to a future central government.[91] U.S. Army Major Erwin W. Bard in the Civil Administration Division explained to Parkman that the outlines of British policy in the Bremen area were not clear but that the evidence suggested they intended to deflate Bremen's significance economically as a port and politically as a Land. He claimed that if the British gained control of Bremen they would surely eliminate its port as the only competition to Hamburg's port for overseas traffic to serve their own agenda. Bard's conclusion was that British control of Bremen would harm American interests in the long run.[92]

Summarizing his findings for General Clay, Parkman argued for American control of Bremen to preserve the port's importance for the German economy and, more importantly, to protect American interests in Europe: "I reached the conclusion that the proper solution is for the U.S. to resume full Military Government responsibility in the Enclave, with the eventual prospect of creating a new Land government for the area with certain additions and modifications."[93] In view of Parkman's assessment, General Clay and his British counterpart, General Robertson, decided it was essential to come to a timely and mutually satisfactory arrangement with regard to Bremen. They agreed that Parkman, who was already familiar with the situation in Bremen, should work with his British colleague Austin Albu, deputy president, Governmental Sub-Commission of the Control Council for Germany (British Element), to make recommendations for a solution. Following a fact-finding mission to Bremen, Parkman and Albu submitted their report. Their unanimous opinion was that the progressive development of German governmental institutions and the creation of states in the British Zone made a clarification of Bremen's status essential. They identified four major problem areas that needed to be addressed:

1. Territorial Boundaries. Land Bremen should consist of Stadt [city] Bremen, Land Gebiet [state area] Bremen and Stadtkreis [city] Wesermünde.
2. Economic Problem. Land Bremen should be represented on the bi-zonal committees equally with Hamburg. . . .
3. Political Problems.
   a. Bremen should provisionally have the full powers of a Land government.
   b. Bremen should be directly represented at the Zonal Advisory Council, but informal representation should be continued at the Laenderrat [Council of States].
4. Military Government Problems.
   a. An integrated staff is not desirable.
   b. The December 10 agreement should be reviewed.
   c. U.S. Military Government should operate under U.S. Military Government rules.
   d. It is not desirable to extend the area of jurisdiction of U.S. Military Government to include the intermediary ports on the Weser because of the problems of German civil administration involved.[94]

Clay and Robertson approved the findings and instructed Parkman and Albu to draft an agreement for the military governors to sign. Within Parkman's Civil Administration Division, however, his and Albu's recommendations were controversial. U.S. Army Colonel William Whipple was concerned that the United States would have to assume full responsibility for the economic supply of the state of Bremen in case "anything should happen" and the U.S.-UK Bizonal Economic Agencies should not materialize. He also feared that Bremen would naturally vote with the other North German states in the Council of States and that this would be detrimental to American interests. Whipple's particular concern was that the state governments in the U.S. Zone might become less compliant with the wishes of the U.S. military government as a result.[95] In response, Parkman agreed with some of Whipple's concerns but was on the whole more optimistic about Germany's economic and political unification. The principle, he believed, should be to let Germany act as Germany with elections reflecting the interests of the constituent units.[96]

On 5 November 1946, Bremen's OMG informed the newly elected senators that the city would become a state within the U.S. Zone very shortly. By the end of the month, however, the Allies had not taken any steps in that direction. Meanwhile, delegates from the other states in the British and American zones held meetings to prepare for the establishment of new Bizonal agencies for the impending merger of the two zones. Impatient to have the city's interests represented in these meetings, Kaisen pressed Dunn on the matter.[97] Despite the mayor's best efforts, however, Bremen's status remained unchanged for another two months.[98]

Bremen's Denazification Program at a Crossroads

In the second half of 1946, developments in Bremen's denazification policy were also critical. On 7 September 1946, the British Military Government issued Zone Policy Instruction No. 38 for the Disposal and Categorization of War Criminals, Nazis, and militarists. The instruction was designed to clear the way for thousands of internment camp inmates' discharge.[99] In light of Bremen's uncertain future status, officers from Special Branches, Bremen, and Hanover met and discussed whether this policy should be implemented in the city. At the conference, they compared the Law for Liberation from National Socialism and Militarism as implemented in the U.S. Zone[100] and ZPI No. 38. The law introduced five new and different categories of defendants instead of the previous two, nominal and active Nazis, and it instituted a system of tribunals that meted out sanctions keyed to offenses, instead of demanding permanent exclusion in every case. The categories were designed to distinguish between those who should be punished for their crimes, including major offenders and offenders, and those who should be rehabilitated, including lesser offenders, followers, and exonerated. The schedule of punishment included up to ten years of prison for major offenders; up to five years for offenders; fines up to ten thousand reichsmarks for lesser offenders; and fines up to ten thousand reichsmarks for followers. The American delegation criticized the British approach as too lenient. They found that the most egregious flaws of ZPI 38 were the lack of sanctions against lesser offenders in category III and the fact that only persons applying for supervisory positions would be subjected to denazification.[101] After careful study of the differences, the conference delegates decided not to implement ZPI No. 38 in Bremen until sanctions had been greatly revised.[102] In the end, American officers in Bremen judged ZPI No. 38 as too lenient—one even called it "the Law for Liberation of National Socialists"—but British Special Branch officers agreed, leading to the decision not to implement it at all.[103]

This decision left the Bremen enclave, as well as the British Zone, without an Amnesty for Youthful Ex-Nazis. Effective July 1946 in the U.S. Zone, the amnesty applied to youth born after 1 January 1919. British Military Government Headquarters released its own amnesty legislation on 17 October, when it ordered an "Exoneration of Youth born after 1 January 1919" to be implemented in Bremen and the rest of the British Zone. Since only persons applying for supervisory positions had to undergo denazification, this exoneration did not automatically apply to all persons born after 1 January 1919 but only to those appearing before the German Denazification Panel. As in the American Zone, those in Class I and II were not eligible to apply.[104] In January 1947, the British Military Government issued ZPI No. 54 based on Control Council Directive No. 38 of 12 October 1946, which basically embraced the principles of the Law for Liberation.[105] With negotiations about Bremen's status as a state within the American Zone still ongoing, the enclave did not adopt ZPI No. 54.[106]

Preparing for Another Change

Denazification panels, committees, and boards in Bremen increased their activities under ZPI No. 3 in the waning days of British control at the end of 1946. In the process, the military government and German officials took a close look at all agencies involved in denazification with a view to improving their work if possible. In a conference on 27 November 1946, Kaisen and Oberlander discussed the slow handling of appeals in Bremen. Kaisen was under the impression that the Special Branch was at fault, based on information he had received from the former chair of the Denazification Panel.[107] Oberlander retorted that progress and speed of appeals was entirely up to the

German Denazification Panel. Kaisen assured Oberlander that he would do everything in his power to assist the panel to expedite the appeals process. To this end, Kaisen declared he would put out an order to the effect that all Nazis, including those in the category of ordinary labor employed by the city, had to be removed from their positions as soon as replacements could be found.[108]

As it turned out, however, procedural mishandling, incompetence, and also obstruction were not the only reasons for the slow processing. Winter had set in suddenly, and the German Denazification Panel experienced an extraordinary shortage of coal hindering its work. In addition to the cold temperatures, the committees made only little progress because they lacked forms such as summaries, file cards, and opinion sheets.[109] Nonetheless, the Special Branch and German Denazification Panel made efforts to complete denazification as quickly as possible. To guarantee a thorough and speedy denazification, the panel established thirty-eight additional denazification committees in Bremen alone.[110] The panel itself also underwent a complete reorganization under its new chair, Georg Ziegler. He set up a system in which each of the twelve members had to supervise a department within the organization of the panel. Furthermore, each member was charged with supervising several denazification committees to ensure uniformity in the decision of the committees.[111] By the end of 1946, Bremen's boards, panels, and committees had vetted 81,304 persons since the occupation, and 17,232 persons had been dismissed from their positions.[112]

Before adoption of the Law for Liberation in March 1947, the backlog of appeals cases for Bremen amounted to four thousand. In conference, the Special Branch and the chairman of the German Denazification Panel established a priority list for handling appeals: "a. Persons born after 1 January 1919, falling under the terms of the Youth Amnesty; b. Persons with temporary retention pending appeal; c. Simple and clear appeal cases; and lastly, d. Complicated appeal cases."[113] Beginning in February 1947, provisions of the Christmas Amnesty of 24 December 1946 also applied in consideration of appeals.[114] This amnesty was an extension of the Youth Amnesty and applied to persons in low-income groups who were not chargeable as major offenders or offenders. To be eligible, a person's yearly income during the calendar years 1943 and 1945 could not exceed 3,600 reichsmarks and his taxable property had to be below 20,000 reichsmarks in 1945. Another group included under the Christmas Amnesty were those who were more than 50 percent disabled.[115] Soon it became apparent, however, that this provision lent itself to abuse by Germans eager to evade the denazification process altogether. Captain Morse, the new chief of the Denazification Division, alerted the German authorities to the creative ways numerous wealthy individuals employed to bring themselves within the provisions of the Christmas Amnesty. They paid medical doctors to certify that they were 50 percent or more disabled or rewarded health workers for supporting their claim that their advanced age, illness, or various chronic deficiencies made them eligible. To curtail this activity, Morse declared that only legally recognized disabled persons, receiving social insurance, pension, or public relief, were to be accepted.[116]

Augmenting the practice of the original appeal boards, names of appellants in the appeal procedure were announced every evening over Radio Bremen. At first, 120, and later 350, names were announced weekly. In response to this program, the military government received on average 150 letters weekly. The procedure proved to be so successful that the Office of Military Government of the United States (OMGUS) recommended it to all radio stations in the U.S. Zone.[117]

As useful as soliciting the public's help was, it had its pitfalls when it involved prominent citizens. The appeal case of Franz Stapelfeldt, the former chairman of the board of directors of the Deutsche Schiff- und Maschinenbau Aktiengesellschaft (Deschimag) Shipyard was an example. Stapelfeldt had been in the shipbuilding business since before World War I and presided over the Deschimag's expansion into one of the Nazi's premier warship, submarine, and plane producers. At the height of the war in 1943, the Deschimag employed nearly twenty thousand workers, among them approximately two thousand forced laborers and concentration camp inmates. As director of this important war industry, the Nazi regime bestowed on him the rank of *Wehrwirtschaftsführer*, or leader of the war economy, reporting directly to the Office of War Economy of the German Wehrmacht. While his position suggested he had been a major supporter of the Nazis, Stapelfeldt's contacts to a circle of conspirators led by Carl Goerdeler, the former mayor of Leipzig and a leader of the July 1944 conspiracy to kill Hitler, suggested otherwise. In May 1945, American forces arrested him and held him in an internment camp until February 1946.[118] When the Denazification Panel sought information about Stapelfeldt in special broadcasts of Radio Bremen and an announcement in the daily *Weser-Kurier*, it received nearly two hundred letters, with a majority in favor of the appellant. The result took the Special Branch by surprise because it had expected incriminating responses. When Stapelfeldt appeared before a special committee of the Denazification Panel on 18 February 1947, his appeal was approved by a vote of four to one. Prüser, a former dockworker, cast the only dissenting vote. He protested against Stapelfeldt's exoneration and declared that the panel obviously engaged in "whitewashing the past of various responsible and big Nazis." He resigned from the panel the following month.[119]

While lenient treatment of prominent citizens such as Stapelfeldt raised doubts about the fairness of the denazification program, the continuing

British practice of reemploying persons who had been dismissed from their positions by the American Military Government was even more damaging to its credibility. One such case involved Dr. Hans Herrmann, another former Deschimag director who had been a favorite in Albert Speer's armament ministry for his unscrupulous handling of slave workers. When the Americans dismissed Herrmann according to the provisions of Law No. 8, he left Bremen and settled in the British Zone. By November 1946, British authorities had rehabilitated him, and he found a leadership position in the firm Reinhausen Stahlbau, responsible for building all bridges in the British Zone. Special Branch chief Morse protested against the decision and pointed out that a case such as Herrmann's confirmed to many Germans that nobody takes denazification seriously. He warned that opinion polls indicated that the public believed "the big Nazis have been allowed to go free and obtain leading positions in the administration of the country, while the 'little man' is unduly punished."[120]

Complaints and warnings notwithstanding, the British Military Government continued to welcome Bremen's dismissed and demoted skilled workers and leadership personnel to rehabilitate them and to put them to work for the better part of 1947. Nearing the end of the year, the British and the American authorities finally established a set of ground rules regarding denazification cases involving concurrent jurisdiction and recognition of clearance. Both sides agreed to "(a) the fact that the provisions of Control Council Directive No. 24 are recognized namely that an individual who is mandatory in one occupation zone will be considered mandatory in all other zones, and (b) the fact that a prior denazification decision made in Bremen will not be reversed by British denazification tribunals without a consultation with OMG Bremen."[121]

Appeal Boards in Wesermünde

While Bremen's Military Government was satisfied with the German denazification efforts in general, it severely criticized the work of appeal boards in Bremerhaven. These boards, established in October 1945 according to the provisions of Law No. 8, reported to the mayor of then Wesermünde. The mayor in turn delegated his authority to Dr. Rosemary Ambrosius, an economist who likely possessed excellent English-language skills because she had lived for a while in New York City.[122] In the fall of 1946, Wesermünde's Special Branch grew increasingly impatient with the boards' performance because they approved over 85 percent of appeals cases. According to the American officers, many of the boards' members were "as incapable of denazifying as an out and out Nazi would have been." Ambrosius, the board's "organizing talent," drew Special

Branch's particular wrath. It faulted her for seeming to be "preoccupied with the procurement of temporary retention permits and legal loophole escapes for Nazis," instead of dismissing "these dubious elements."[123]

At the beginning of 1947, Special Branch's criticism of the Wesermünde appeal boards became even more scathing. It condemned their work as a travesty of denazification. As an illustration, the branch's officers pointed to the boards' record of finding over 90 percent of the cases involving "Mandatory Removal" categories to be no more than nominal Nazis. The officers also stated that there was evidence that members of the boards advised those whose appeals were rejected to withdraw their appeals and wait for a more favorable time to resubmit. To make matters worse, the appeal boards' inefficient methods of processing appeals created a huge backlog of cases that posed considerable problems for Special Branch.[124]

As a result of the military government's mounting criticism of the old appeals boards, on 10 January 1947 Wesermünde established a new denazification panel and subcommittees. Ernst Karstaedt, a former concentration camp prisoner, became the panel's new chairman. Under his leadership, approval of appeals dropped from 90 to 50 percent, and many cases approved by the old boards were retried and rejected. The panel and committees continued to function until 15 June 1947, when they were dissolved and their personnel and records became the nucleus for the newly created Office of the Senator for Political Liberation.[125]

1947: The Americans Again

Land Bremen

On 23 January 1947, the U.S. Military Governor General Joseph T. McNarney formally announced Bremen's statehood in Proclamation No. 3, which went into effect retroactively on 1 January 1947.[126] As a result, Bremen's days as a field for Anglo-American experimentation with different approaches for military government and denazification were over. For the U.S. occupation forces, however, major changes in their organization and training had just begun. With troop levels dropping rapidly through 1946, the army eliminated nonessential requirements that were drains on manpower. It sold surplus property in occupied and liberated countries rather than guarding it. It released prisoners of war as fast as it could process them. It returned captured enemy stocks to the German economy for civilian use, destroyed fortifications and military installations, closed clubs and recreational facilities that it deemed unessential to the occupation mission, and eliminated small, scattered installations and troop concentrations in order to reduce overhead and simplify logistics.[127]

In March, General Clay succeeded General McNarney as military governor and commander in chief. One of his first initiatives was to create separate headquarters for the U.S. tactical forces, called European Command, and for the OMG. Clay assigned Lieutenant General Clarence R. Huebner, his deputy and chief of staff, responsibility for the European Command.[128] By this time, approximately 120,000 U.S. troops in Germany and Austria were under Huebner's command. The U.S. 1st Infantry Division provided the main body of the occupation force and deployed its three regiments throughout the American Zone in garrisons of battalion and company size. The 16th Infantry sent one battalion to Berlin while the remainder of the regiment moved to the U.S. Zone in Austria. The 18th Infantry provided one battalion to the U.S. enclave that encompassed Bremen and Bremerhaven. The remainder moved to Frankfurt in October to become the honor guard for the European Theater's headquarters. The third regiment, 26th Infantry, moved to the state of Württemberg-Baden, while the Division Artillery transferred to Hesse. Under these circumstances, the division ceased all training.[129]

The new Land Bremen encompassed the city and its surrounding area, the harbor of Bremerhaven, and the town area of Wesermünde, which had been part of the state of Prussia. The following month, on 7 February, the city council of Wesermünde decided to rename the town "Bremerhaven" after the adjacent harbor.[130] Bremen's democratically elected administration continued as a state government until a new constitution could be ratified. Meanwhile, the enclave remained in place, and the United States reserved control of the harbor and all facets of the shipping industry. As a state within the U.S. Zone, the city attained direct representation in the Council of States while at the same time becoming informally affiliated with the Zonal Advisory Council for the states within the British Zone. It also became a member with full rights in all Bizonal agencies. The practical implication of the creation of Bizonal agencies and the Joint Export-Import Agency (JEIA) was that the military government relinquished control over traffic, economic issues, and finance as well as export-related matters.[131] After a prolonged period of legal and administrative uncertainty, Bremen entered the end phase of military government with stabilized borders, democratically elected governmental agencies, and a clear relationship with the occupying powers.

The new Land Bremen needed a constitution. To speed up the process, the director of Bremen's Military Government, Dunn, requested that OMGUS waive the requirement for an election of a constitutional assembly and instead accept Bremen's Bürgerschaft as a constitutional assembly. OMGUS approved and the council began drafting a new constitution.[132] Bremen's new status also brought changes for the military government. In April 1947, the Office of Military Government for Bremen Enclave was redesignated the Office of

Military Government for Bremen (OMG Bremen).[133] At the same time, the Bremerhaven Detachment became a Liaison and Security Detachment.[134]

From Guard to Protector

Following the merger of the Anglo-American zones in the beginning of 1947, deliberations began in London and Washington regarding rebuilding the economy. Meanwhile, the political relationship between the United States and the Soviet Union had deteriorated to a point of mutual mistrust over motives in treatment of Germany and policy toward Europe in general. In this charged atmosphere, George F. Kennan, an American diplomat stationed in Moscow, sent his now famous "Long Telegram" confirming suspicions about the Soviet Union's expansionist tendencies. Ensuing discussions in Washington caused a reorientation of American foreign policy from cooperation with to containment of the Soviet Union.[135] President Harry S. Truman and his administration realized that the threat the Soviet Union posed to Western Europe was as much economic as military. To counter and contain Soviet expansionism, the United States pursued a two-pronged policy of economic aid to European countries and military assistance to free nations that resisted communist takeover attempts. One of the first manifestations of the policy shift was the president's decision on 12 March 1947 to ask Congress for four hundred million dollars in military and economic assistance for Greece and Turkey. It established an approach later known as the Truman Doctrine that would guide U.S. diplomacy for the next forty years. The Cold War had begun in earnest.[136]

In Germany, financial experts began preparing for currency reform because the reichsmark had become completely devalued. Across the Atlantic, U.S. Secretary of State George C. Marshall convinced the U.S. Congress to allot funds for a Europe-wide recovery program. Marshall intended the program, which became known as the Marshall Plan, to be more than just seed money and goods donated by the United States. He wanted to foster European cooperation and create a system that would permanently link the national economies—make them interdependent.[137]

This profound shift in foreign policy increased already tense relations between the Western Allies and the Soviet Union to a point that the newly established European Command decided to reconstitute the U.S. Army in Europe as an effective tactical force. On 1 May 1947, General Huebner as commanding general, U.S. Ground and Service Forces in Europe, ordered the 26th Infantry to move to Grafenwöhr to prepare the area for use as a training center. He also wrote letters to the various post commanders, the commanding officers at the BPC, and the Berlin Military District announcing his intention to reassemble at the earliest possible moment the various scattered elements of the U.S. 1st Infantry Division. In effect, he was serving notice that the 1st Division was again a combat unit and that military posts where the division then served would have to find replacements to carry out the static missions it had thus far performed. Shortly thereafter, posts and agencies of the European Command began to eliminate jobs wherever possible, to make better use of German labor and to close out at the quickest possible rate the secondary missions that had grown up since the war. The 1st Battalion, 18th Infantry, withdrew from duty in Bremen in late summer. No combat unit remained now in Bremen. Instead, in case of an emergency, U.S. forces would reinforce the service troops there by passing through the British Zone to the mouth of the Weser River.[138]

The Law for Liberation Comes to Bremen

The beginning months of 1947 marked another period of transition in Bremen's denazification program. As in the first half of 1946, when review and appeal boards set up under American rules continued their work until British-mandated bodies were ready to take over, the existing denazification panels and committees carried on for nearly six months until the Bürgerschaft began setting up trial tribunals as required by the Law for Liberation from National Socialism and Militarism. With the denazification rules once again in flux, "cross-border" cases of postal workers were caught in the middle. The postal service or Reichspost, by its very nature, operated across the boundaries of the American and British zones, and many of its employees worked in Bremerhaven but lived outside of the city in the district or Landkreis Wesermünde in the British Zone. As residents of the British Zone, these postal employees submitted their Fragebogen to British authorities. The British evaluated the information according to their denazification policies and dismissed employees categorized as M (mandatory). If the workers appealed their cases successfully, the British reinstated them. Since the postal employees worked in the enclave, however, the American Military Government also investigated them and again demanded their dismissal from the postal service. The case of Ewald Friedhoff of Dorum, a fishing village about twenty-six miles northeast of Bremerhaven near Cuxhaven, was a typical example. The British dismissed him in July 1946 and reinstated him after his successful appeal in November. In spring 1947, the Americans reinvestigated him and again called for his dismissal. In May, the British officer in charge of postal and telegraph service in Lower Saxony intervened on Friedhoff's and the Reichspost's behalf and requested that Bremen's Military Government recognize British denazification certificates to avoid future complications.[139]

Meanwhile, Bremen's OMG and civil administration prepared during this transition period to write the legislation and to make the organizational changes necessary for implementing the law. Changes in the OMG concerned mainly the Special Branch but had ripple effects for other sections and branches involved in the denazification program. At the end of March 1947, the Special Branch became a Denazification Division reporting directly to the director. Captain Morse, who had led the old branch, stayed on as acting chief of the new division.[140] In other reorganizations, the military government's Operations Section became the new Special Branch, Stadt Bremen, with a branch office in Bremerhaven designated as Special Branch Bremerhaven, Liaison and Security Detachment. Further, Special Branch Bremen enclave's old Investigation Sections and Special Branch Office, Bremerhaven, were consolidated into a new Inspection Branch responsible for carrying out sanctions imposed by the law.[141]

While Bremen's OMG was in the midst of restructuring its offices to fit the pattern of the other military governments in the U.S. Zone, the Bürgerschaft sent Aevermann and his fellow panelists on fact-finding missions to Bavaria, Hesse, and Württemberg-Baden to learn from the southern states' experiences. As the legislators waited for the panel members to return before drafting Bremen's version of the Law for Liberation, anxiety about the changeover grew among Bremen's denazification officers. Their concerns were similar to those they had a year ago before British rules began to apply in Bremen. Since, in the fall of 1946, the officers noted a trend among citizens to delay filing their appeals until the more lenient British policies were in effect, in February 1947, they feared a run on the panel and committees before the policies ceased to apply. Oberlander, then chief of the Denazification Section, even believed that Germans residing in Land Bremen would flock to have themselves cleared by a denazification panel in the British Zone before the establishment of Spruchkammern in Land Bremen.[142] George Dehn, military government operations officer and future head of Special Branch for Stadt Bremen, agreed that a large percentage of those citizens who lived in Land Bremen but had business interests or jobs outside of the state could easily have themselves denazified under the more lenient British system and could not be touched by the more severe American system.[143] The British Military Government announcement to complete denazification by May 1947 lent special urgency to an early introduction of the Law for Liberation in Bremen.

Becoming increasingly impatient, on 25 February 1947, Captain Morse, Dehn, Oberlander, and other Special Branch officials met with the Bremen lawmakers. Morse urged the Bürgerschaft to pass the Law for Liberation as soon as possible with as few changes as possible because that would guarantee immediate approval by OMGUS.[144] When the council had not taken action nearly a month later, Dunn added his admonishment that the new state had the responsibility to make its basic laws conform to those enacted in the other states of the U.S. Zone of Occupation. Specifically, this entailed passing the Law for Liberation.[145] On 26 March, Bremen's Senat presented a draft of the Law for Liberation to the Denazification Division. The division reviewed and approved of the draft the following day.[146] After final approval by OMGUS, the Bremen Senat adopted the law on 9 May 1947.[147]

The implementation of the law required the creation of a host of new agencies. Responsibility for administration rested with the minister or in Bremen's case the Senator for Political Liberation, who would be appointed by the minister president or the president of the Senat, respectively. Discussions between military government officials and the president of the Senat about suitable candidates for this pivotal post began in early March. All agreed that impeccable credentials were a minimum requirement. When Kaisen mentioned Aevermann, however, Oberlander objected on the grounds that he was a poor organizer and had been generally unable to handle his job as chairman of the denazification panel. Oberlander also asserted that, as a result of Aevermann's inadequacy, the process of the denazification procedure had been set back by six months.[148] Notwithstanding the military government's doubts, the Bürgerschaft elected Aevermann as Senator for Political Liberation on 27 March 1947, since he had carried out much of the groundwork for adoption of the law.[149]

Creating the Instruments

The main bodies for the implementation of the Law for Liberation were trial tribunals or *Spruchkammern* and appellate tribunals. In the South German states each county established a *Spruchkammer.* Bremen and Bremerhaven planned to base the number of tribunals on the number of electoral districts.[150] Each *Spruchkammer* was comprised of a chairman, two to four lay assessors, and a public prosecutor assisted by a staff of investigators. The Senator for Political Liberation appointed the chairpersons of the *Spruchkammer* as well as public prosecutors. Bremen's political parties had the right to recommend their members as lay assessors for selection by the *Spruchkammer* chairs. Citizens could appeal their *Spruchkammer* decisions to appellate tribunals. Judicial experience was mandatory only for the persons chairing an appellate tribunal.[151]

A new *Meldebogen,* or registration form, replaced the *Fragebogen* as the primary instrument for vetting the population. Every person above the age of eighteen had to fill one out and submit it to a local police station or other administrative agency that served as collection offices for the public prosecutor. To ensure compliance, the city's government required citizens to show the receipt for a filed *Meldebogen* before it issued a new ration card.[152] The public prosecutor's office evaluated each *Meldebogen*, and based on the information tentatively assigned persons to one of five groups: Class I: major offender; Class II: offenders (activists, militarists, and profiteers); Class III: lesser offenders (probationers); Class IV: followers; and Class V: exonerated. Final classification rested with the *Spruchkammer* that would decide cases either through a hearing or based on written statements. Only persons falling within Class II and I required an obligatory hearing.[153] The same two classes were also excluded from provisions under Article 60 of the Law for Liberation that empowered the Senator for Political Liberation with the important right to grant temporary and revocable licenses for employment of persons in Class III who were considered essential personnel for maintaining public health or safety.[154] In theory, the role of the military government denazification agencies was supposed to be limited. Their orders were to cooperate in every possible manner with the German agencies and to exercise their right to supervise and to control only to the extent necessary to ensure proper administration of the law.[155] In practice, however, the Denazification Division and Special Branch offices devised bureaucratic instruments such as Delinquency and Error Reports to steer the German agencies to a stringent interpretation of the law.

In April 1947, Aevermann's first challenge in his new position was to procure approximately five tons of paper for the printing of the new *Meldebogen* and other forms necessary.[156] By the third week of June, his office had distributed approximately 356,000 *Meldebogen*, of which 96,000 had already been returned. The senator estimated that, at that time, about 70,000 persons were chargeable and about 285,000 not chargeable under the law. On 30 June, Aevermann published the first list of 1,006 persons not chargeable for the required eight days of public posting, before he issued certificates of nonincrimination.[157]

A far greater test for the senator was the recruitment of personnel to staff the *Spruchkammern*, his own office, and the position of public prosecutor. Shortly after the adoption of the law on 9 May, Bremerhaven's mayor rebuffed Aevermann's call for assistance in staffing his office with the explanation that the city personnel strength had been depleted through denazification so that it could not sacrifice any of the remaining personnel to fill in the vacant positions.[158] Despite this early setback, by the middle of June the senator had recruited enough personnel to operate four of the projected twelve *Spruchkammern* for Bremen, and two out of six for Bremerhaven. Commenting on his experiences with recruitment of personnel to the military government's Denazification Division, he pointed out that persons were generally willing to become judges or assessors for *Spruchkammern* but hesitated when asked to take the job of a public prosecutor. In the same report, Aevermann was pleased to announce that Karstaedt, former chair of the Denazification Panel in Bremerhaven, had agreed to become a public prosecutor.[159] By the beginning of July, personnel recruitment in Bremerhaven had increased.[160]

In Bremen, however, it still lagged behind expectations in the OMG. This situation prompted OMG director Dunn, at the end of the month, to vent his frustration about the new state's passive attitude with regard to denazification to Kaisen. He reminded the mayor that Article 56 of the law gave him authority to draft personnel if necessary "to arrange that suitable persons in sufficient numbers are available to fill positions as public prosecutors, chairmen of Tribunals and assessors." Dunn also left Kaisen in no doubt that he expected him to use it to ensure expeditious implementation.[161]

A month later, Joseph F. Napoli, the newly appointed chief of the Denazification Division, had similar discussions with Aevermann. After serving in the Army Intelligence Corps in North Africa and Italy, Napoli came to Berlin in early 1946, where he again worked as an intelligence officer. The following year, he accepted a position as a budget and fiscal officer in Bremen. In the beginning of August, Napoli became the head of the Denazification Division when Captain Morse, its old chief, returned to the United States.[162] Shortly before the opening of the first *Spruchkammer* trial in Bremen, Aevermann and Napoli disagreed strongly about the priority of cases to be tried and recruitment of suitable personnel for these trials. Napoli insisted on trying major offenders first. Aevermann declared it impossible because he could not recruit enough competent judges and prosecutors. To support his point, he referred to experiences in the southern German states that were just now beginning to try major offenders, eighteen months after they had adopted the law. Napoli remained adamant, however, and reminded Aevermann several times during their meeting that *Bürgermeister* Kaisen had the power to draft personnel if needed.[163] In the end, Napoli's viewpoint prevailed. Aevermann accepted the priority of Class I cases. On 28 August 1947, Dr. Selmar Seemann, a physician classified as a major offender, appeared before the first *Spruchkammer* procedure.[164]

Before the trial began, Dunn, Kaisen, and Aevermann attended an opening ceremony. Dr. Alexander Lifschütz, representing the group of tribunal judges, explained in an opening address how he understood the deeper sense of the Law for Liberation. According to his interpretation, the law's purpose was not only to liberate Bremen's citizens politically "but [also] to rectify the spirits of all guilty respondents by making them recognize that they had failed."[165] Seemann's *Spruchkammer* hearing then commenced with Dr. Arminius Lürmann as chair; Friedrich Buschmann, a German employee of the Denazification Division, as his deputy; Dr. Heinrich Borchers as public prosecutor; and

Dr. Pohl serving as defense counsel. During the daylong proceedings, the prosecution and defense called thirty-seven witnesses. Based on the evidence, the *Spruchkammer* assigned Seemann to Class III: lesser offenders, enabling him to reopen his medical practice. Sanctions against him included paying a fine of four thousand reichsmarks and serving a probation period of two years, during which he was barred from assuming a supervisory position. Buschmann was appalled about the outcome. Summarizing his impressions, he submitted a scornful report about the first trial to his employer. In it, he criticized the chairman for not controlling the proceedings sufficiently and blamed the result on the "entirely incompetent" public prosecutor for failing to cross-examine witnesses for the defense.[166]

Criticism of Aevermann Mounts

From the first *Spruchkammer* trial, the Denazification Division monitored the work of Senator Aevermann's office closely. Growing increasingly dissatisfied with the outcomes of proceedings and the slow pace in establishing new tribunals over the course of September, the division's chief aired his grievances about Aevermann in a report to the director of OMG Bremen in the beginning of October. Napoli began by stating that the senator's administrative incompetence had resulted in a painful slowdown in the progress of denazification in Bremen. To illustrate his point, Napoli compared the performance of Bremerhaven's three *Spruchkammern* to Bremen's nine. Since August, Bremerhaven had disposed of twenty-five cases whereas Bremen handled only three. Napoli explained the difference with the fact that the Bremerhaven office functioned independent of the senator's office so that weaknesses in his organization had little or no effect. Napoli continued that the serious shortcomings in discharging his obligations had been the subject of Denazification Division weekly meetings with the senator since the middle of August but that Aevermann had not made any appreciable progress in addressing these problems.[167] If left in his position, Napoli predicted dire consequences:

> In the next few weeks the disproportion in the number of cases tried in Bremen and Bremerhaven will become even greater. This development will cause considerable speculation and dissatisfaction outside of Denazification Division, because Bremerhaven will have 6 Spruchkammern to try its 25,000 odd cases and Bremen will have about 9 Spruchkammern to try its 75,000 cases. The quixotic relation between Bremen and Bremerhaven is another case of the tail wagging the dog.[168]

Among other major problems in Senator Aevermann's job performance, Napoli mentioned his "loose interpretation" of Article 60 of the Law for Liberation by granting temporary permits to individuals who had been removed from their positions by the military government. He also pointed out that the senator had failed to issue proper instructions to the public prosecutors. The "weak prosecution" of the Seemann trial was in Napoli's opinion a direct result of Aevermann's inability to recruit suitable personnel for Bremen's *Spruchkammern*.[169] The acting division chief concluded his summary recommending the replacement of Senator Aevermann as well as his deputy Ziegler. Even though Napoli described Aevermann as "a fine sincere person," he felt it best to appoint a new senator in the interest of "a more expeditious and efficient denazification."[170]

At the end of October, Aevermann asked to be relieved of his duties. In his letter of resignation to Kaisen, he accepted full responsibility for the lack of *Spruchkammer* personnel but explained that the disproportion between Bremen and Bremerhaven denazification efforts was due to its smaller size and better quality personnel. He also blamed Bremen's poor performance on the military government's insistence to try major offenders first.[171] The following day, Kaisen met with Dunn and announced Aevermann's resignation. *Bürgermeister* Kaisen explained that he had asked Aevermann to remain in office until a suitable replacement could be found.[172]

New Leadership, Old Challenges

In the end of November 1947, Lifschütz was elected as the new Senator for Political Liberation. During the years of the Weimar Republic, Lifschütz was a partner in one of the most successful law practices in Bremen. His career ended abruptly when the Nazis came to power in 1933. Unable to prove his grandparents' "Aryan" descent to their satisfaction, they classified him as a Jew and disbarred him. Left without a way to support himself and his family, Lifschütz went into exile to Switzerland and two years later to the Netherlands. He remained in Amsterdam where he eked out a living in a small law practice until the end of the war. He returned to Bremen in 1945 but kept the office in Amsterdam open until 1949.[173] In his first newspaper interview, Lifschütz announced that he would soon implement a number of "revolutionary plans." Very critical about the way denazification had been conducted in Bremen, he promised to streamline the procedure. He also stated his determination to finish tribunal trials by the summer of the next year.[174]

In assuming office, Lifschütz and his new deputies Karstaedt and Josef Daubach first had to deal with problems they had inherited from their predecessors. Among the most pressing were opening new and reforming existing trial tribunals and denazifying the German railroads or *Reichsbahn*. Aware of the importance of its services for the community and the strictures the unique status and insular geography placed on an already limited pool of replacements, the reichsbahn's cooperation with the Denazification Division and the Office of the Senator for Political Liberation in the removal of Nazis from their ranks was unforthcoming at best. When the U.S. enclave Bremen became Land Bremen in January 1947, its population of more than 750,000 decreased by nearly 70,000 because of the loss of the county of Osterholz, which became part of the British Zone.[175] With Bremen's labor force reduced even further, the *Reichsbahn* management concluded that it could deal with the military government from a position of strength.

Denazifying the *Reichsbahn*

Serious efforts to denazify the railroads began in June 1947, when then Senator Aevermann demanded dismissals of officials according to Article 58 of the Law for Liberation.[176] According to this provision, all individuals chargeable under the law had to be dismissed from their positions and could only be reemployed in positions of ordinary labor at places geographically distant from their former places of work. At the time of Aevermann's investigation, 382 individuals in supervisory positions fell under the provision. The Senator's Office supported by the *Reichsbahn*'s works councils took for granted that the dismissals would not disrupt the railroad operations. Relying on the *Reichsbahn*'s management, Aevermann assumed that everything "reduced itself to pure routine."[177]

It did not become routine. In the end of October, the Senator's Office had to revisit the issue. As one of his last actions in office, Aevermann admonished the *Reichsbahn* management to implement denazification immediately. The managers balked and warned that denazification would lead to a breakdown of the railway system. The senator backed by his reichsbahn advisory committee and all works councils countered that it would not result in serious slowdowns.[178] Another month without discernible progress had passed when the *Reichsbahn* leadership sent some of its representatives on a goodwill visit to Bremen to stem the tide of criticism. In the beginning of November, the president of the *Reichsbahn* Hanover met the director of the military government, and a representative of the Denazification Division complained that considerable time had been lost because the *Reichsbahn*'s managers deliberately avoided dismissing personnel and instead simply transferred them to other positions. The denazification officer criticized that managers continued their efforts to make denazification as painless as possible. Showing remarkable creativity, he observed that they circumvented actually dismissing or demoting politically tainted supervisors to positions of common labor by merely detailing them with a promise to keep their former positions open for them. He continued that the *Reichsbahn* obviously disregarded Bremen's Senator for Political Liberation because his only recourse was to protest against this practice and to demand compliance with the provisions of the law.[179] The session concluded with a general agreement to complete the railroad employees' denazification by 15 February 1948.[180]

In the beginning of December, *Reichsbahn* managers met with all works councils in Land Bremen. After an address by a vice president about the status of denazification, the floor was open for discussion. Works council members took this opportunity to severely criticize the management's slow handling of denazification. A common complaint was that the leadership always seemed to spare personnel in higher positions. Responding, the *Reichsbahn* management representatives defended their policies and blamed delays that might have occurred in the British Military Government for prohibiting a general purification.[181]

Napoli later summarized the results of the meetings for General Clay. He concluded that the *Reichsbahn* would doubtlessly complete denazification by the specified deadline but only in such a way that no official of the higher brackets would suffer financial loss or find his position occupied after the Spruchkammer trial. He attributed this apparent failure of denazification to the lack of effective means of inspection and enforcement for the Senator for Political Liberation but vowed to continue to pursue denazification of the reichsbahn "notwithstanding the dilatoriness and reluctance of the railroad management to participate."[182]

More Spruchkammern

With regard to improving existing tribunals, one of Lifschütz's first measures was to prohibit *Spruchkammer* chairmen from appearing as defense counsels in cases before other tribunals because it created conflicts of interest. Aevermann had authorized this practice in July, but the new senator was convinced that it discredited denazification in the eyes of the public. The military government feared that the senator's pronouncement might lead to the resignation of seven out of eight chairmen who were professional lawyers, but the chairmen continued.[183]

The senator's next priority was to find enough personnel to open additional Spruchkammern. At the time Aevermann resigned, the seeming unwillingness of city government offices and political parties to cooperate with the Senator's Office in the recruitment of new Spruchkammern personnel had already reached crisis level. To support the Senator's Office, the liberal Bremer Demokratische Volkspartei (BDV) issued an urgent plea to the citizens of Bremen to volunteer their services. In the interest of a speedy conclusion of denazification, the BDV urged all men and women who were decent citizens and had an anti-Nazi record to come forward regardless of their professional background. The appeal warned against counting on persons from the legal professions because the number of politically untainted lawyers was negligible. In concluding, the BDV admonished the citizens of Bremen not to try to evade their responsibility to participate in denazification because this would force the democratic parties in the *Bürgerschaft* to approve conscription of personnel.[184] While politicians considered the drafting of citizens a tool of last resort, it was the only condition under which some eligible groups in the population would serve in a *Spruchkammer*. After nearly three years of denazification according to three different sets of rules, they were extremely reluctant to participate in the largely unpopular program. Speaking for the members of the cotton exchange, Fritz Entholt, the director of the Boden & Haac sock factory, explained to Napoli that "the large majority of those with clean political records have expressed the wish that they would prefer to be conscripted into serving on the Denazification Courts."[185]

By the middle of December 1947 the situation showed no improvement. Concerned that he might have no other recourse but to draft personnel, Kaisen demanded to know whether city government agencies and political parties had done their part and provided lists of persons for *Spruchkammern* and other positions. When he found out that parties and industry had submitted a list of four hundred names a few months earlier, he assumed that the military government was responsible for the delay in screening personnel and sent a letter to that effect to Napoli.[186] The military government's investigation led to the Office of the Senator for Political Liberation and revealed that the cause for the holdup was part of Aevermann's legacy of inefficiency. The newly elected German denazification officials reported that they had just found a list of three hundred names, dated 23 September 1947, among the papers of Ziegler, the former deputy of the senator. Senator Lifschütz submitted the list to the military government with the request for expedited processing so that he could set up ten new *Spruchkammern* by 15 January 1948.[187]

Expedite!

By the end of 1947, the military government and state governments in the U.S. Zone alike shared the desire to finish denazification in the speediest fashion to concentrate fully on rebuilding the economy. In October, the military government approved amendments to the Law for Liberation designed to expedite procedures, involving unimportant persons categorized as Class II major offenders against whom there appeared to be no evidence warranting a finding higher than follower.[188] The measure was supposed to free public prosecutors and tribunals to concentrate their efforts against the more highly incriminated and influential Nazis, militarists, and profiteers who were within the incriminated groups of the organizations declared criminal by the International Military Tribunal. To be able to charge a person in a Class II category as a follower, pubic prosecutors had to fulfill the following conditions:

1. There must have been an investigation;
2. The evidence must indicate that the respondent falls within the definition of a follower (Article 12);
3. Approval of Military Government must be obtained prior to the submission of the charge to the Tribunal.[189]

An unintended effect of the expedited procedure was that public prosecutors tended to concentrate their efforts on the disposition of unimportant cases and to postpone the investigation and trial of the principal offenders.[190] To counter this trend, Bremen's Military Government ordered public prosecutors to draw up a list of highly incriminated persons by 15 January 1948 and use it to establish a court calendar of trials, to be finished by 30 May. Publication of this court calendar would also allow for ample notice to respondents and their defense and, in theory, should remove any justification for further postponements of trials.[191]

To the expedited procedure for major offenders Senator Lifschütz added in the first week of December his own suggestion to speed up denazification of the group of lesser offenders. His proposal was a procedure that would allow members of that category to submit to a sanction voluntarily. In his explanation to the military government, he referred to the good experiences Bremen had had with this type of procedure in tax and customs affairs and in matters of foreign exchange. Lifschütz expected from the introduction of the submission procedure a considerable moral and practical success for the Law for Liberation.[192] This innovative suggestion for the expedited handling of the denazification of the large group of lesser offenders as well as the successful reorganization of his section convinced Kaisen that Lifschütz "had been a very good choice."[193] The military government approved the measure a week later.[194]

In spite of the expedited procedure and the new senator's best efforts to improve the efficiency and correct past mistakes, Bremen's citizens displayed an unmistakable desire for an early and painless end of denazification. The military government's denazification officers observed that the general feeling of opposition affected the whole population and even the ranks of the staff of the Office of the Senator for Political Liberation. They went so far as to accuse Lifschütz's employees of producing poor results because of laxity, lack of conviction, and absence of wholehearted enthusiasm. According to the officers, tribunal chairmen also had a hostile attitude toward denazification as exemplified by their efforts to hamper the work of public prosecutors.[195]

Chief public prosecutor Heinrich Hollmann complained in a meeting with Denazification Division representatives that the new emphasis on rebuilding the economy overshadowed everything. As a result, employers made every effort to hold on to their workers, making it nearly impossible for prosecutors to obtain evidence against respondents. Hollmann illustrated his point with the example of Bremen's Borgward plant. While its owner, Carl F. W. Borgward, was still in American detention, a skeleton crew of four hundred workers and managers had returned to their old factory, repaired it as best they could, and begun manufacturing simple items such as pushcarts and horse-drawn vehicles from what materials they could collect. By the end of 1947, Borgward's workforce had grown to nearly two thousand again and was of great importance to the economy of the city. So important, in fact, that Hermann Wolters, Senator of Economics and former Borgward worker, took extraordinary steps to ensure its continued operation. According to Hollmann, Wolters deliberately undermined prosecutorial work at the plant by handing affidavits of clean political records, or *Persilscheine*, to employees who had to appear before a tribunal. All in all, the chief public prosecutor's prognosis for the future of the denazification program was dire. His prosecutors were severely demoralized because they were not able to count on any cooperation in finding evidence for their cases. Even their traditional allies among Social Democrats and Communists had abandoned them, Hollmann concluded.[196]

1948: The Beginning of the End

Scandals and Strains

Borgward's tribunal trial confirmed Hollmann's and the Denazification Division's worst fears that the goal to rebuild the economy superseded denazification. Borgward had joined the Nazi Party in 1938 and quickly rose to high positions in industrial organizations supporting the Nazi war effort. His automobile factories retooled and became one of the most important suppliers for Hitler's war machine. At the height of the war, Borgward employed nearly twenty-three thousand workers, among them about one thousand forced laborers. As a profiteer and activist in the Nazi regime, the public prosecutor charged Borgward as a Class II offender in his tribunal trial on 22 December 1947. At the end of two days of hearings, the tribunal classified him as a lesser offender with three months' probation and a sanction of fifty thousand reichsmarks. The local daily *Weser-Kurier* ridiculed the decision as "the greatest tribunal procedure Bremen has ever seen."[197] Hollmann was appalled. Shortly after the turn of the year, he announced to Lifschütz that he intended to appeal. The senator agreed and, in March 1948, decided to quash the tribunal's decision altogether. Without mentioning Borgward's classification, the senator reasoned in his ruling that three months' probation was insufficient to reform a person.[198]

Hollmann's successful intervention in the Borgward case was one of his last as Bremen's chief public prosecutor. Appointed by Aevermann, the previous Senator for Political Liberation, Hollmann's performance was closely watched by the Denazification Division and by the new senator. As early as the beginning of December 1947, Napoli raised concerns to Lifschütz about the prosecutor's lack of thoroughness in his investigations of cases of internment camp inmates and called for his replacement. Lifschütz agreed with Napoli but decided to wait for an opportune moment. He worried that another important personnel change in the denazification machinery only two months after he had replaced Aevermann might fuel public opinion against the program and against his own organization.[199] In the middle of January, Lifschütz's patience was rewarded. Hollmann became involved in a controversy.

In an effort to build up a complete dossier on the Sturmabteilung (SA) in the Bremen area, Hollmann dispatched two of his coworkers to cover a criminal trial of an SA man accused of murdering three Jews. Even though he had obtained the court's approval before sending the investigators, when they arrived in the courtroom the judge denied them permission to take notes.[200] Hollmann was deeply offended by this action, more so because Dr. Georg Heimann-Trosien, the presiding judge, allowed a representative of the Jewish community, press and radio reporters, and a historian writing a book on the history of Germany through the Nazi regime to record their impressions.[201] On 21 January, Hollmann addressed an official complaint about Heimann-Trosien and his court to Spitta, Bremen's Senator for Justice and Constitution and deputy mayor. In his letter, the chief public prosecutor explained his grievances and raised doubts about the political reliability of the jurists involved in this case: "I am officially bownd [*sic*] to do everything to enforce the Law for Liberation from National Socialism and Militarism. It is known to me which judges in office are subject to this law and I ask you, Herr Bürgermeister, to review the decision of this court and to take steps if you deem this necessary."[202] When Spitta informed the court of Hollmann's complaint, a storm of protest against him erupted in the court itself, in the Free Democratic Party (FDP) of which he was a member,[203] and in Bremen's Lawyers' Association. The court protested that Hollmann obviously tried to influence proceedings by exercising pressure on the witnesses and defense counsels.[204] The FDP asked him to resign his membership, claiming he had repeatedly violated the principles for which it stood and that, as a result, he had sullied the party's reputation.[205] Hollmann's professional colleagues finally passed a resolution on 29 January 1948, condemning his action against the court and asking Spitta to take disciplinary action against him.[206]

On 31 January, Hollmann decided to offer Lifschütz his resignation because he did not feel he could "bear the burden" of his office any longer. Subsequently, Lifschütz chaired a Bürgerschaft committee to examine the incident thoroughly and determine if criminal investigation was warranted. In its final report, the committee concluded that not only was Hollmann justified in taking steps the way he did but also his position as chief prosecutor even demanded that course of action. The report further determined that Hollmann's allegations about the Nazi past of some members of the court were apparently also right as evidenced by the resignation of one of the jurors. To exonerate Hollmann fully in the eyes of the public, the committee even offered him his old position back. He respectfully declined.[207]

In another case involving German denazification personnel, Lifschütz and Napoli did not see eye to eye. Ernst Ahlers was the public prosecutor for Spruchkammer I in Bremerhaven. His seemingly inadequate performance had come to the attention of Bremerhaven's Special Branch and Bremen's Denazification Division in November 1947, when both agencies submitted their first Delinquency and Error Reports about Ahlers to the Senator's Office.[208] During the following month, eight additional Delinquency and Error Reports about Ahlers's failure to investigate cases properly—letting star witnesses withdraw written statements, passing on cross-examinations of crucial witnesses, and failing to present evidence or prosecution witnesses—were on file. Without a reaction from the Senator's Office by the beginning of January 1948, Napoli addressed a letter directly to Lifschütz stating that Ahlers was not suitable for his position and advocating that he be released immediately.[209]

Yet, Lifschütz kept Ahlers in his position. Consequently, over the course of the following two months, the relationship between Burrows, the acting chief of Special Branch, Bremerhaven, and Ahlers turned into personal animosity. On several occasions, Ahlers charged that the American denazification agencies "countermanded" decisions of some *Spruchkammern* while playing favorites with others. To illustrate his point, he claimed he knew that the chairmen and public prosecutors of *Spruchkammern* III and IV were personal friends of the acting chief of Special Branch. These friendships, Ahlers continued, biased Special Branch against decisions made by *Spruchkammern* I and II and led the others to render overly severe ones—so much so, that he accused them of employing "Gestapo methods" in their treatment of former Nazis that made them little more than the contemporary equivalent of the infamous Nazi *Volksgerichtshof*, or People's Court.[210]

On 17 March, Napoli tried once again to convince Senator Lifschütz of the evils of keeping Ahlers as public prosecutor. This time, he pointed out that Ahlers not only failed to discharge his obligations as a prosecutor in conformity with the Law for Liberation but also warranted another Delinquency and Error Report because of the attitude he expressed in the course of official business. Warning the senator about the detrimental and unhealthy effect of the sniping among the *Spruchkammern* about their efficiency, Napoli concluded his argument with the dire prediction that the internal difficulties served to provide "Nazis with additional ammunition."[211] Again, Lifschütz ignored Napoli's wishes, and Ahlers remained as public prosecutor.

A few days later, the SPD, the Deutsche Partei, and the Christian Democratic Union invited all German denazification personnel, representatives from the military government, and the press for a special meeting in Bremerhaven. Burrows attended for the Special Branch. At the outset, it was not quite apparent to him what the sponsors intended to accomplish. Only after the opening remarks by the SPD representative did Burrows realize that the purpose of the meeting was to "criticize those Spruchkammer members" considered "to be at fault" and to introduce "necessary" reforms. One speaker who struck him as "either insane or 'possessed'" was Ahlers. As Burrows detailed in a report of the meeting, Ahlers criticized "everything and everybody." His speech, clearly meant to insult, compared American internment camps to Nazi concentration camps in Dachau and Mauthausen, called *Spruchkammern* III and IV "cursed" and "diabolical instruments," derided American denazification policies, and accused Special Branch of using "Gestapo tactics." In response, Senator Lifschütz's deputy Karstaedt, the chairmen of *Spruchkammern* III and IV, and Burrows took the floor to defend denazification practices. The meeting adjourned without result.[212] The following day, Burrows confessed amazement that Ahlers had not decided on his "voluntary separation from *Spruchkammer* affairs."[213]

The scandal that led to the resignation of former chief public prosecutor Hollmann and the tension Ahlers's outspokenness caused between the Denazification Division and Senator Lifschütz's office highlighted the strain all personnel involved in the program experienced. After nearly three years of denazification, political parties on both sides of the aisle openly attacked the continued effort, and public opinion had turned cynical. Beyond that, the incidents exposed conflicts simmering within the German denazification bureaucracy that further eroded what trust the public still had in the process. Most importantly, however, the incidents demonstrated that the German denazification apparatus under the leadership of Senator Lifschütz was in firm control of the program. The American agencies only grudgingly yielded the powers they had held more than a year longer than their counterparts in the southern German states.

The Last Phase Begins

In the midst of refereeing the sparring between factious tribunal personnel and holding the demanding American denazifiers at bay, Senator Lifschütz's office opted for a simplified *Meldebogen* processing system and completed instructions for cases falling under the expedited procedure. In February, the senator reported to the Denazification Division that his office received approximately 387,000 *Meldebogen* of which 276,000 belonged to nonchargeable persons and 110,000 to chargeable persons. He stated that about 87 percent of nonchargeable persons and 70 percent of all persons covered by amnesties had already been notified. Lifschütz expected that the remaining cases could be expedited in writing leaving only five hundred cases of a severe or Class I nature. With the new expedited procedure in place, the senator's staff expected to be able to finish Class II cases by June 1948. A trial calendar for Class I cases forecasted completion of these trials in Bremerhaven for April and in Bremen for June.[214] Bremen's Military Government was delighted with Lifschütz's report. Napoli praised the senator and his assistants for completing tasks in twelve weeks that surely would have taken former Senator Aevermann and his deputy Ziegler thirty-five weeks.[215] Director Dunn even extended his office's "warmest congratulations for a most important job well done" to Bürgermeister Kaisen.[216]

By March the deteriorating relationship between the Anglo-American powers and the Soviet Union added urgency to a rapid conclusion of the denazification program. The Allied Control Council was never effective in agreeing on policies for Germany as a whole—excepting those of a punitive nature—and it broke down completely when the Soviet delegation walked out in protest over American, British, and French steps toward rebuilding the German economy. Concurrently, negotiations of the Council of Foreign Ministers that met in 1946 and 1947 to decide the shape of a German state and a final peace treaty were unsuccessful. The main problem was that American, British, and French visions of Germany's future could not be reconciled with those of the Soviet Union. While the Western powers were determined to rehabilitate Germany—if necessary at the expense of division—the Soviet side initially hoped that Germany would remain unified and "neutral" but vulnerable to the Moscow-controlled German Communists. With a four-power agreement on Germany seemingly impossible, both sides forged ahead with plans for separate German states.[217]

To concentrate fully on planning an East German state, Marshal Vassily Sokolovsky, the supreme commander of the Soviet Military Administration in Germany, ordered the termination of the Soviet denazification program for 10 March 1948. Committees and commissions handling appeals and complaints were to be dissolved a month later.[218] At the end of the month, the OMGUS followed suit. It released amendments to the Law for Liberation designed to decrease the number of pending tribunal cases to hasten the end of the denazification program. The office's rationale for the drastic speedup was that the program had fulfilled its purpose because "persons chargeable under the Denazification Law have been removed and excluded from positions of responsibility in German life."[219] The most important of these amendments dramatically increased the discretionary powers of public prosecutors. They gained the authority to allocate persons to the group of lesser offenders or followers without trial if an investigation of the person's political past did not unearth evidence to the contrary. OMGUS issued orders to all local military governments to make personnel, office space, and equipment available to German denazification agencies to ensure prompt implementation. The target date for handling of all cases not requiring trial was 1 May 1948.[220]

In practice, the amendments reversed the principle of presumptive classification that had been the base for the denazification program since the International Military Tribunal at Nuremberg. In fact, the changes resulted in the paradoxical situation of German denazification agencies objecting to the leniency of the changes in allowing almost everyone to be eligible for an expedited procedure, or *Schnellverfahren.* In Bremen, Senator Lifschütz and his deputy Karstaedt felt that these changes made it almost impossible to carry out any effective denazification.[221] Karstaedt's misgivings went to the heart of the new expedited procedure. In his opinion, the door was opened too wide for those who were not activists, or "Nürnberger," referring to members of organizations declared criminal by the International Military Tribunal, but still did not belong on the list of expedited procedures.[222] These shortcomings of the procedure notwithstanding, Senator Lifschütz took full advantage of it and ordered cessation of all oral cases after 1 May 1948.[223]

At Bremen's Military Government headquarters, Director Dunn issued the necessary instructions to all U.S. personnel engaged in denazification operations. He declared that in the upcoming months relatively few highly incriminated cases would remain for trial. All others were subject to the expedited procedure. To prevent loss of time in disputed cases, Dunn commanded the Denazification Division to suspend the practice of issuing Delinquency and Error Reports on actions by public prosecutors. In the future, Senator Lifschütz's office would settle differences of opinion.[224]

Tribunals Try Ardent Nazis

While the military government and Senator Lifschütz calculated how fast they could complete denazification, Bremen and Bremerhaven's tribunals began trying the cases of major offenders and activists that had been postponed in favor of processing Class III cases quickly. As expected, the trials tended to be time consuming because they required hearing a number of witnesses for and against the defendant. Another factor slowing the pace at which these cases moved through the tribunals was, once again, Bremen's unique geography and resulting questions of jurisdiction. Even in its new configuration as a Land with clearly defined borders, trials of persons who lived in the British Zone but worked in Bremen defied simple solutions. An example of the kinds of complications that could arise was the case of an officer of the *Schutzstaffel* (SS), Hitler's "Praetorian Guard."

Heinrich Schuchmann was a SS-Obersturmführer, a rank equivalent to that of a first lieutenant, who was active in the National Socialist movement in Bremerhaven even before the Nazis came to power.[225] He lived in Cuxhaven in the British Zone on a boat called *Seebär* that he registered with the shipping bureau in Bremerhaven. His business, a shipping company by the name of Schuchmann Reederei, was also in Bremerhaven. In May 1947, when a Cuxhaven denazification committee tried all seamen living in the city, he had a routine preliminary hearing. In September, with his British denazification still in progress, Schuchmann also submitted a *Meldebogen* in Land Bremen. His case was assigned to Robert Stoffers, the public prosecutor of Bremerhaven's *Spruchkammer* III. In his investigation, the prosecutor worked closely with the denazification committee in Cuxhaven, which "readily forwarded the requested documents." Everything, including the trial, "was functioning smoothly," according to Stoffers, until 18 November when the tribunal sentenced Schuchmann in his absence to seven years in a labor camp.[226]

Shocked by the verdict, Schuchmann pleaded with the British Military Government in Cuxhaven to intervene on his behalf with American authorities in Bremerhaven. The British agreed to take up his case and in the second week of January 1948 filed a complaint about his sentence with Special Branch Bremerhaven. Arguing the Spruchkammer displayed an "unheeding rush" in bringing the subject to justice and that the decision was "very stringent," the British denied Bremerhaven's jurisdiction in the case. Instead, they claimed that right for Cuxhaven.[227] The dispute over whether residence or business determined jurisdiction in denazification procedures between Military Government Bremen and British authorities lasted through January into the middle of February. Finally, Denazification Division Chief Napoli referred the issue to the Public Safety Division at the OMGUS headquarters in Berlin for adjudication.[228] The following week, Theo E. Hall, chief of the Public Safety Branch, responded that the case was indeed in *Spruchkammer* Bremerhaven's jurisdiction. It was also his opinion that the Cuxhaven panel's categorization of Schuchmann should be set aside and Bremerhaven's sentence of seven years at a labor camp be upheld. To prevent future incidents of this nature in the Bremen area, Hall recommended that as a "rule of thumb" the tribunal or panel "possessing the bulk of the evidence relevant to the case should assume final jurisdiction."[229]

Another area of friction between the two military governments, though less time consuming, was the extradition of persons from the British Zone to stand trial in Bremen. Even if generally cooperative, British authorities denied Bremen's requests if panel proceedings, as in the case of Class I major offender Friede Frieden, a former Gestapo agent, had already begun. Although Bremen's Denazification Division officials, in particular Napoli, were convinced that the trial would result in "a gross miscarriage of justice" because of the more lenient policies in the British Zone, they accepted the refusal.[230]

The Cold War Grows Colder

With tribunals hearing the first cases of major offenders, militarists, and activists, the denazification of persons categorized as Class II and III offenders, by way of processing their paperwork, continued at "top speed."[231] It progressed so well that, by the end of April 1948, Director Dunn declared denazification of Bremen completed except for 1,500 "heavily incriminated cases."[232] In a letter addressed to the president of the Senat, he praised the work of the Office of the Senator for Political Liberation and expressed confidence that "the hard nut of the 1500 cases still to be tried will be treated as thoroughly as it has been the case in Dr. Lifschütz' office during the past."[233]

A few months earlier, on the diplomatic front, the four-power administration of Germany collapsed rapidly. The Allied Control Council broke down completely in January 1948, when the Soviet delegation walked out in protest over American, British, and French steps toward establishing a West German state. The following month, the already strained relations between the Western powers and the Soviet Union reached another low point when Communists staged a coup d'état in Czechoslovakia. At the end of March, the Soviet Military Government declared that it intended to search all military rail traffic passing through their zone on the way to Berlin. Rather than allowing the searches to occur, the U.S. Military Government suspended rail transports and airlifted supplies. This airlift lasted only eleven days. On 12 April, American military rail traffic resumed. In June, when the American, British, and French zones introduced a new currency, the deutsche mark, in their zones, Soviet premier Joseph Stalin ordered a blockade of all land and water access routes to western Berlin to either force the Allies back to the negotiating table or out of Berlin or both. The Americans and British responded with an unexpectedly successful airlift, handing the Soviets a humiliating diplomatic defeat and forcing them to lift the blockade in May of the following year.[234]

In the time between the end of the first and the beginning of the second airlift, on 4 May, OMGUS in Berlin issued further directives designed to eliminate all obstacles for the speedy completion of denazification. It instructed the Land offices to discontinue the system of Delinquency and Error Reports effective immediately because it was deemed "unnecessary." If the Land military government received reports about errors in tribunal trials, they had orders to notify the Senator for Political Liberation in individual letters. The same directive also repealed Military Government Law No. 8.[235] Thus, the military government had in effect withdrawn from denazification. All efforts were on rebuilding the economy and preparing the ground for a West German national government.

Meanwhile, Borgward, one of Bremen's most prominent businessmen, was still barred from setting foot in his own factory. There had been no developments in his case since Senator Lifschütz annulled his original tribunal sentence in March. In the intervening time, anxiety grew in Bremen and in the United States about Borgward's prospects to return to his business soon in order to lead its recovery. As Napoli recalled, one American businessman thought the matter urgent enough to offer the Denazification Division chief a handsome bribe to speed up the process:

> Carl Borgward came to see me, after having made an appointment, which was unusual for him because he was one of the most important people in Northern Germany. He had 5,000 employees in his factory. He brought a letter from Walter Chrysler—and I really am sorry that I threw it out by the window in rage. It said, "Dear Mr. Napoli, Carl Borgward is an old and trusted friend. I hope that you can find a way to release him, putting him though the denazification process as soon as possible, restoring him to his factory. The German democracy needs him badly. [Second paragraph.] This is Mr. Borgward's authority to offer you a position anywhere in the world with a lifetime contract." I declined.[236]

An appeal board finally upheld Borgward's original tribunal ruling classifying him as a lesser offender on 6 July. The board also rescinded his three months' probation as time served and lowered his fine from the original sum of fifty thousand to five thousand reichsmarks.[237] Barely two weeks after the beginning of the Berlin airlift, Borgward's sentence reflected the new reality. The U.S. strategic goal of building a West German state and economy as fast as possible into a bulwark against Soviet-style communist expansion dwarfed all other occupation objectives, including the denazification program.

Denazifying the Lawyers

If Bremen's captains of industry were the beneficiaries of the new U.S. emphasis on rebuilding rather than punishing, so were its lawyers and judges. From the beginning, implementing the denazification program in the courts and legal practices was particularly difficult. Not only was it nearly impossible to replace highly trained professionals who were removed because of their ties to the former Nazi regime, but also most court officers had had some affiliation with it by virtue of enforcing its laws and belonging to its professional organizations. As a result, judicial officials procrastinated or refused the military government's demands for removal of all implicated personnel. In February 1948, with his division's influence on the denazification process fading fast, Napoli complained to Kaisen that Nazis who should have been removed two and a half years ago were still working in the courts. He urged the mayor to give this matter the highest priority.[238] Kaisen's administration ignored his plea.

Six months later, Napoli complained bitterly to the director of the military government about the sad state of the denazification of Bremen's judiciary. In exasperation, he accused Spitta, the deputy mayor and Senator for Justice and Constitution, of committing "political fraud" and actively engaging in "subterfuge." According to Napoli, Spitta and his colleagues obviously believed that "the dismissals in the early days of this occupation completed the cleansing of the Bremen judiciary." Summing up his charges against Spitta, Napoli stated that the pervasive attitude in the Senator's Office was "obviously that denazification is to be avoided as though it were a plague."[239]

In 1945, in the "early days" after the end of war, the military government detachments faced great difficulties when they implemented the denazification policies in the judiciary. They soon discovered that most judges and attorneys had been members of the Nazi Party or one of its affiliated orders and had to be dismissed. Replacing them proved nearly impossible. The experiences of two local detachments were typical for the enclave. In Brake, which later became part of the British Zone, I1C2 detachment had dismissed all available lawyers and judges by September because of their ties to the Nazi regime. To enable the detachment to reopen Brake's German courts, Bremen's detachment sent two qualified judges. The situation in Wesermünde was slightly better. The local G1C2 detachment had admitted twelve of the approximately forty-five judges and attorneys practicing law in the city before the occupation. In addition, the detachment was able to recruit several refugees who had fled from Russian-occupied territory.[240]

As time passed, so did the American fervor of radical denazification of the legal profession. Reconstituting a functioning German court system as soon as possible was a necessity that dictated that most lawyers and judges in the enclave receive temporary work permits because they were irreplaceable personnel. When neither refugees nor other replacements in Bremen and Wesermünde could be found in sufficient numbers to fill their positions, the temporary permits in effect became permanent. In light of that reality, the quixotic nature of Napoli's late efforts was lost on Kaisen, Dunn, or Spitta.

The Waning Months, Years

On 11 August 1948, OMGUS issued a directive for the withdrawal of the military government from denazification operations. All Land OMGs were instructed to eliminate Special Branch Offices and rescind all supervision and control of denazification as carried out by German agencies. The directive further ordered Land military governments to appoint denazification advisors to assist with denazification questions and maintain liaison with the ministers or Senators for Political Liberation.[241]

Napoli's reaction to this directive was to try to keep his office staff employed as long as possible. He explained to the executive officer at military government headquarters that it was impossible for him to dismiss more than three officers because his division still had important functions. These included screening of key personnel of American units, screening of applicants for immigration to America, maintenance, and investigation of dossiers, as well as inspections to prevent Nazi infiltrations. To fulfill all of these tasks satisfactorily, Napoli requested a minimum staff of twenty-six persons, including eighteen investigators and inspectors, three stenographers, four clerks, and one translator.[242] At the end of the month, Napoli was able to announce that he had succeeded in extending the time of employment of the personnel of this division until 1 December. Still, he cautioned everyone to start looking for new positions since this notification was equivalent to a three months' notice. He assured his coworkers that they would receive preferential treatment for jobs with American military installations and with the German *Arbeitsamt* (Labor Office).[243]

The German denazification agencies took similar steps to ease the transition for their personnel. With completion of the denazification program expected for the end of the year, discussions about the dismissal of personnel began in July. As a precaution, all states in the U.S. Zone had passed an Assurance Law, or *Sicherungsgesetz*, for denazification personnel. This law stated that persons who had served at least twelve months in the Senator's Office would be taken into other administrative positions; be transferred into vacant positions in private economy; be supported in establishing themselves in business; or be paid an indemnity. The personnel in the Office of the Senator for Political Liberation received their notices according to time of service.[244]

The target date for the end of denazification was 31 December 1948. Article 154 of Bremen's constitution provided the legal framework for the continuation of the program. It stipulated that laws deviating from rules set by the constitution could be passed until that date to allow for effective denazification. The article also allowed for an extension of that period.[245] In the beginning of November, Senator Lifschütz announced that 1,891 cases remained, of which 956 were already scheduled for tribunal hearings and 773 for appellate hearings. He estimated that an extension until March 1949 was "the utmost time limit for Land Bremen" and that there would be "only liquidating activities, in particular the execution of decisions" after that time.[246] Together with Senator Spitta, he decided to introduce a law for the prolongation of the Law for Liberation "to remove all doubts, if the liberation law with respect to the regulations of article 154, paragraph 2 of the constitution will remain in force beyond 31 December 1948."[247] At the end of December, the Bürgerschaft decided to extend the Law of Liberation for six months.[248]

In the military governor's office at OMGUS headquarters, Lifschütz's data on pending cases in Bremen raised eyebrows. On 14 December, General Clay expressed his reservations in a letter to Captain Jeffs, U.S. Navy, Dunn's successor as director of the military government for Bremen. He was particularly concerned about "an unusually large percentage of cases which have been on the calendar from periods prior to 1 June, the date we had estimated for the completion of the denazification program."[249] Though conceding that there might have been "a large number of new registrations which have hampered the German denazification authorities in completely disposing of all pending cases," Clay added that "it appears to me that we may expect the program to last indefinitely." Concluding, he urged Jeffs to discuss this matter with Kaisen and help him develop a program that would bring denazification to an early completion.[250] A few days later, Jeffs called a meeting with Kaisen and Lifschütz to discuss how to speed up the processing of pending cases. Senator Lifschütz explained, however, that the nature of cases that made up most of the backlog defied faster handling: "It has to be considered that these old cases are concerning mostly SS-captains, majors, a.s.o. and that, after having passed the court of 1st instance, they mostly file an appeal which means a repeated lot of work."[251] He further stated that his colleagues in the three southern states also expected that they "will need at least one or two more years to complete denazification" and therefore refused "to accept a final termination date."[252]

Consequently, the denazification program continued in 1949. At the end of February, Jeffs once again summoned Kaisen to query him about the remaining 430 unfinished trials. Growing rather impatient, the director speculated that one of the obstacles to the completion of the denazification program was the fear of some of the *Spruchkammer* members of working themselves out of a job.[253]

Kaisen referred Jeffs to Senator Lifschütz. On 15 March, about two weeks before expiration of the self-imposed denazification deadline, the senator addressed Jeffs's charges of deliberate procrastination. He pointed out that the target date was not binding and that not meeting it did not imply that it was the fault of anyone in his office. On the contrary, everybody involved had pledged to intensify his or her efforts to the utmost to finish the last trials in Bremerhaven by the end of April and in Bremen by the end of June. Finally, Lifschütz reiterated his earlier argument about the serious and time-consuming nature of the cases:

> The delay must not, in the last place, be ascribed to the incriminated individuals themselves; for the law provides them with legal remedies postponing the conclusion of the individual procedure. . . . The serious cases are being dealt with now. In these cases the law calls for a legal procedure, this, besides, mostly stipulating oral proceedings. Even with the best intentions it is impossible to cope with hundreds of trials in so short a time as would be desirable.[254]

In June 1949, when the Bürgerschaft's six-month extension period drew to a close, OMGUS reversed its earlier position and decided instead that the "Military Government cannot allow any action which would interfere with the completion of the Denazification Program." Accordingly, Bremen's OMG received instructions to inform the president of the Senat that the denazification trials had to continue. Furthermore, OMGUS called attention to the fact that the Law for Liberation "contained no time limit on its effectiveness" and was also included in a list of laws which could not "be amended, supplemented or repealed except at Laenderrat or higher level."[255]

Ultimately, the time frame for the completion of denazification extended far beyond any of Senator Lifschütz's or the military government's estimates. On 4 April 1950, the Bremen Bürgerschaft passed a Law for the Conclusion of the Political Liberation that classified all respondents as followers, except 21 cases in the category of major offenders and 165 cases in the category of offenders. In a departure from the procedure of the three southern states that summarily declared all remaining cases to be followers, Bremen's administration decided on individual pardons. By May 1954, the president of the Senat had pardoned all but three of the remaining persons classified as either a major offender or an offender. They received their pardons in 1956 when they were released from prison after serving their sentences.[256]

Notes

1. Michael Scherer, "Freie Hansestadt Bremen," *Der Bürger im Staat* 1, no. 2 (1999): 2–4 (Landeszentrale für politische Bildung Baden-Württemberg); Herbert

Schwarzwälder, *Das große Bremen-Lexikon*, 2 vols. (Bremen, Germany: Edition Temmen, 2002), 128.

2. Scherer, "Freie Hansestadt Bremen," 5; Herbert Schwarzwälder, *Die Machtergreifung der NSDAP in Bremen 1933* (Bremen, Germany: Carl Schünemann Verlag, 1966), 24–29, 35.

3. Karel Margry, "The Capture of Bremen," *After the Battle* 135 (February 2007): 2–4; Jörg Friedrich, *Der Brand: Deutschland im Bombenkrieg 1940–1945* (München, Germany: Propyläen Verlag, 2002), 195–98; Herbert Schwarzwälder, *Bremer Geschichte* (Bremen, Germany: Johann Heinrich Döll, 1993), 251.

4. Andreas Röpke, "Entstehung, Status und Verwaltung der amerikanischen Enklave Bremen," *Bremisches Jahrbuch* 66 (1988): 432–33; *Conquer: The Story of the Ninth Army, 1944–1945* (Washington, DC: Infantry Journal Press, 1947), 335; *History of the XVI Corps: From Its Activation to the End of the War in Europe* (Washington, DC: Infantry Journal Press, 1947), 85; George M. Fuermann and F. Edward Cranz, *Ninety-Fifth Infantry Division History 1918–1946* (Nashville, TN: Battery Press, 1988).

5. Margry, "The Capture of Bremen," 4.

6. Margry, "The Capture of Bremen," 33–34.

7. Military Government Report, 0001–2400 hour, 27 April 1945, Headquarters Detachment E2C2, ECAD, p. 1, 329–5.1, 27 April–22 May 1945, World War II Operations Reports, 1940–1948, 29th Infantry Division, Box 8657, Record Group (RG) 407, National Archives and Records Administration (NARA).

8. Almuth Meyer-Zollitsch, *Nationalsozialismus und Evangelische Kirche in Bremen* (Veröffentlichungen aus dem Staatsarchiv der Freien Hansestadt Bremen, Band 51, 1985), 314.

9. Secret Report No. L-360 from OSS Concerning Erich Vagts, Lord Mayor of Bremen, Luther Stevens Smith, Director, Civil Administration Division for Deputy Military Governor, USGCC/G, 9 August 1945, n.p., OMGUS Adjutant General 1945–1946, Box 57, RG 260, NARA.

10. Schwarzwälder, *Das große Bremen-Lexikon*, 749.

11. Röpke, "Entstehung, Status und Verwaltung der amerikanischen Enklave Bremen," 439.

12. Historical Report (undated), pp. 1–3, Records of the Bremerhaven Liaison and Security Detachment, Central Office, Subject File, Box 546, RG 260, NARA. Davis stayed in command of this detachment until the arrival of Lieutenant Colonel Luther S. Diggs on 7 August 1945.

13. Historical Report (undated), pp. 1–3.

14. Joseph H. Ewing, *29 Let's Go! A History of the 29th Infantry Division in World War II* (Washington, DC: Infantry Journal Press, 1948), 262; *Conquer*, 335–37.

15. Summary of the Enclave Military District, 30 July 1945, p. 1, Headquarters 29th Infantry Division, 329-5.0 G-5 Special Report Summary and Survey of German Civil Administration—Enclave Military District—Occupation of Germany, 29th Infantry Division, 15 Jun–30 Jul 1945, Box 8657, RG 407, NARA.

16. Summary of the Enclave Military District, 30 July 1945, 1; Military Government Report, 27 April 1945.

17. Röpke, "Entstehung, Status und Verwaltung der amerikanischen Enklave Bremen," 437; Ewing, *29 Let's Go!* 262; *Conquer*, 335–37; FHMG, 10 December 1945–31 January 1946, Records of the Public Information Office, Functional Histories of Military Government in Bremen, April 1945–March 1948, pp. 1, 3–4, Box 69, RG 260, NARA.

18. Military Government Summary No. 2, 28 April 1945, Headquarters Detachment E2C2, ECAD, pp. 3–4, 329–5.1, 27 April–22 May 1945, 29th Infantry Division, Box 8657, RG 407, NARA; Hans Hesse, *Konstruktionen der Unschuld: Die Entnazifizierung am Beispiel von Bremen und Bremerhaven 1945–1953* (Bremen, Germany: Selbstverlag des Staatsarchivs Bremen, 2005), 36.

19. Der Regierende Bürgermeister to Regierungskanzlei, 30 May 1945, Entnazifizierung 3-B.10.29, 2, Staatsarchiv der Freien Hansestadt Bremen (StAB); FHMG, October 1945–June 1946, p. 1.

20. Historical Report (undated), pp. 8–9 (the report does not give information about the number of civil servants and other employees in Wesermünde).

21. FHMG, 26 April–30 September 1945, p. 15, Records of the Public Information Office, Functional Histories of Military Government in Bremen, April 1945–March 1948, Box 68, RG 260, NARA.

22. FHMG, October 1945–June 1946, p. 3; cf. Robert F. Knox, Major CE, Deputy, to All Branches, DET. G1C2, ECAD, 20 August 1945, Records of the Denazification Division, Box 159, RG 260, NARA.

23. FHMG, October 1945–June 1946, p. 2.

24. G-3 Journal, 3, 4, and 10 July 1945, 29th Infantry Division, 1–31 July 1945, 329-3.2 to 329-3.4, 29th Infantry Division, Box 8645, RG 407, NARA.

25. Earl F. Ziemke, *The U.S. Army in the Occupation of Germany 1944–1946*, Army Historical Series (Washington, DC: United States Army Center of Military History, 2003), 318–19; G-3 Journal, 20 July 1945 and 23 July 1945, p. 2.

26. FHMG, October 1945–June 1946, p. 2.

27. FHMG, October 1945–June 1946, pp. 2–3; Information contained in Military Government of Germany *Fragebogen und Lebenslauf* (Questionnaire and Personal Data Sheet, trans. Adams), 23 August 1945; Report on Student No. R663, 3 October 1945; Military Government of Germany Fragebogen Action Sheet, 2 March 1946, Records of the Denazification Division, Box 174, RG 260, NARA.

28. Meyer-Zollitsch, *Nationalsozialismus und Evangelische Kirche*, 315; Lutz Niethammer, ed., *Walter L. Dorn: Inspektionsreisen durch die U.S.-Zone. Notizen, Denkschriften und Erinnerungen* (Stuttgart, Germany: R. Oldenbourg Verlag, 1973), 41.

29. Karl-Ludwig Sommer, *Wilhelm Kaisen: Eine politische Biographie* (Bonn, Germany: Dietz, 2000), 122.

30. Schwarzwälder, *Das große Bremen-Lexikon*, 678.

31. Niethammer, *Walter L. Dorn*, 40; Meyer-Zollitsch, *Nationalsozialismus und Evangelische Kirche*, 314.

32. Secret Report No. L-360.

33. Röpke, "Entstehung, Status und Verwaltung der amerikanischen Enklave Bremen," 440; Aussage aus der Senats-Sitzung vom 3., August 1945, Seite 267ff, Verhandlungen über den Erlaß eines bremischen Gesetzes wegen ihrer Zugehörigkeit

zur NSDAP und über Neueinstellung 1945, Mai 8-, Entnazifizierung 3-B.10.b.29,2, Staatsarchiv der Freien Hansestadt Bremen, pp. 2–4.

34. Weekly Military Government Report to Commanding General, Seventh Army, 4 August 1945, MGSUM No. 94, p. 1, Headquarters Military Government, Detachment E2C2, Bremen, Records of the European Theater of Operations, U.S. Army, Historical Division, Program Files, Office of Military Government for Germany, U.S., Bremen Enclave Reports, Box 1, RG 498, NARA.

35. Aussage aus der Niederschrift über die Besprechung mit Capt. Bard vom 10.8.1945, in Beamtenentlassungen, betr. Richtlinien für das Berufungsverfahren und das Vorstellungsverfahren bei Beamtenentlassungen wegen Zugehörigkeit zur NSDAP, Entnazifizierung 3-B.10.b.21, StAB.

36. Besprechung mit Bard 11.9.1945, Entnazifizierung 3-B.10.b.21, StAB.

37. Berufungsverfahren für die Beamten, Angestellten und Arbeiter der bremischen Verwaltung, 19 September 1945, Entnazifizierung 3-B.10.b.21, StAB.

38. Charles M. G. Heldebrant, Capt. FA, Administration Officer, to Commanding Officer, Office of Military Government for Bremen, 26 November 1945, Records of the Bremerhaven Liaison and Security Detachment, Records of the Central Office, Subject Files 1945–1949, Box 543, RG 260, NARA.

39. Ordinance, Wesermünde, 17 December 1945, signed Dr. Koch, Records of the Bremerhaven Liaison and Security Detachment, Records of the Central Office, Subject Files 1945–1949, Box 536, RG 260, NARA.

40. FHMG, 26 April–30 September 1945, pp.19–20.

41. Military Government—Germany, U.S. Zone, Law No. 8 and Regulation No. 1 Under Law No. 8, Nachrichtenblatt Wesermünde, Monday, 15 October 1945, Records of the Denazification Division, Box 162; FHMG, October–November 1945, 1–10 December, p. 6, Records of the Public Information Office, Functional Histories of Military Government in Bremen, April 1945–March 1948, Box 68, RG 260, NARA; Hesse, *Konstruktionen der Unschuld*, 41. The number of review boards in Wesermünde was not recorded.

42. Addendum to General Denazification Report Det. G1C2, November 45, p. 1, Records of the Bremerhaven Liaison and Security Detachment, Records of the Central Office, Subject Files 1945–1949, Box 543, RG 260, NARA.

43. FHMG, October–November 1945, 1–10 December, p. 9.

44. FHMG, October–November 1945, 1–10 December, p. 10.

45. Functional History, October 1945, p. 2, Headquarters Military Government Detachment G1C2 Wesermünde, Records of the Public Information Office, Functional Histories of Military Government in Bremen, April 1945–March 1948, Box 68, RG 260, NARA. The uninhabited dock area, during the early period of the occupation called Bremerhaven, always belonged to Bremen.

46. Raymond M. Davis, Major, Inf., Commanding, to Lt. Col. B. C. Welker, Commanding Officer, Mil. Gov. Det. E2C2, Bremen, 20 July 1945, Records of the Bremerhaven Liaison and Security Detachment, Central Office, Subject File, Box 541, RG 260, NARA.

47. Der Oberpräsident der Provinz Hannover to the Oberbürgermeister, Wesermünde, the Landrat Dr. Arps, Lokstedt, Wesermünde-Land, the Regierungsvizepräsi-

dent Dr. Benken, Stade, 6 September 1945, Records of the Bremerhaven Liaison and Security Detachment, Central Office, Subject File, Box 541, RG 260, NARA.

48. Historical Report (undated), p. 7.

49. Röpke, "Entstehung, Status und Verwaltung der amerikanischen Enklave Bremen," 437; Bryan L. Milburn, Brigadier General, GSC, Chief of Staff to Secretary General, USGrCC, 30 July 1946, OMGUS Adjutant General 1945–1946, Box 54, RG 260, NARA.

50. FHMG, October–November 1945, 1–10 December, p. 11.

51. FHMG, October–November 1945, 1–10 December, p. 6.

52. FHMG, October–November 1945, 1–10 December, p. 8.

53. FHMG, October–November 1945, 1–10 December, pp. 1–2. According to the report, Berlin had been under the impression that Stadt Wesermünde was a part of Bremerhaven.

54. Agreement of Military Government Responsibility in the Bremen Enclave, p. 1, OMGUS Adjutant General 1945–1946, Box 54, RG 260, NARA.

55. FHMG, October–November 1945, 1–10 December, p. 2.

56. Röpke, "Entstehung, Status und Verwaltung der amerikanischen Enklave Bremen," 443.

57. FHMG, 10 December 1945–31 January 1946, p. 3.

58. FHMG, 10 December 1945–31 January 1946, p. 4.

59. FHMG, 10 December 1945–31 January 1946, pp. 8–9. Bremen's military government had great difficulty fulfilling this particular order because Bremen's population grew steadily due to an influx of refugees and returning soldiers. By the end of October 1946, a British census showed Bremen's population at 753,518 residents (German Census, 29 October 1946, British Zone, Records of the Bremerhaven Liaison and Security Detachment, Records of the Central Office, Subject Files 1945–1949, Box 558, RG 260, NARA).

60. FHMG, 10 December 1945–31 January 1946, p. 16.

61. FHMG, 10 December 1945–31 January 1946, p. 17.

62. As quoted in Röpke, "Entstehung, Status und Verwaltung der amerikanischen Enklave Bremen," 445.

63. Röpke, "Entstehung, Status und Verwaltung der amerikanischen Enklave Bremen," 445.

64. Occupation Forces in Europe Series, 1945–1946, *Troop Basis and the Disposition of Forces* (Frankfurt am Main, Germany: European Command, Office of the Chief Historian, 1947), 10, 11, and 18; Occupation Forces in Europe Series, 1945–1946, *The United States Constabulary* (Frankfurt am Main, Germany: European Command, Office of the Chief Historian, 1947), 6–8, 12, 57.

65. FHMG, 10 December 1945–31 January 1946, p. 61.

66. FHMG, 27 April 1945–30 June 1946, pp. 85–87, Records of the Public Information Office, Functional Histories of Military Government in Bremen, April 1945–March 1948, Box 68, RG 260, NARA; Hesse, *Konstruktionen der Unschuld*, 41–42. As Hesse points out, this practice was very similar to the procedure adopted in spring 1946 by denazification tribunals implementing the Law for Liberation from National Socialism and Militarism in the U.S. Zone.

67. FHMG, 27 April 1945–30 June 1946, p. 85.

68. FHMG, 10 December 1945–31 January 1946, p. 65.

69. Hesse, *Konstruktionen der Unschuld*, 35–36; Historical Report on denazification, 8 January 1947, signed Ambrosius, p. 6, Records of the Bremerhaven Liaison and Security Detachment, Records of the Special Branch, Denazification Records, 1945–1949, Box 601, RG 260, NARA. The boards remained in existence until January 1947, when Bremen became a state within the U.S. Zone of Occupation.

70. Zone Policy Instruction No. 3 of 17 January 1946, p. 1, Main Headquarters, Control Commission For Germany (British Element), De-Nazification Measures in the British Zone, Records of the Office of Military Government for Bremen, Records of the Denazification Division, Box 159, RG 260, NARA.

71. A list of Bürgerschaft members from April until September 1946 is printed in "Eine Dokumentation für die Ausstellung Antifaschistischer Widerstand in Bremen," 28.4.74–19.5.74, Rathaushalle Bremen, p. 95.

72. Historical Report (undated), pp. 9–11; Kenneth R. Moul, Captain, Adm. O. for The Oberbürgermeister Gerhard van Heukelum, 1 July 1946, Records of the Bremerhaven Liaison and Security Detachment, Central Office, Subject File, Box 541, RG 260, NARA.

73. FHMG, October 1945–June 1946, p. 5.

74. FHMG, 1 January–31 March 1947, p. 24, Records of the Public Information Office, Functional Histories of Military Government in Bremen, April 1945–March 1948, Box 72, RG 260, NARA.

75. Standing Operating Procedure for Denazification in the Bremen Enclave, pp. 3–10, Records of the Public Safety Division, General Correspondence and Other Records, 1945–1949, Box 224, RG 260, NARA.

76. Main Hq. Control Commission for Germany (British Element) Zone Policy Instruction No. 3 of 17th January 1946, De-Nazification measures in the British Zone, p. 5, Records of the Denazification Division, Box 170, RG 260, NARA.

77. Der Senator für Schulen und Erziehung, Hauptausschuß für Entnazifizierung, 7 June 1946; Report of Meeting of the German Denazification Panel and members of the Bremen Nominated Representative Council, 3 June 1946, signed Burghardt; Ernest B. Smith, 1st Lt. Inf., Adm. Officer, Internal Affairs and Communication Division, Office of Military Government for Bremen Enclave (U.S.) to President of the Nominated Representative Council for Hansestadt Bremen, 31 May 1946, pp. 1–2 and appendices 1 and 2, Records of the Denazification Division, Box 175, RG 260, NARA. In 1947, Aevermann became the first Senator for Political Liberation for the state of Bremen (Schwarzwälder, *Das große Bremen-Lexikon*, 1: 52).

78. FHMG, 1 July–31 August 1946, p. 11, Records of the Public Information Office, Functional Histories of Military Government in Bremen, April 1945–March 1948, Box 70, RG 260, NARA.

79. FHMG, 1 July–31 August 1946, p. 13.

80. FHMG, 1 September–31 December 1946, pp. 39–40, Records of the Public Information Office, Functional Histories of Military Government in Bremen, April 1945–March 1948, Box 71, RG 260, NARA. One of the defendants, Fritz Hackmann,

was convicted of bribery and sentenced to five years in prison and a fine of ten thousand reichsmarks.

81. FHMG, 1 September–31 December 1946, p. 1; FHMG in Land Bremen, 1 July 1946–30 June 1947, pp. 1–2, Records of the Public Information Office, Functional Histories of Military Government in Bremen, April 1945–March 1948, Box 74, RG 260, NARA. Captain Jeffs succeeded Dunn as director of the Office of Military Government for Bremen on 30 November 1948.

82. FHMG, 1 September–31 December 1946, p. 30; cf. FHMG, 1 July 1946–30 June 1947, p. 41, Records of the Public Information Office, Functional Histories of Military Government in Bremen, April 1945–March 1948, Box 74, RG 260, NARA.

83. Memorandum, Arthur J. Waterman Jr., City Administration Officer, and Robert A. Fletcher, Political Affairs Officer, for Director, Information Control Division, City Administration History, 1 September–31 December 1946, p. 5–7, Records of the Bremerhaven Liaison and Security Detachment, Records of the Central Office, Subject Files 1945–1949, Box 532, NARA.

84. "Bremen Today and Tomorrow," Speech by Bürgermeister Kaisen after the Election of the New Senate, translated from *Weser-Kurier*, 30 November 1946, pp. 4–5, Records of the Bremerhaven Liaison and Security Detachment, Records of the Central Office, Subject Files 1945–1949, Box 532, RG 260, NARA.

85. "Bremen Today and Tomorrow," 5.

86. Röpke, "Entstehung, Status und Verwaltung der amerikanischen Enklave Bremen," 447–48.

87. John W. Boyd, Major CMP, Communications Officer to Director, Office of Military Government for Bremen Enclave (U.S.), 15 July 1946, Records of the Public Safety Division, General Correspondence and Other Records, 1945–1949, Box 234, RG 260, NARA.

88. Robert W. Johnson, Chief Legal Officer, to Col. Welker, Director of OMG for Bremen Enclave (U.S.), p. 8, Records of the Denazification Division, Box 168, RG 260, NARA.

89. Memorandum, Henry Parkman, Director, Civil Administration Division, for the Secretary General, 27 November 1946, OMGUS Adjutant General, 1945–1946, Box 54, RG 260, NARA.

90. Memorandum, Views of Colonel Welker in Respect to Bremen, Henry Parkman, Director, Civil Administration Division, 16 September 1946, OMGUS Adjutant General, 1945–1946, Box 88, RG 260, NARA.

91. Memorandum, Views of Bürgermeister Kaisen on the status of the Free City of Bremen, Henry Parkman, Director, Civil Administration Division, 18 September 1946, OMGUS Adjutant General, 1945–1946, Box 88, RG 260, NARA.

92. Erwin W. Bard, Major AUS, to Director, Civil Administration Division, OMGUS, 19 August 1946, pp. 3, 5, OMGUS Adjutant General, 1945–1946, Box 88, RG 260, NARA.

93. Henry Parkman for Deputy Military Governor (DMG), 18 September 1946, OMGUS Adjutant General, 1945–1946, Box 88, RG 260, NARA.

94. Memorandum, Austin Albu and Henry Parkman for General Robertson and General Clay, Military Government Administration in the Bremen Enclave, 29 October 1946, OMGUS Adjutant General, 1945–1946, Box 109, RG 260, NARA.

95. Memorandum, William Whipple, Colonel, GSC, Secretary General, for Chief of Staff, Administration of Bremen, 25 November 1946, OMGUS Adjutant General, 1945–1946, Box 54, RG 260, NARA.

96. Memorandum, Henry Parkman, Director, Civil Administration Division, for the Secretary General, Administration of Bremen, 27 November 1946, OMGUS Adjutant General, 1945–1946, Box 54, RG 260, NARA.

97. Kaisen, Bürgermeister, for Director, OMGUS Bremen Enclave, Bremen Participation in Bizonal Administrative Committees [*sic*], 23 November 1946, Records of the Bremerhaven Liaison and Security Detachment, Records of the Special Branch, Denazification Records, 1945–1949, Box 601, RG 260, NARA.

98. *Weser-Kurier*, Thursday, 23 January 1947, Records of the Bremerhaven Liaison and Security Detachment, Records of the Central Office, Subject Files 1945–1949, Box 546, RG 260, NARA.

99. HQ/06101/SecG, 12 August 1946, Zonal Executive Offices Control Commission for Germany (British Element), Zone Policy Instruction No. 38, Disposal and Categorization of War Criminals, Nazis and Militarists, Records of the Office of Military Government for Bremen, Records of the Denazification Division, Box 170, RG 260, NARA.

100. Erich Schullze, ed., *Gesetz zur Befreiung von Nationalsozialismus und Militarismus vom 5: März 1946 mit Ausführungsvorschriften, Formblättern, der Anweisung für die Auswerter der Meldebogen und der Rangliste in mehrfarbiger Wiedergabe* (München, Germany: Bierstein Verlag, 1946).

101. Jesse S. Morse, Capt. QMC, Chief of Special Branch, Office of Military Government for Bremen Enclave (U.S.), for Director, Office of Military Government for Bremen Enclave (U.S.), 11 September 1946, pp. 1–2, Records of the Denazification Division, Box 166, RG 260, NARA.

102. Jesse S. Morse, Capt. QMC, Chief of Special Branch, Office of Military Government for Bremen Enclave (U.S.), for Internal Affairs and Communication Division, 2 October 1946, Records of the Denazification Division, Box 166, RG 260, NARA.

103. FHMG, 1 September–31 December 1946, p. 33.

104. FHMG, 1 September–31 December 1946, p. 33; cf. Jesse S. Morse, Capt. QMC, Chief of Special Branch Bremen Enclave, for Special Branch Officers Bremen Enclave (U.S.), 26 October 1946, Records of the Denazification Division, Box 167, RG 260, NARA.

105. G. H. Garde, Lieutenant Colonel, AGD, Adjutant General, Office of Military Government for Germany (U.S.), for Directors, 19 October 1946, Records of the Denazification Division, Box 168, RG 260, NARA.

106. FHMG, 1 January–31 March 1947, p. 23.

107. Henry J. Oberlander, U.S. Civilian, Chief Denazification Division, Office of Military Government for Bremen Enclave (U.S.), for Chief of Special Branch, 29 November 1946, Records of the Denazification Division, Box 166, RG 260, NARA.

108. Henry J. Oberlander, for Chief of Special Branch, 29 November 1946.

109. Engel for Military Government c/o Mr. Oberlander, 23 December 1946, Records of the Denazification Division, Box 166, RG 260, NARA.

110. FHMG, 1 January–31 March 1947, p. 22.

111. FHMG, 1 January–31 March 1947, p. 23.

112. FHMG, 1 September–31 December 1946, pp. 42–43.

113. FHMG, 1 January–31 March 1947, p. 23.

114. FHMG, 1 January–31 March 1947, p. 26.

115. Office of Military Government for Germany (U.S.), Public Relations Office, 24 December 1946, Records of the Denazification Division, Box 167, RG 260, NARA.

116. Jesse S. Morse, Capt. QMC, Chief Denazification Division, Office of Military Government for Bremen, for Senator for Political Liberation for Land Bremen, 2 July 1947, Records of the Denazification Division, Box 177, RG 260, NARA.

117. FHMG, 1 January–31 March 1947, pp. 25–26.

118. Schwarzwälder, *Das große Bremen-Lexikon*, 2: 849; United States Holocaust Memorial Museum, "Non-Jewish Resistance: Overview," Holocaust Encyclopedia, Photography, p. 1, at www.ushmm.org/wlc/media_ph.php?lang=en&ModuleId=10005420&MediaId=1552 (accessed 22 October 2008); Peter Müller, "Die A.G.-'Weser' in Bremen," p. 3, at http://werften.fischtown.de/archiv/agweser1.html (accessed 22 October 2008); Werften und Stadtgeschichte Bremerhavens, "Franz C. H. Stapelfeldt," p. 1, at http://werften.fischtown.de/archiv/stapelfeldt.html (accessed 22 October 2008).

119. FHMG, 1 January–31 March 1947, p. 26; Weekly Detachment Report, Office of Military Government for Bremen, 27 March 1947, p. 1, Records of the Denazification Division, Box 167, RG 260, NARA.

120. Jesse S. Morse, Capt., QMC, Chief of Special Branch, Office of Military Government for Bremen Enclave (U.S.), for Area Intelligence Officer, British Area Security Officer, 29 November 1946, p. 1, Records of the Denazification Division, Box 161; cf. also Lieutenant J. A. Garrett, Area Intelligence Officer, 202 A.I.O., for Denazification Division, OMG Bremen, 7 July 1947, Records of the Denazification Division, Box 161, RG 260, NARA.

121. FHMG, 1 October–31 December 1947, p. 20, Records of the Public Information Office, Functional Histories of Military Government in Bremen, April 1945–March 1948, Box 73, RG 260, NARA.

122. Hesse, *Konstruktionen der Unschuld*, 87.

123. FHMG, 1 September–31 December 1946, p. 40.

124. FHMG, 1 January–31 March 1947, pp. 27–28.

125. FHMG, 1 January–31 March 1947, p. 29; FHMG, 1 July 1946–30 June 1947, p. 43.

126. *Weser-Kurier*, Thursday, 23 January 1947, Records of the Bremerhaven Liaison and Security Detachment, Records of the Central Office, Subject Files 1945–1949, Box 546, RG 260, NARA.

127. Occupation Forces in Europe Series, 1947–1948, *The Evolution of the Occupation Forces in Europe*, by Joseph R. Starr and Francis Chase (Frankfurt am Main, Germany: European Command, Historical Division, 1948), 252–53.

128. Hans Jürgen Schraut, "U.S. Forces in Germany, 1945–1955," in *U.S. Military Forces in Europe: The Early Years, 1945–1970*, ed. Simon W. Duke and Wolfgang Krieger (Boulder, CO: Westview Press, 1993), 154–62. The arrangement was formalized in 1952 when the U.S. Army, Europe (USAREUR) took command of the European Theater's U.S. Army forces.

129. Occupation Forces in Europe Series, 1950, *Reorganization of Tactical Forces, VE-Day to 1 January 1949*, by Francis S. Chase (Karlsruhe, Germany: Historical Division, European Command, 1950), 15. The numbers for the years 1946–1947 are based on *Directory of the Army of the United States (Outside Continental Limits of the United States)*, AG 461 AO-I-M, and *Strength of the Army*, Department of the Army, Strength Accounting Branch, Office of the adjutant general under direction of Statistical Division, Office of the Army Comptroller, O.C.S.

130. G. v. Heukelum for American Military Government Wesermünde, Alteration of the name of the City of Wesermünde, 10 February 1947, Records of the Bremerhaven Liaison and Security Detachment, Records of the Central Office, Subject Files 1945–1949, Box 532, RG 260, NARA.

131. Annual Functional History of Military Government in Land Bremen, January–December 1948, p. 5, Records of the Public Information Office, Functional Histories of Military Government in Bremen, April 1945–March 1948, Box 75, RG 260, NARA.

132. Thomas F. Dunn, Director, Office of Military Government for Bremen Enclave (U.S.), for the Deputy Military Governor, Office of Military Government for Germany (U.S.), Constitutional Assembly of Land Bremen, 10 March 1947, OMGUS Adjutant General, 1947, Box 173, RG 260, NARA. Bremen's constitution passed into law on 21 October 1947.

133. C. K. Gailey, Brigadier General, GSC, Chief of Staff, Office of Military Government for Germany (U.S.), General Orders, 14 April 1947, OMGUS Adjutant General, 1947, Box 173, RG 260, NARA.

134. Röpke, "Entstehung, Status und Verwaltung der amerikanischen Enklave Bremen," 452.

135. George F. Kennan, *Memoirs: 1925–1950* (London: Hutchinson, 1968), chap. 11, annex C.

136. Norman Friedman, *The Fifty-Year War: Conflict and Strategy in the Cold War* (Annapolis, MD: Naval Institute Press, 2000), 69–76; *Foreign Relations of the United States. Diplomatic Papers. 1947. Volume III: The British Commonwealth, Europe*, 8 vols. (Washington, DC: United States Government Printing Office, 1972), 237–39; Occupation Forces in Europe Series, 1946–1947, *The Second Year of the Occupation* (Frankfurt am Main, Germany: European Command, Office of the Chief Historian, 1947), 69.

137. George C. Marshall, "Remarks by the Secretary of State: European Initiative Essential to Economic Recovery," *Department of State Bulletin* 16, no. 415 (15 June 1947): 1159–60; David W. Ellwood, "The Marshall Plan: A Strategy That Worked," *U.S. Department of State EJournal USA* (April 2006): 17–22; Act of April 3, 1948, European Recovery Act (Marshall Plan); Enrolled Acts and Resolutions of Congress, 1789–1996, General Records of the United States Government, RG 11, National Archives, Washington, D.C.

138. Occupation Forces in Europe Series, 1950, *Reorganization of Tactical Forces*, 21–26. Grafenwöhr was a former Wehrmacht training and maneuver ground that U.S. Army units used in 1945 and 1946 for artillery firing and other live fire activities.

139. C. F. Shapley, DAC for Senior P&T Officer (British), OPD Bremen, for PS (SB) Stade, 8 May 1947, Records of the Denazification Division, Box 161, RG 260, NARA.

140. FHMG, 1 July 1946–30 June 1947, p. 41; cf. Memorandum, Jesse S. Morse, Capt. QMC, Chief Denazification Division, Office of Military Government for Bremen, 24 March 1947, Records of the Denazification Division, Box 169, RG 260, NARA.

141. FHMG, 1 July 1946–30 June 1947, pp. 44–48.

142. Henry J. Oberlander, U.S. Civilian, Chief Denazification Division, Headquarters Office of Military Government for Bremen Enclave (U.S.), for Capt. Jesse S. Morse, Chief of Special Branch, 1 February 1947, Records of the Denazification Division, Box 169, RG 260, NARA.

143. George Dehn, U.S. Civilian, Operations Officer, Headquarters Office of Military Government for Bremen Enclave (U.S.), for Capt. Jesse S. Morse, Chief of Special Branch, 5 February 1947, Records of the Denazification Division, Box 168, RG 260, NARA.

144. Minutes, Meeting at Special Branch, Room 530 of Haus des Reichs, 25 February 1947, p. 3, Records of the Denazification Division, Box 169, RG 260, NARA.

145. Thomas F. Dunn, Director, Office of Military Government for Bremen Enclave (U.S.), for President of the Senate for Land Bremen, Bürgermeister Wilhelm Kaisen, 10 March 1947, Records of the Denazification Division, Box 169, RG 260, NARA.

146. Weekly Detachment Report, 27 March 1947, p. 3.

147. FHMG, 1 July 1946–30 June 1947, p. 42.

148. Conference between the Director of Bremen Military Government and the President of the Senate of Land Bremen, 7 March 1947, p. 2, Records of the Denazification Division, Box 169, RG 260, NARA.

149. FHMG, 1 July 1946–30 June 1947, p. 42.

150. Morse made this suggestion at the conference on 25 February 1947 (Minutes, Meeting at Special Branch, 25 February 1947, p. 2).

151. Memorandum, G. H. Garde, Lieutenant Colonel, AGD, Adjutant General, OMGUS, 29 April 1946, Records of the Denazification Division, Box 179, RG 260, NARA; Schullze, *Gesetz zur Befreiung*, 21–22.

152. Director Dunn requested OMGUS to amend the law to require every German above the age of nineteen to register in order to take into consideration the fact that the law was adopted in Bremen one year later than in the other Länder (Dunn, Director, Office of Military Government for Bremen, for Commanding General, OMGUS, 10 June 1947, Records of the Denazification Division, Box 168, RG 260, NARA).

153. Memorandum, G. H. Garde, 29 April 1946, pp. 2–3.

154. Memorandum, G. H. Garde, 29 April 1946, p. 6; cf. Schullze, *Gesetz zur Befreiung*, pp. 42–43.

155. Memorandum, G. H. Garde, 29 April 1946, p. 3.

156. Weekly Information Letter No. 1, 1 April 1947, p. 1, Office of Military Government for Bremen, Denazification Division, Records of the Denazification Division, Box 166, RG 260, NARA.

157. FHMG, 1 July 1946–30 June 1947, pp. 43–44.

158. Weekly Information Letter No. 8, 19 May 1947, Office of Military Government for Bremen, Denazification Division, p. 1, Records of the Denazification Division, Box 166, RG 260, NARA.

159. Weekly Information Letter No. 12, 16 June 1947, pp. 1–2, Office of Military Government for Bremen, Denazification Division, Records of the Denazification Division, Box 166, RG 260, NARA.

160. Weekly Information Letter No. 15, 7 July 1947, Office of Military Government for Bremen, Denazification Division, p. 1, Records of the Denazification Division, Box 166, RG 260, NARA.

161. Thomas F. Dunn, Director, Office of Military Government for Bremen, for President of the Bremen Senate, 28 July 1947, Records of the Denazification Division, Box 172, RG 260, NARA.

162. Joseph F. Napoli, interview by Adams, Bethesda, Maryland, 10 July 1990.

163. Minutes of the Conference regarding Denazification, 19 August 1947, pp. 1–2, Records of the Denazification Division, Box 169, RG 260, NARA.

164. "At First Only Procedures against Major Offender," *Weser-Kurier*, 23 August 1947, Records of the Denazification Division, Box 169, RG 260, NARA.

165. "New Phase in Denazification," *Weser-Kurier*, 30 August 1947, Records of the Denazification Division, Box 169, RG 260, NARA.

166. Tribunal Procedure against Selmar Seemann on August 28, 1947, signed Buschmann, German Deputy, 2 September 1947, Records of the Denazification Division, Box 157, RG 260, NARA. Dr. Pohl's first name does not appear on the documents.

167. Joseph F. Napoli, U.S. Civilian, Acting Division Chief, Denazification Division, for Director, Office of Military Government for Bremen, 10 October 1947, p. 1, Records of the Denazification Division, Box 168.

168. Joseph F. Napoli, 10 October 1947, p. 3.

169. Joseph F. Napoli, 10 October 1947, p. 2.

170. Joseph F. Napoli, 10 October 1947, p. 3.

171. Aevermann, Senator for Political Liberation, Bremen, for President of the Senate, Bürgermeister Kaisen, 30 October 1947, Records of the Denazification Division, Box 177, RG 260, NARA.

172. Conference between the Director of Bremen Military Government and the President of the Senate of Land Bremen, 31 October 1947, p. 2, Records of the Denazification Division, Box 169, RG 260, NARA.

173. Walther Richter, "Dr. Alexander Lifschütz, Senator für politische Befreiung in Bremen (27.11.1947 bis 31.12.1949)," in *"Denazification" Zur Entnazifizierung in Bremen*, ed. Wiltrud Ulrike Drechsel and Andreas Röpcke, 40 (Bremen, Germany: Edition Temmen, 1992); Hesse, *Konstruktionen der Unschuld*, 99–100; Schwarzwälder, *Das große Bremen-Lexikon*, 2: 546.

174. "Senator Dr. Lifschütz Had Prepared 'Revolutionary Plans,'" *Weser-Kurier*, 22 November 1947, Records of the Denazification Division, Box 169, RG 260, NARA.

175. German Census, 29 October 1946, British Zone, Records of the Bremerhaven Liaison and Security Detachment, Records of the Central Office, Subject Files 1945–1949, Box 558, RG 260, NARA.

176. Schullze, *Gesetz zur Befreiung*, 41–42.

177. Jesse S. Morse, Captain, QMC, Chief, Denazification Division, Office of Military Government for Bremen, Weekly Information Letter No. 10, 2 June 1947, pp. 1–2, Records of the Denazification Division, Box 166, RG 260, NARA.

178. Edward E. Harriman, U.S. Civilian, Acting Chief Special Branch, Stadt Bremen, Office of Military Government for Bremen, Report on Denazification of the German Railroads, Land Bremen, 4 December 1947, pp. 1–2, Records of the Denazification Division, Box 158, RG 260, NARA.

179. Edward E. Harriman, 4 December 1947, p. 3.

180. Edward E. Harriman, 4 December 1947, p. 2.

181. Beobachtung der Betriebsräteversammlung der Reichsbahn am 3 December 1947 (signed Buschmann), pp. 1–2, Records of the Denazification Division, Box 158, RG 260, NARA.

182. Joseph F. Napoli, Chief, Denazification Division, Office of Military Government for Bremen, for Commanding General, OMGUS, 5 December 1947, p. 3, Records of the Denazification Division, Box 165, RG 260, NARA.

183. Edward E. Harriman, U.S. Civilian, Acting Chief Special Branch, Stadt Bremen, for Chief Denazification Division, Office of Military Government for Bremen, 14 November 1947, Records of the Denazification Division, Box 158, RG 260, NARA. An example of the kind of conflict of interest Lifschütz intended to prevent occurred when *Spruchkammer* chairman Fritz Kölling, acting as defense counsel in a tribunal trial, interfered with the investigation of an employment sanction against the respondent he defended. FHMG, 1 October–31 December 1947, p. 29.

184. "Befreit Bremen von den Nazis," Bremer Demokratische Volkspartei, 29 October 1947, pp. 1–2, in Maßnahmen zur beschleunigten und erleichterten Durchführung der Entnazifizierung im Lande Bremen sowie Betrachtungen zur Entwicklung der Entnazifizierung und ihre Auswirkung—Bremisches Gesetz zum Abschluß der politischen Befreiung vom 4.4.50, Entnazifizierung 3-B.10.b Nr.132, I, StAB.

185. Letter, Fritz Entholt, Boden & Haac, Bremen, for Mr. Napoli, 8 December 1947, Records of the Denazification Division, Box 168, RG 260, NARA.

186. Der Präsident des Senats, Kaisen, for Mr. Napoli, 16 December 1947, in Einsetzung von Juristen für die Durchführung der Maßnahmen nach dem Befreiungsgesetz. Personelle Besetzung der Spruchkammern. Entnazifizierung 3-B.10.b Nr.106, StAB.

187. Bernard J. Ilson, U.S. Civilian, Liaison and Adv. Section, Office of Military Government for Bremen, for Mr. Napoli, 29 December 1947, p. 1, Records of the Denazification Division, Box 168, RG 260, NARA.

188. Memorandum, Joseph F. Napoli, U.S. Civilian, Acting Division Chief, Denazification Division, Office of Military Government for Bremen, 18 November 1947, p. 1, Records of the Denazification Division, Box 183, RG 260, NARA.

189. Quarterly Report for the Period of 1 October to 31 December 1947, Office of Military Government for Bremen, 5 January 1948, p. 1.

190. Memorandum, Thomas F. Dunn, Director, Office of Military Government for Bremen, 10 December 1947, p. 1, Records of the Denazification Division, Box 168, RG 260, NARA.

191. Memorandum, Thomas F. Dunn, 10 December 1947, p. 2.

192. Dr. Lifschütz, Der Senator für die Politische Befreiung, Bremen, for Military Government, 8 December 1947, Records of the Denazification Division, Box 177, RG 260, NARA.

193. Conference between the Director of Bremen Military Government and the President of the Senate of Land Bremen, 9 December 1947, p. 4, Records of the Denazification Division, Box 169, RG 260, NARA.

194. Memorandum, Joseph F. Napoli, U.S. Civilian, Division Chief, Denazification Division, Office of Military Government for Bremen, 16 December 1947, Records of the Denazification Division, Box 177, RG 260, NARA.

195. Quarterly Report for the Period of 1 October to 31 December 1947, Office of Military Government for Bremen, 5 January 1948, pp. 6–8, Records of the Denazification Division, Box 158, RG 260, NARA.

196. Peter Kurze, "115 Jahre Carl F.W. Borgward," *Oldtimer Info* 3 (2005): 4–5; Andreas Falkenhagen, Christoph W. O. Matthies, and Maik Ziemann, "Die Automobilindustrie im Nationalsozialismus: Drei biographische Beispiele" (Referat, Historisches Seminar TU Braunschweig, January 2000), 11, at www.millennum.de/referate/autonazi/ (accessed 10 November 2008); Sitzung mit den Klägern der Spruchkammer, Herrn Hollmann und Herrn Borchers, Monday, 27 October 1947, p. 6, Records of the Denazification Division, Box 159, RG 260, NARA. "Persilscheine" were named after a popular German brand of laundry detergent.

197. "Borgward—Lesser Offender: Top Positions No Incrimination—RM 50,000-Sanction," *Weser-Kurier*, 27 December 1947, Records of the Denazification Division, Box 169, RG 260, NARA; cf. Intelligence Report, Joseph F. Napoli, Chief, Denazification Division, Office of Military Government for Bremen, 6 January 1948, p. 2, Records of the Denazification Division, Box 184, RG 260; FHMG, 1 January–31 March 1948, p. 38, Records of the Public Information Office, Functional Histories of Military Government in Bremen, April 1945–March 1948, Box 73, RG 260, NARA.

198. Hesse, *Konstruktionen der Unschuld*, 426–31.

199. Hesse, *Konstruktionen der Unschuld*, 102.

200. "Chief Prosecutor Hollmann Resigns Position," *Weser-Kurier*, 31 January 1948, p. 1, Records of the Denazification Division, Box 180, RG 260, NARA.

201. Memorandum, Joseph F. Napoli, Chief, Denazification Division, Office of Military Government for Bremen, 2 February 1948, p. 1, Records of the Denazification Division, Box 177, RG 260, NARA.

202. "Chief Prosecutor Hollmann Resigns Position," 2.

203. The FDP in Bremen had a political program similar to the Bremen Democratic People's Party. Both parties represented the interests of Bremen business groups and based their programs on "free enterprise in economics and the 'rule of law' in politics" (Office of Military Government for Bremen, Supplementary Information on Civil Administration for the Congressional Committee, Robert A. Fletcher, Political Affairs Officer, 26 September 1947, p. 2, Records of the Denazification Division, Box 137, RG 260, NARA).

204. "Chief Prosecutor Hollmann Resigns Position," 2.

205. Intelligence Report, Joseph F. Napoli, Chief, Denazification Division, Office of Military Government for Bremen, 4 February 1948, p. 2, Records of the Denazification Division, Box 184, RG 260, NARA.

206. Intelligence Report, Joseph F. Napoli, p. 2.

207. "Chief Prosecutor Hollmann Resigns Position," 1; "Heinrich Hollmann rehabilitiert," *Weser-Kurier*, 23 March 1948, Records of the Denazification Division, Box 158, RG 260, NARA.

208. Office of Military Government for Bremen, Liaison and Security Office Bremerhaven, Tribunal Supervision Worksheet No. 64, Delinquency and Error Report, Joseph F. Napoli, Land Chief, Denazification Division, 20 November 1947, Records of the Denazification Division, Box 184, RG 260, NARA.

209. Joseph F. Napoli, Chief Denazification Division, Office of Military Government for Bremen, for Senator for Political Liberation for Land Bremen, 8 January 1948, Records of the Denazification Division, Box 177, RG 260, NARA.

210. Walter V. Burrows, Special Branch, Bremerhaven, for Mr. Ilson, Chief, Liaison Section, Denazification Division, Office of Military Government for Bremen, 6 March 1948, pp. 1–2, Records of the Denazification Division, Box 177, RG 260, NARA. The *Volksgerichtshof*, or People's Court, was a vehicle the Nazi regime created for the sole purpose of dealing with politically undesirable persons in show trials presided over by Ronald Freisler, an ill-famed judge.

211. Joseph F. Napoli, Chief, Denazification Division, Office of Military Government for Bremen, for Senator for Political Liberation for Land Bremen, 17 March 1948, p. 2, Records of the Denazification Division, Box 177, RG 260, NARA.

212. Walter V. Burrows, Special Branch, Bremerhaven, for Mr. Napoli, Chief Denazification Division, Office of Military Government for Bremen, 19 March 1948, pp. 1–4, Records of the Denazification Division, Box 182, RG 260, NARA.

213. Walter V. Burrows, Special Branch, Bremerhaven, for Denazification Division, Office of Military Government for Bremen, 20 March 1948, Records of the Denazification Division, Box 182, RG 260, NARA.

214. FHMG, 1 January–31 March 1948, pp. 20–21; Memorandum, the Senator for Political Liberation, Bremen, 4 February 1948, pp. 1–2, Records of the Denazification Division, Box 188, RG 260, NARA.

215. Joseph F. Napoli, Chief, Denazification Division, Office of Military Government for Bremen, Historical Report for the Period of 1 January 1948 to 31 March 1948 for Land Bremen, 16 April 1948, p. 3, Records of the Denazification Division, Box 168, RG 260, NARA.

216. Thomas F. Dunn, Director, Office of Military Government for Bremen, for Bürgermeister Wilhelm Kaisen, 17 February 1948, Records of the Denazification Division, Box 177, RG 260, NARA.

217. Friedman, *The Fifty-Year War*, 77–80; Report by Secretary of State Marshall on the Fourth Session of the Council of Foreign Ministers, 28 April 1947, in *Documents on Germany, 1944–1959. Background Documents on Germany, 1944–1959, and a Chronology of Political Developments Affecting Berlin, 1945–1956*, Senate Committee on Foreign Relations, 43–51, 49 (Washington, DC: United States Government Printing Office, 1959). For the full account of the proceedings of the Fourth and Fifth Session of the Council of Foreign Ministers, cf. United States of America, Department of State, *Foreign Relations of the United States. Diplomatic Papers. 1947. Volume II: Council of Foreign Ministers, Germany and Austria*, 8 vols. (Washington, DC: United States Government Printing Office, 1972), 139–576; Memorandum, G. H. Garde, Lieutenant Colonel, AGD, Adjutant Gen-

eral, Office of Military Government for Germany (U.S.), 27 March 1948, p. 1, Records of the Denazification Division, Box 180, RG 260, NARA.

218. "Denazification Finished," *Weser-Kurier*, 28 February 1948, Records of the Denazification Division, Box 180, RG 260, NARA.

219. Edward H. Litchfield, Director, Civil Administration Division, Office of Military Government for Germany (U.S.), for the Chief of Staff, 25 March 1948, TAB F, OMGUS Adjutant General 1948, Box 489, RG 260, NARA.

220. Memorandum, Lieutenant Colonel, AGD, Adjutant General, Office of Military Government for Germany (U.S.), March 1948, OMGUS Adjutant General 1948, Box 489, RG 260, NARA.

221. Intelligence Report, Investigation and Inspection Section, Week of 15 to 21 March 1948, Irving H. Saxe, Chief, Investigation Section, Denazification Division, Office of Military Government for Bremen, 23 March 1948, p. 3, Records of the Bremerhaven Liaison and Security Detachment, Records of the Special Branch, Denazification Records, 1945–1949, Box 600, RG 260, NARA.

222. E. Karstaedt, Stellvertreter, Der Senator für die Politische Befreiung, Bremen, for die Militär-Regierung, 11 March 1948, Records of the Denazification Division, Box 171, RG 260, NARA.

223. FHMG, 1 January–31 March 1948, p. 24.

224. Instructions for Expediting the Completion of Denazification Trials in the U.S. Zone, Thomas F. Dunn, Director (undated), pp. 1–2, Records of the Denazification Division, Box 177, RG 260, NARA.

225. Joseph F. Napoli, Chief, Denazification Division, Office of Military Government for Bremen, for British Area Intelligence Officer, 13 February 1948, Records of the Denazification Division, Box 183, RG 260, NARA.

226. Walter V. Burrows, Special Branch Office Bremerhaven, to Mr. Ilson, Chief, Liaison Section, Denazification Division, Office of Military Government for Bremen, 8 January 1948, pp. 1–2; Walter V. Burrows, Special Branch Office Bremerhaven, to Mr. Ilson, Chief, Liaison Section, Denazification Division, Office of Military Government for Bremen, 24 January 1948, p. 3, Records of the Denazification Division, Box 183; Joseph F. Napoli, Chief, Denazification Division, Office of Military Government for Bremen, for British Area Intelligence Officer, 16 January 1948, Records of the Bremerhaven Liaison and Security Detachment, Records of the Special Branch, Denazification Records, 1945–1949, Box 596, RG 260, NARA.

227. Minutes of the weekly discussion with officials of the Spruchkammer on 8 January 1948, p. 9, Records of the Denazification Division, Box 180; cf. also Walter V. Burrows, Special Branch Office Bremerhaven, for Mr. Ilson, Chief, Liaison Section, Denazification Division, Office of Military Government for Bremen, 8 January 1948, p. 1, Records of the Denazification Division, Box 183, RG 260, NARA.

228. Joseph F. Napoli, 13 February 1948.

229. Memorandum, Theo E. Hall, Chief of Branch, Public Safety Branch, OMGUS, 18 February 1948, pp. 2–3, Records of the Denazification Division, Box 183, RG 260, NARA.

230. Joseph F. Napoli, Chief, Denazification Division, Office of Military Government for Bremen, for British Area Intelligence Officer, 17 March 1948, Records of the

Denazification Division, Box 177, RG 260, NARA; cf also Bernard J. Ilson, Liaison and Adv. Section, Office of Military Government for Bremen, for Commanding General, OMGUS, 17 March 1948, Records of the Denazification Division, Box 177, RG 260, NARA.

231. "Denazification Going Top Speed," *Weser-Kurier*, 17 April 1948, Records of the Denazification Division, Box 180, RG 260, NARA.

232. Outgoing Message, Dunn, Office of Military Government for Bremen Enclave (U.S.), for Commanding General, OMGUS, 27 April 1948, Records of the Denazification Division, Box 177, RG 260, NARA.

233. "Thanks to Senator Dr. Lifschütz," *Weser-Kurier*, 11 May 1948, Records of the Denazification Division, Box 180, RG 260, NARA.

234. For a detailed account of the effort, cf. Elizabeth S. Lay, *The Berlin Airlift, Part I: 21 June–31 December 1948, Part II: 1 January–30 September 1949*, Special Studies Series, vols. 100, 102 (Karlsruhe, Germany: Headquarters, Historical Division, European Command, 1952). For the first airlift, cf. 1: 2–3.

235. Memorandum, Rescission of Portions of Title 2 and Part 8 of Title 9, MGR, G. H. Garde, Lieutenant Colonel, AGD, Adjutant General, 4 May 1948, Records of the Denazification Division, Box 179, RG 260, NARA.

236. Napoli, interview.

237. Hesse, *Konstruktionen der Unschuld*, 431.

238. Joseph F. Napoli, Chief, Denazification Division, Office of Military Government for Bremen, for the President of the Senate, Land Bremen, 17 February 1948, Records of the Denazification Division, Box 177, RG 260, NARA.

239. Memorandum, Joseph F. Napoli, Chief, Denazification Division, Office of Military Government for Bremen, 10 August 1948, pp. 1, 3, Records of the Denazification Division, Box 178, RG 260, NARA.

240. Distribution of History for Period 26 April–30 September 1945, pp. 19 and 21, Records of the Public Information Office, Functional Histories of Military Government in Bremen, April 1945–March 1948, Box 68, RG 260, NARA.

241. Directive, Withdrawal of Military Government from Denazification Operations, G. H. Garde, Lieutenant Colonel, AGD, Adjutant General, OMGUS, 11 August 1948, Records of the Denazification Division, Box 178, RG 260, NARA.

242. Joseph F. Napoli, Chief, Denazification Division, Office of Military Government for Bremen, for Executive Officer, 23 August 1948, pp. 1–2, Records of the Denazification Division, Box 177, RG 260, NARA.

243. Joseph F. Napoli, Chief, Denazification Division, Office of Military Government for Bremen, for Indigenous Personnel of Denazification Division, 31 August 1948, Records of the Denazification Division, Box 177, RG 260, NARA.

244. "Denazification Personnel," *Weser-Kurier*, 3 July 1948, Records of the Denazification Division, Box 180, RG 260, NARA.

245. Article 154, Landesverfassung der Freien Hansestadt Bremen vom 21, October 1947, Landeszentrale für politische Bildung in Zusammenarbeit mit der Verwaltung der Bremischen Bürgerschaft, Bremen, 1977, p. 94.

246. "Denazification not to last much longer," *Weser-Kurier*, 4 November 1948, Records of the Denazification Division, Box 161, RG 260, NARA.

247. Dr. Spitta, Senator for Law and Constitution, for Senator for Political Liberation, Bremen, 4 November 1948, p. 2, Records of the Denazification Division, Box 171, RG 260, NARA.

248. Conference between the Director of the Office of Military Government for Bremen and the President of the Senate of Land Bremen, 20 December 1948, Records of the Denazification Division, Box 171, RG 260, NARA.

249. Lucius D. Clay, General, U.S. Army, Military Governor, OMGUS, for Captain Charles R. Jeffs, USN, Director, Office of Military Government for Bremen, 14 December 1948, Records of the Denazification Division, Box 171, RG 260, NARA.

250. Lucius D. Clay, 14 December 1948.

251. Conference, 20 December 1948.

252. Conference, 20 December 1948.

253. Charles R. Jeffs, Captain, USN, Director, Office of Military Government for Bremen, for the President of the Bremen Senate, Bürgermeister Kaisen, 26 February 1949, Records of the Denazification Division, Box 171, RG 260, NARA.

254. Dr. Lifschütz, Senator for Political Liberation, for President of the Senate, Herr Bürgermeister Wilhelm Kaisen, Bremen, 15 March 1949, Records of the Denazification Division, Box 171, RG 260, NARA (emphasis in the original).

255. Telegram Received, OMGUS, signed Hays, 27 June 1949, Records of the Denazification Division, Box 171, RG 260, NARA.

256. Vorlage für die Ministerpräsidenten-Konferenz am, 3–4 May 1956, pp. 1–2, in Maßnahmen zur beschleunigten und erleichterten Durchführung der Entnazifizierung in Lande Bremen sowie Betrachtungen zur Entwicklung der Entnazifizierung und ihre Auswirkung—Bremisches Gesetz zum Abschluß der politischen Befreiung vom 4.4.50 nebst Änderungen, 1950, May 25–, Entnazifizierung 3-B.10.b Nr.132, II, StAB.

5

Bremen's Schools and Teachers

Reopening the Schools

To democratize the Germans, the Allies used a two-pronged approach of punitive measures such as the denazification program on the one hand and teaching democratic values through propaganda and school reform on the other. While the removal of Nazis from influential positions in society had first priority, constructive actions such as licensing newspapers and radio stations, reviving political parties and labor unions, disseminating propaganda films to cinemas, and establishing libraries soon followed. Among the various elements that shaped a program to reeducate the German public, reforming the education system was the most important. In addition to scrutinizing and rewriting school curricula and procuring suitable textbooks, U.S. Military Government officers tried to reform teacher training and, finally, the education system itself.

Before Captain Erwin W. Bard, the education officer of Bremen's Military Government, could begin to make any of the desired changes, he closed all schools and took stock. The aerial bombings of the city and docks had left many school buildings damaged or destroyed; there was a shortage of suitable books; and, most importantly, many teachers and school superintendents had to be dismissed because they had been members of the Nazi Party or its organizations. Six weeks after the beginning of the occupation, on 6 June 1945, Bard began the rebuilding process from the top. In his search for suitable candidates, he relied on a group of educators who had taught in progressive *Versuchsarbeitsschulen*, or experimental schools. These schools were a peculiarity of the Bremen school system before 1933. After World War I, school reformers founded several such schools based on experimental programs and new methods. The underlying democratic philosophy for these schools redefined the role of the teacher, teaching, and learning. Accordingly, schoolwork was more than mere training of the brain or an accumulation of knowledge; it also aimed to develop both body and soul. The teachers' task was not one of drilling and cramming like the corporal on the drilling ground. Instead, the teacher was supposed to be a personality who realized his or her task of harmoniously developing the physical, intellectual, and social qualities of the children, stressing education instead of teaching.[1] The schools featured democratic constitutions such as student councils and school papers and introduced coeducation throughout all grades. Funded exclusively out of contributions from participating parents, the instruction alternated with manual work and practice of the arts. To acquaint students with rural life and work, the schools also acquired or built *Schullandheime* or houses outside of the city to move the whole school to from time to time. When the Nazis came to power, they closed down the experimental schools immediately and dismissed most of the teachers.[2]

For the important post of Senator for Education, Captain Bard chose Christian Paulmann, a former experimental schoolteacher and Socialist Party politician. Paulmann had been elected a member of Bremen's Bürgerschaft, and his work in an education committee had gained him a reputation as a brilliant advocate of advanced ideas in educational and cultural policy. Initially imprisoned by Hitler's regime, he had continued his fight for modern education and against what he saw as the barbarism of the Nazis. His first act in office was to select new superintendents. The group of teachers he assembled had, like him, worked with or in experimental schools. Friedrich Aevermann, the new chief superintendent of elementary schools, had been the founder and principal of one of the experimental schools; Wilhelm Blanke, the superintendent of elementary schools in charge of buildings and school supplies, had been chairman of Bremen's Teacher Association; Karl Kircher, the acting superintendent of boys' secondary schools, had been a principal of a secondary school; Dr. Johanna Lürssen, the superintendent of girls' secondary schools, had held the same position until the Nazis dismissed her in favor of a leading Nazi candidate; Dr. Alfred Nawrath, the superintendent of arts and science, was an ethnographer and photographer who had authored numerous books on a wide variety of subjects such as ancient Roman architecture, Indian landscape and folk life, and the landscapes of Iceland; Johann Osterloh, the superintendent of elementary schools, had been a leading teacher before 1933; and Dr. Bernhard Rossmann, the chief superintendent of vocational schools, was also reinstated in his former office, which he had held until the Nazis removed him. Osterloh soon received an appointment to serve in the mayor's office.

His replacement was Hans Warninghoff, another experimental schoolteacher. Together with the senator, the new appointees formed a Board of Education charged with implementing military government directives.[3]

The new leadership's most urgent task was to repair schools and to reopen them as soon as possible. The children's education had suffered during the war, and the schools had to make up for lost time. Also, reopening the schools would serve to provide Bremen's youth with a semblance of normalcy and structure during the day—and perhaps even a meal. A survey of school premises indicated that about 60 percent of school buildings were totally destroyed or severely damaged. Even slightly damaged buildings required extensive repairs before they would be ready to receive children. Moreover, the lack of building materials severely hampered efforts to make the schools habitable, and military units occupied many of those that were in good shape. Further complicating the board's rebuilding efforts was the fact that Bremen Port Command, not the city's military government, controlled access to building materials. Considering schools and education "a strictly German problem," the officer in charge of material allotments at first denied Bard's requests. Only protracted negotiations convinced the officer to grant a small number of materials.[4]

The next challenge was the shortage of suitable textbooks. All Nazi-era textbooks and literature in libraries had been impounded. In lieu of help from the U.S. Group Control Commission in Berlin, the Education Branch conducted a search throughout the enclave for untainted textbooks for possible school use. Members of the school board and Education Office inspected each discovery. The next steps included investigating printing facilities, to search for existing plates, and requesting assistance from the British education officer at the 21st Army Group. The search resulted in finding a primer for elementary schools that Bard sent to Berlin for approval. By the time it arrived in Bremen, in July 1945, he had located the printing plates for the primer and a supply of paper at a Bremen publishing house. He instructed Senator Paulmann to have thirty thousand copies printed. With much of the work already completed, the Education Branch received orders to halt production because the author of the primer was found "not politically acceptable." A new order informed the education officer that ninety thousand "emergency" textbooks would be printed at Munich and that Bremen would receive an adequate supply. The promised shipment arrived in Bremen during the week of 10 September 1945, covering the needs for the first four grades.[5]

By far the greatest problem was the denazification and recruitment of teachers. When Allied troops entered Bremen in April 1945, the city had a total of 1,736 teachers, a number that was already inadequate at the time. Of those, more than a third had had close ties to the Nazi Party and were dismissed. In October, when the denazification program reached its peak, the percentage climbed to over 50 percent. Nevertheless, the Education Branch in cooperation with the school board managed to recruit enough teachers among retirees and married women who had stayed home with their children to open the first four grades of elementary schools within the main schools on 10 September 1945. To make up for the shortage of personnel and buildings, every available instructor, including secondary school teachers, taught enlarged elementary school classes in shifts. The teacher-to-student ratio was on average 1:74. Later that same fall, grades 5 through 8 of the main schools also opened. Secondary schools followed in December 1945. Finally, vocational and trade schools and special schools for children with learning disabilities reopened in February 1946.[6]

By this time, almost all of Bremen's approximately sixty thousand school-age children had returned from evacuation camps in the countryside and were enrolled in school. At any given time, between 70 and 90 percent of them attended school regularly. Chief among the reasons for missing class during the cold winter months were the lack of shoes and respiratory diseases. Want and poverty at home also played a role when parents sent their children on trips to the country to supplement meager food supplies with potatoes and other root vegetables they could find in the fields or beg or pilfer from farmers.[7] To ease the food shortages for families, Bremen's Military Government together with the city's civil authorities and help from the British Military Government Region Hanover began providing school meals in the middle of March for children between the ages of six and fourteen. Initially, about 15,600 children received a warm soup made of peas, beans, meat extract, milk, and biscuits in various combinations six times a week. The main obstacle for an expansion of the program was the lack of containers and other cooking utensils. Alerted through announcements in the press and on the radio, mothers contributed dishes from their own kitchens, and businesses donated enough cook pots to set up thirteen kitchens close to schools. As a result, at the beginning of April, the number of children receiving a warm lunch increased to nearly forty thousand. Most schools did not have dining halls, so the children ate at makeshift tables set up in corridors or in classrooms. Mothers volunteered their time cooking and serving the lunches, and each child brought his or her own utensils.[8]

Lasting Problems: Textbooks for a Democratic Future

While the military government and the German authorities were able to reopen schools in Bremen at the earliest practical date, they had done so at the expense of lowering the standard of education. The quantity of the shipment of textbooks from Munich was not nearly sufficient, and the quality left much to be desired. In secondary schools the situation was worse. Teachers had to rely entirely on provisionally approved textbooks that were mostly published before 1933.[9] All existing teaching texts for history lessons were banned from classrooms. Instead, Senator Paulmann's office issued detailed guidelines to history instructors for incorporating democratic values such as love of freedom, peace, justice, and mankind into their course materials. Once teachers completed their syllabi, they had to submit them to the military government for approval. On the subject of wars, Paulmann's guidelines were particularly strict:

> Wars have to be dealt with in an unbiased way in so far as they represent part of a historical development in general, this includes that the study of the strategic and tactical details of the various wars (Schemes of operations, sketches of battle-fields) is not allowed. In exactly the same way the glorification of war and the deliberate emphasis of soldier ship contradicts the general educational aim of the historical instruction and is on principle not allowed. Lessons have to be free from chauvinistic imperialistic, fascistic or military tendencies.[10]

In December 1945, the military government established textbook committees of qualified teachers to write new books for every subject taught in grades 1 through 8 in Bremen's elementary schools. In their work, the authors followed detailed curricula guidelines for the integration of democratic values into every subject. For the first four grades of elementary school, subjects included object lessons (knowledge of the native district), German language, arithmetic, writing, drawing, singing, and gymnastics. For the upper grades, they covered German language, arithmetic and geometry, geography, history, biology, natural science, biblical lessons, drawing, singing, gymnastics, and needlework and handicraft.[11] Half a year later, in June 1946, the committees had produced three textbooks—a German Primer *Bremer Fibel*, and parts 1 and 2 of *I Learn English*—that the Senator for Schools and Education published. Several other textbooks dealing with local history, arithmetic, and English literature were still under development.[12] After this good start, the work of the committees slowed, and the number of textbooks was still very limited in the beginning of 1947. Except for English-language classes that were held with books donated from the United States, there were only enough new and usable old textbooks for every second student. The Education Branch officers had hoped for faster progress and blamed the committees' poor leadership and insufficient number of capable writers but also the shortage of materials for the slowdown.[13] In June 1948, authors, textbook writers, illustrators, teachers, and publishers founded the Bremen Workshop for Textbooks that replaced the original textbook committees. At the end of the year, the workshop had published twelve textbooks that were in use in schools in Land Bremen.[14]

Libraries were another institution important for the reeducation of Germans. Many of the school libraries were destroyed during the war, leaving only one professional library, the beginnings of another, and the public library. The military government slowly expanded these existing facilities mainly through the donation of books.[15] On 11 December 1947, the military government opened the Bremen Curriculum and Textbook Center. Consisting of two rooms in a school building, it housed approximately three thousand books and offered services to teachers, textbook writers, and publishers. In June 1948, the collection of books in the center had grown to eight thousand volumes. This center later became the nucleus for an Amerika Haus (which provided information about American politics and culture) in Bremen.[16] All in all, the Americans founded more than twenty centers in larger cities in their occupation zone. In over seventy smaller communities, they opened reading rooms or small libraries of eight hundred to three thousand volumes. To reach people in rural areas, the military government equipped bookmobiles with small libraries, periodicals, and magazines. In addition to English-language books, the libraries also offered sizable collections of translated American books and provided numerous cultural services such as lectures, language classes, or book loans to educational institutions. The information centers were very popular with Germans who had been denied access to many works of literature and news media under strict Nazi censorship.[17] During the Cold War years and until the late 1990s, the Amerika Häuser continued to operate under the auspices of the Department of State U.S. Information Service.

Training New Teachers

The Nazis' distrust of the teaching profession made teachers' membership in at least one of the National Socialist German Workers' Party organizations practically compulsory—and their employment under occupation rules impossible. During the summer months, Education Branch continuously screened applicants for positions in schools but found that about 50 percent of them were unsuitable because of their political past. In September, the lack of suitable teachers continued to be a big problem. In these dire circumstances, mobilizing so-called teacher reserves of retirees and married women teachers who had stayed at home after they had children was a desperate but effective measure that enabled the authorities to open schools in the fall of 1945. To augment the pool, they also recruited refugee teachers, but differences in professional training, general academic standards, and in some cases doubts about their political reliability soon ended that practice.[18] Lack of professional training was also the reason for the Board of Education's refusal to accept untrained lay teachers, as was the practice in the neighboring British Zone. The board members argued that the Nazis had undermined the foundation of the professional training of teachers to such an extent that any proposal making for a further decline had to be turned down, even as an emergency solution. As a result, Bremen's pool of educators in the fall of 1945 was mostly older and female. Their average age was fifty-one years and that of male teachers was fifty-five years. The military government worried about the "greatly advanced feminization of the teaching profession" and decided to counter the trend with retraining of younger, dismissed teachers.[19]

But since education in general and training of teachers in specific were of little interest to the Nazi regime, only one institution, the *Lehrerbildungsanstalt*, or Teacher Training Institute, existed in Bremen at the end of the war. Designed for quick training of politically acceptable candidates, it required no proof of a general education such as a high school diploma for entry, and the training consisted of indoctrination and rote memorization rather than academic lectures and discussions. Early on, the Education Branch and the Board of Education agreed not to revive this institution.[20] Instead, the military government founded a Teacher Training College, or *Pädagogisches Seminar*, for elementary school teachers. Making the Abitur,[21]or German high school diploma, a prerequisite for admission, the new college opened its doors on 1 December 1945. Its new director was Klaus Böttcher, another leader of the experimental school movement. In 1930, he had spent a year working at the International Institute of Columbia University, New York, where he prepared a thorough study of the most progressive schools in the United States. After his return to Bremen, he headed one of the experimental schools that were closed in 1933.[22] For the first yearlong emergency training course, more than four hundred candidates applied. Böttcher selected the one hundred most qualified applicants and began their program on 3 December. As an experiment and a necessity, he also admitted older applicants who possessed "practical knowledge of life" but no high school diploma.[23] In December 1946, sixty-two students passed their final examinations. This first course was a learning experience for the students as well as for the Board of Education and for the military government. The main difficulty the college faculty members encountered was trying to tailor their instruction to accommodate students' different levels of knowledge in the sciences.[24] A second course, again with one hundred participants, commenced in the beginning of March 1946.[25] To train badly needed secondary school teachers, a *Studienseminar* opened on 8 February 1946. The prerequisite for enrollment in the institute was a university degree. The first two-year course had twenty-four participants with sixteen of them women. Five months later, the Board of Education expanded training capacity for secondary teachers. It converted a provisional Teacher Training

College into a Pedagogical Academy, or *Pädagogische Hochschule*, which offered complete professional training in four to six terms.[26]

In June 1946, the board also established a course to retrain younger teachers in the Mandatory Dismissal category. The new course was the first of its kind in Germany and began on 20 August 1946 with forty-four "carefully selected" participants between the ages of twenty and forty-three years. All students met ideological and scientific requirements of the course and passed a final exam on 15 November. On graduation day, the participants received certificates of attendance that made them eligible for provisional employment in the Bremen public school system.[27] In addition to training for new teachers, the Board of Education insisted on a "refresher" course for all of Bremen's teachers. This course consisted of a series of lectures that were mostly delivered by the mayor and other prominent members of the Bremen Senate and school board on the political, economic, and educational problems of the day.[28]

With teacher training programs still in their beginning stages in the spring of 1947, schools in Bremen and Bremerhaven had to put politically tainted teachers back into the classroom. Many of them taught without certificates because Land Bremen had not yet established enough *Spruchkammern* to hear their cases, according to George Freimarck, the military government's chief of intelligence in the Information Control Division. Researching German reactions to the problems of education for a report, Freimarck interviewed a grammar school principal in Bremerhaven about temporarily reinstated teachers. In the principal's experience, the teachers generally behaved extremely cautiously, and they tried to camouflage their attitudes. The school director feared that the combined effects of these teachers' nationalistic slant in their teaching and the scarcity of textbooks would result in a new generation of young Nazis. Not every cautious teacher, however, had something to hide. Some of the younger reinstated educators were well intentioned but lacked training in how to teach in a democratic system, so they were very guarded around their colleagues and in their classes. In his investigation, Freimarck spoke to one of the reinstated teachers. She was a young woman who had been a member of the Bund Deutscher Mädchen, the Nazi youth organization for girls. Telling the intelligence officer how very grateful she was to be allowed to work again, she stated that she considered it her highest duty to educate the children "along the desired lines." She confessed, however, that her work was infinitely more complicated under the current circumstances than it had been under the Nazis because of the lack of available teaching material. Faculty meetings and a daily issue of directives through the principal were poor substitutes for directive material for the teacher.[29]

The parents, Freimarck pointed out, were for the most part not troubled about the state of public education because they were too concerned with the more immediate things of daily life:

> If the child has shoes with which to go to school, gets a noon-day meal at school, is kept off the streets and out of his parents' way for a sufficient time each day, then school is [a] good thing and education is fulfilling its purpose. Those parents who find either the time or the interest to wonder whether their children are getting a democratic education satisfy themselves with the belief that the teachers are adequately supervised by their superiors, both among the German and American authorities.[30]

Not surprisingly, Freimarck concluded that the state of public education in Bremerhaven was "deplorable" and that the only acceptable solution was more teacher training and "the introduction of new blood in the staff."[31] In February 1948, almost a year after Freimarck's analysis, Bremerhaven's Special Branch was still dissatisfied with the situation in public schools. In a report to Bremen's Denazification Division, Walter V. Burrows declared that too many former Nazis and militarists taught young children in Bremerhaven's elementary schools.[32] Five months later, Harold H. Crabill, chief of the Education Division, repeated the same complaint to Senator Paulmann and threatened that noncompliance with orders to dismiss politically undesirable teachers might even result in possible prosecution of superintendents for failure to comply with military government orders.[33] By this time, however, the military government had withdrawn from the denazification program and was fully engaged in helping to rebuild Germany's economy and keep the city of Berlin supplied by air. As a result, no superintendent was prosecuted, and politically tainted teachers remained in their jobs because they were needed.

Long-Term Effects of U.S. Reeducation Efforts

The Old School System Survives

In December 1945, the military government made plans to reorganize Bremen's traditional three-tiered school system, which distributed students according to their abilities after they completed elementary school and was part of Volksschule or main school. Under this system, children who remained in main school spent the next four years, grades 5 through 8, focusing on reading, writing, and arithmetic in preparation for an apprenticeship in a trade. The second tier was the *Realschule*, a technical high school that graduated students after tenth grade and qualified them for white-collar jobs. The third tier was the *Gymnasium*, or high school, which taught a strictly academic curriculum and prepared students for university. Students graduated from *Gymnasium* with an *Abitur* or high school diploma after the thirteenth grade. There was virtually no interchange between the three school types, making it impossible for students to go on to the next higher school even if they excelled in main school, or *Realschule*. The decisions teachers and parents made about the type of school a fourth grader should attend determined that child's future as a blue-collar worker, white-collar employee, or academic. In order to open up the possibility for a higher education to a larger number of children, the Education Branch proposed to leave grades 5 and 6 undivided, to be followed by upper grades that would lead the gifted children in a four-year course to the *Mittlere Reife* (middle school diploma), while the remaining pupils would pass to vocational schools after a two-year course.[34]

Discussions between the military government and German authorities on this proposal lasted for two years. In March 1947, both sides agreed in principle on a reorganization plan that included a six-year elementary school with a common curriculum, a three-year junior high school, or *Mittelschule*, with some common subjects for all children, and a three- or four-year high school, or *Oberschule*, separated according to various branches such as modern languages or the natural sciences. The plan also stipulated coeducation for all schools, free tuition for all students at all schools, as well as a three-year program for teacher training at a teachers, college or *Pädagogische Hochschule*. The officers and politicians agreed to implement the reform at the beginning of the new school year in the fall, at first in two sectors of the city with approximately one-third of the school children. The military government hoped to implement the program for the entire Land Bremen in the beginning of 1948.[35]

When details of the planned reform became public, however, teachers and parents in the affected school districts opposed the reforms. They based their objections on the argument that any reform that increases the number of years a child had to spend in elementary school automatically would inevitably decrease the achievement level of the secondary school. Not wanting to be seen as deliberately lowering standards of German schooling, the Education Division took this opposition very seriously, and in the face of continued resistance, the military government and Bremen's school leaders abandoned reform plans in 1948.[36]

Reformers who had worked on the plans, however, did not give up on their desire for a fundamental restructuring of Bremen's schools and pursued their cause with dogged determination. In the next two and a half decades, they chipped away at public mistrust of a high school concept that combined the three types of schools. In 1970, the *Gesamtschule* or comprehensive school, officially replaced the traditional school system in Bremen.[37]

International University Bremen

In the summer of 1947, while still engaged in the effort to reform primary and secondary schools, the military government and German authorities also began developing a concept for an international university for Bremen. On 29 September, the Senate, the city's administration, adopted the idea as its own and appointed a planning committee.[38]

The committee's proposal broke the boundaries of German university traditions by suggesting a campus university with a student population of 30 to 40 percent foreigners—studying, working, and living together at the university. This new university would be located on the premises of the barracks at Bremen-Grohn, which would be turned back over to the German government during the first six months of 1948. It would house a medical school, a pedagogic college, and a school of social studies.[39]

Despite wide support and practical assistance from the American and British Military Governments and Bremen's population for the project, progress came to an abrupt halt when it became clear that the barracks would not be available because they were needed as a camp for displaced persons. With its momentum lost, the university project became a mainstay of Senate debates and the subject of study for successive committees. Along the way, the original idea of an international university gave way to a more traditional approach to an institution of higher learning. At the end of this more than two decades–long process, the city of Bremen inaugurated its new university in October 1971. The concept of an international university, however, was not forgotten. In the late 1990s, it resurfaced as the basis for a private university that would fund itself through student tuition and corporate sponsorship. The city's administration closely cooperated with Rice University in Houston, Texas, and founded the International University Bremen in 1999 on the grounds of the Grohn barracks.[40]

Notes

1. Functional History Military Government (FHMG), 27 April 1945–30 June 1946, part 2, appendix 46, p. 1, Records of the Public Information Office, Functional Histories of Military Government in Bremen, April 1945–March 1948, Box 68, RG 260, NARA.

2. FHMG, 27 April 1945–30 June 1946, part 2, appendix 46, p. 2.

3. FHMG, 27 April–30 September 1945, pp. 35–36, 174–75; FHMG, October–November 1945, 1–10 December, p. 45, Records of the Public Information Office, Functional Histories of Military Government in Bremen, April 1945–March 1948, Box 68; FHMG, 10 December 1945–31 January 1946, part 1, pp. 19–22, Records of the

Public Information Office, Functional Histories of Military Government in Bremen, April 1945–March 1948, Box 69, RG 260, NARA; FHMG 10 Dec 1945–31 Jan 1946, Part I, pp. 19–22, Records of the Public Information Office, Functional Histories of Military Government in Bremen. Apr. 1945–Mar. 1948, Box 69, RG 260, NARA; Personalien, Dr. Alfred Nawrath, *Der Spiegel*, 18.08. 1949, 34/1949, p. 24.

4. FHMG, 27 April–30 September 1945, pp. 37–39.

5. FHMG, 27 April–30 September 1945, pp. 40–41.

6. FHMG, 27 April–30 September 1945, pp. 41–43, 168.

7. FHMG, 27 April–30 September 1945, pp. 180–81. The experiences of Bremen's school-age children were typical for the whole region. My father, who grew up in Cäciliengroden, a small village about sixty-five miles northwest of Bremen, was eight years old at the end of the war. Talking about the immediate postwar years, he recalled that his mother sent him regularly to nearby farms to "collect" potatoes. Occasionally, he and his friends also made their way to a local train yard to pilfer potatoes from British Military Government freight railcars.

8. FHMG, 27 April–30 September 1945, p. 182–83; FHMG, 1 February–31 March 1946, part 1, p. 2, Records of the Public Information Office, Functional Histories of Military Government in Bremen, April 1945–March 1948, Box 70, RG 260, NARA.

9. FHMG, 10 December 1945–31 January 1946, p. 34; FHMG, 27 April 1945–30 June 1946, p. 184.

10. FHMG, 10 December 1945–31 January 1946, part 2, appendix 7, Curricula for Primary Schools, Curriculum for the upper grades of the Elementary Schools, pp. 10–17, here p. 10.

11. FHMG, 10 December 1945–31 January 1946, part II, appendix 7.

12. FHMG, 27 April 1945–30 June 1946, pp. 166, 185.

13. FHMG, 1 January–31 March 1947, p. 99, Records of the Public Information Office, Functional Histories of Military Government in Bremen, April 1945–March 1948, Box 72, RG 260, NARA.

14. Annual FHMG in Land Bremen, January–December 1948, p. 83, Records of the Public Information Office, Functional Histories of Military Government in Bremen, April 1945–March 1948, Box 76, RG 260, NARA.

15. FHMG, 1 January–31 March 1947, p. 101.

16. FHMG, 1 October–31 December 1947, p. 68, Records of the Public Information Office, Functional Histories of Military Government in Bremen, April 1945–March 1948, Box 73, RG 260, NARA; Annual FHMG in Land Bremen, January–December 1948, p. 83.

17. "Amerika Haus: US Information Centers in Germany," *Information Bulletin* 148 (November 1948): 19–21 (Office of Military Government for Germany [U.S.], Control Office, Berlin, Germany, APO 742, U.S. Army).

18. FHMG, 27 April 1945–30 June 1946, pp. 19–21, 177.

19. FHMG, 10 December 1945–31 January 1946, p. 29.

20. FHMG, 27 April 1945–30 June 1946, p. 178.

21. The *Abitur* is a secondary school diploma equivalent to Great Britain's university entrance exam or an associate's degree from a college in the United States.

22. FHMG, October–November 1945, 1–10 December, p. 46.

23. FHMG, 10 December 1945–31 January 1946, part 2, appendix 23, Plans for the Bremen Board of Education for Future Training of Teachers of Primary Schools, pp. 1–3, here p. 2.

24. FHMG, 1 September–31 December 1946, part 2, appendix 60, Experiences Made in the First Course of the Teachers' Training College Bremen, pp. 1–2, here p. 1, Records of the Public Information Office, Functional Histories of Military Government in Bremen, April 1945–March 1948, Box 71, RG 260, NARA.

25. FHMG, 27 April 1945–30 June 1946, p. 179.

26. FHMG, 10 December 1945–31 January 1946, p. 30.

27. FHMG, 1 July–31 August 1946, p. 38, Box 70; see also FHMG in Land Bremen, 1 July 1946–30 June 1947, p. 106, Box 74; FHMG, 1 September–31 December 1946, part 2, appendix 61, First Teachers' Retraining Course in Bremen, p. 1, Records of the Public Information Office, Functional Histories of Military Government in Bremen, April 1945–March 1948, Box 71, RG 260, NARA.

28. FHMG, 27 April 1945–30 June 1946, p. 180. The date for this "refresher" course remained unspecified.

29. George Freimarck (USC), Chief of Intelligence, Information Control Division, Office of Military Government for Bremen, Special Report No. 32: German Reactions to the School and Youth Program in Bremerhaven—Preliminary Report, 1 April 1947, pp. 2–4, Records of the Bremerhaven Liaison and Security Detachment, Records of the Central Office, Subject Files 1945–1949, Box 532, RG 260, NARA.

30. George Freimarck, Special Report No. 32, p. 4.

31. George Freimarck, Special Report No. 32, p. 5.

32. Walter V. Burrows, Special Branch, Bremerhaven Liaison and Security Detachment, for Napoli, Chief, Denazification Division, Office of Military Government for Bremen, 17 February 1948, Records of the Denazification Division, Box 182.

33. Harold H. Crabill, Chief of the Education Division, Office of Military Government for Bremen, for Senator for Schools and Education, 10 July 1948, p. 1, Records of the Denazification Division, Box 178.

34. FHMG, 10 December 1945–31 January 1946, p. 33.

35. FHMG, 1 January–31 March 1947, pp. 85–86.

36. FHMG, 1 July–30 September 1947, p. 65, Records of the Public Information Office, Functional Histories of Military Government in Bremen, April 1945–March 1948, Box 72, RG 260, NARA.

37. FHMG in Land Bremen, 1 October–31 December 1947, p. 62, Records of the Public Information Office, Functional Histories of Military Government in Bremen, April 1945–March 1948, Box 73, RG 260, NARA; Herbert Schwarzwälder, *Das Große Bremen-Lexikon*, 2 vols. (Bremen, Germany: Edition Temmen, 2003), 2: 783, L–Z.

38. FHMG, 1 July–30 September 1947, pp. 66–67.

39. FHMG, 1 July–30 September 1947, pp. 66–67.

40. Schwarzwälder, *Das Große Bremen-Lexikon*, 1: 426, A–K; 2: 901–7. A chronology of the development of the International University Bremen is available on the institution's website at www.iu-bremen.de/about/quickfacts.

Conclusion

THE MILITARY GOVERNMENT OF THE Bremen enclave had to deal with difficulties arising from its insular existence within the British Zone, while facing the same challenges civil affairs detachments encountered in other urban centers in Germany. The confusion over legal and territorial boundaries was often so profound that it prevented the flexible and efficient operation of military government divisions because time-consuming negotiations with local German agencies operating under the direction of state-level offices located in the British Zone preceded any decision or action of significance. The attempts by both military governments to solve the inherent problems by applying American rules in Bremen one year, British rules the next year, and again American in the year after that in effect slowed the development of the city's political institutions and deprived it of representation in the Council of States for a year.

Similar to experiences in the southern states, opposition or support for the denazification program among Bremen citizens depended largely on how it affected them personally.[1] Bremen's geographical situation as an American island within the British Zone, however, led to an increasingly negative perception of the program. Since the British handled denazification in a more lenient fashion, many citizens used this discrepancy in Anglo-American occupation policies to their own advantage and submitted to the British even though the U.S. program applied to them. Furthermore, a number of people the Americans had dismissed from their jobs found employment in their professions in neighboring towns under British rule.

Its geographical situation and the uncertainties and turmoil resulting from changing approaches two times in as many years created its own set of challenges for Bremen's denazification program. The city's civil and military governments spent much of their time and energy setting up denazification bureaucracies according to American or British specifications, making it difficult for them to sustain the program's integrity and credibility in the eyes of its citizens. While one set of agencies heard cases and tried to finish its work, military government and city officials were already searching for personnel for the next set of organizations to be created. At the same time, citizens with a Nazi past used Bremen's peculiar situation to choose the denazification procedure most advantageous to them—usually the British—while others were caught between both systems, further wearing down public trust in the process.

The fits and starts also prolonged and undermined the legitimacy of the program. With each new bureaucracy, the denazification program lost some of its credibility in Bremen. Many of Bremen's citizens reacted with cynicism because it appeared that the "small fry" bore the brunt of the missionary zeal in the beginning, while the "big fish" got away in a new political climate that wanted nothing more than to finish what had become a bureaucratic quagmire. In the end, the U.S. denazification program in Bremen achieved most of its primary objectives. Despite the turmoil created by changing from American to British and back to American control, the program ultimately eliminated Nazi organizations and laws, with most Nazi activists losing their positions of influence in public service and private industry.

In addition to the interzonal complexity, differences of opinion between the German and American denazification agencies and internal American disputes about the correct implementation and extent of the program further complicated the task. While American officers, chiefly Joseph F. Napoli and Walter V. Burrows, literally aimed to remove all former Nazis from positions of influence in public office and the economy, many German denazification officials, among them Dr. Alexander Lifschütz, came to see denazification as a bureaucratic and legalistic process. Accordingly, people had to submit their paperwork so that the authorities could assess the degree to which they had been a Nazi. Once they paid their penalty, they were denazified in the eyes of the public. For a while, the military government officers fought this interpretation of the program with bureaucratic tools such as Delinquency and Error Reports. When the relationship between the United States and the Soviet Union became openly hostile and concerns grew about the crippling effects denazification might have on the rebuilding of the German industry, the German concept ultimately prevailed.

Within the military government, officers charged with denazification also had to overcome resistance and evasive maneuvers by their own colleagues in other divisions. In an internal report, a frustrated investigator pointed out that in the beginning the military government at least made an effort to find politically untainted persons, especially for filling positions in the denazification machinery. Later, however, candidates were selected for their knowledge of the English language rather than their political record.[2] The most outspoken critic of this internal strife in Bremen's Military Government was its principal denazification officer, Napoli. In his view, there were only a few American officers who were truly dedicated to the cause of political purification, and they were ostracized, unpopular, and treated as outsiders by their fellow military government officers. He expressed the sense of futility he and his colleagues felt in the end of 1948:

> Denazification was never enthusiastically accepted by the great body of German public servants, nor has it been accepted completely by the average German. Some flagrant injustices and absurd decisions have convinced the Germans that this one program was as close to being bungled as the German authorities with American help and supervision could manage.[3]

In his judgment, the denazification program was a failure brought on by an overextension of the program, corruption among American officers, and the sheer impossibility of recruiting enough nonincriminated persons to staff trial tribunals that degenerated into whitewashing machinery. But even denazification's most fervent advocate conceded that it was obviously difficult to staff important offices with non-Nazis when technical knowledge and academic background were restricted to those persons who embraced the Nazi faith.[4]

In implementing denazification in the courts, the *Reichsbahn*, the schools, and other fields requiring extensive training, the military government was very aware of the small pool of replacements and ready to make concessions. The field of education in particular, by its very nature, did not lend itself to rapid or easy change. The lifeblood of a school was its teaching staff members who had invested many years of their lives in their own education before they could practice their chosen profession—thus making the replacement of nearly half the members of this select group an extremely difficult task for the American occupiers. When they had exhausted the small number of "reserves," they compromised the ambitious goal of a complete purge for the practical and equally important goal of opening the schools.

The education officers learned very fast that almost every aspect of their job was time consuming and difficult to accomplish. While replacing teachers was hard, trying to convince Bremen's citizens to part with their traditional school system for a more open, less elitist one was impossible. The city's education system had a long tradition, and the military government was not prepared to force a change that had the potential to arouse open rebellion from otherwise obedient parents and teachers. In the end, the military government had to walk a very fine line in its attempts to reeducate Bremen. Reopening the schools meant more than educating children. It brought normalcy to a chaotic situation; it reestablished a familiar rhythm to children's and parents' lives; and it stood for a return of stability to a populace that had been culturally, socially, and emotionally shattered.

What happened in the classrooms and the potential harm it could do to young minds remained a great worry for Bremen's leadership long after 1945. In an April 1949 conversation with Walter Dorn, military governor general Lucius D. Clay's advisor on denazification, Dorn stated that the city's mayor, Wilhelm Kaisen, had admitted that the problem of education touched him most deeply. Kaisen told Dorn about unannounced visits he paid schools from time to time and that the things he had to witness made him cry. A very emotional Kaisen continued that he could deal with the utter destruction the war had brought to Germany but that the ruin of the educational system devastated him. Still, Kaisen conceded that for the moment not much could be done because new teachers could only be trained step-by-step and slowly.[5]

In the end, the denazification program in the Bremen enclave had results similar to those in the other states of the U.S. Zone. Deadlines and waning governmental support forced the bloated denazification bureaucracy to resort to classifying most of the remaining individuals whose cases were still pending as benign "followers" (*Mitläufer*), even when they hardly deserved that label. While the denazification program succeeded in discovering and punishing many of the main functionaries of the Nazi regime, it also fell victim to its own ambition and collapsed underneath the weight of its administrative processes, leaving both the Americans and Germans involved in the program demoralized and disillusioned.

The inglorious conclusion of the program should not be equated, however, with failure. Instead, it all depends on how the success and failure of this remarkable attempt to purge a whole society of its harmful elements by way of a military government is defined. If success is complete removal and exclusion of anyone who was ever more than a nominal member of the Nazi Party or any of its affiliations, denazification was most certainly a failure. But, if the long-term effects of this program on German society are a measure of success, then the denazification was a success.

The absence of attempts to resurrect the Nazi Party or a similar organization in the Federal Republic of Germany, even in times of crisis, is the best indicator of success. Nazi ideology was thoroughly discredited and generally recognized as the primary cause of so much destruction on German society. Despite its obvious flaws, the denazification program permanently removed most members of the Nazi elite from their positions of influence in the public sector. Furthermore, the lingering effects of the program served as a most effective deterrent against political ambitions of former Nazis. While some former Nazis regained a socioeconomic status similar to the one they had occupied before the Nazi regime, they did so in private industry.[6] Even today, the program's lasting effects influence the way German society deals with its history. After initial hesitation,[7] no society in Europe has dealt more candidly with its past in public discourse. That is, perhaps, the most enduring validation of a morally guided and practically implemented denazification policy.

Notes

1. FHMG, October–November 1945, 1–10 December 1945, p. 12, Records of the Public Information Office, Functional Histories of Military Government in Bremen, April 1945–March 1948, Box 68, RG 260, NARA.

2. Bericht Alfred Göbel (undated), pp. 1–2, Records of the Denazification Division, Box 157, RG 260, NARA.

3. FHMG, January–December 1948, p. 31, Records of the Public Information Office, Functional Histories of Military Government in Bremen, April 1945–March 1948, Box 75, RG 260, NARA.

4. Joseph F. Napoli, "Denazification from an American's Viewpoint," *Annals of the American Academy of Political and Social Science* (July 1949): 117–23.

5. Lutz Niethammer, ed., *Walter L. Dorn: Inspektionsreisen durch die U.S.-Zone. Notizen, Denkschriften und Erinnerungen* (Stuttgart, Germany: R. Oldenbourg Verlag, 1973), 169.

6. Ulrich Herbert, *Best: Biographische Studien über Radikalismus, Weltanschauung und Vernunft, 1903–1989* (Bonn, Germany: J. H. W. Dietz, 1996), 472–76.

7. At my high school in Northwest Germany, history teachers studiously avoided broaching the subject of the Holocaust until the American television miniseries *Holocaust* aired in the late 1970s. Ensuing intense public interest and discussion of the Holocaust forced them to cover this subject in class. Before that time, instruction about the Nazi regime ended in 1934. Although my teachers never left a shadow of a doubt as to the evil nature of the regime, concentration camps and the fate of the inmates were off limits.

Glossary of Terms and Abbreviations

Berufungsausschuß. German appeal boards
BPC. Bremen Port Command
Bürgermeister. Mayor
Bürgerschaft. Bremen's city council
CA. Civil affairs
CAD. Civil Affairs Division
CAO. Civil affairs officer
CATS. Civil Affairs Training School
CCS. Combined Chiefs of Staff
CDU. Christian Democratic Union
CIC. Counterintelligence Corps
COSSAC. Chief of Staff to the Supreme Allied Commander
DNVP. German National People's Party
DP. Displaced person
DP. Deutsche Partei, or German Democratic Party
EAC. European Advisory Commission
ECAD. European Civil Affairs Division
ETO. European Theater of Operations
ETOUSA. European Theater of Operations, U.S. Army
flak. Antiaircraft defense
Fragebogen. Questionnaire used by the military government to determine Nazi and militarist associations of Germans
G-1. Personnel section of a divisional or high staff

G-2. Intelligence section
G-3. Operations section
G-4. Supply section
G-5. Civil affairs and military government section
Gauleiter. Regional leader of the Nazi Party
Gemeinde. Municipality
Gestapo. *Geheime Staatspolizei* (the Nazis' secret political police)
JCS. Joint Chiefs of Staff
Land. German state
Landkreis. Rural administrative area similar to a U.S. county
Meldebogen. Questionnaire used under the Law for Liberation from National Socialism and Militarism to determine Nazi and militarist associations of Germans
MG. Military government
Oberbürgermeister. Lord mayor
OMG. Office of Military Government
OMGUS. Office of Military Government of the United States
PMG. Provost Marshal General
Prüfungsausschuß. German review boards
Regierungsbezirk. district
Reichsbahn. German railroads
Reichsbanner Schwarz-Rot-Gold. Reich Flag Black-Red-Gold, a paramilitary group closely linked to the SPD
Reichspost. German postal service
SA. Sturmabteilung (paramilitary organization of the Nazi Party)
SCAEF. Supreme Commander, Allied Expeditionary Force
Senat. Bremen's government/cabinet
senator. Member of Bremen's government/cabinet
SHAEF. Supreme Headquarters, Allied Expeditionary Force
SPD. Social Democratic Party of Germany
Spruchkammer. German denazification tribunals established under the Law for Liberation from National Socialism and Militarism
Stadtkreis. The area within the city limits of a city or town
TALLYHO. USFET raids, July 1945
UNRRA. United Nations Relief and Rehabilitation Administration
USFET. U.S. Forces in the European Theater
Volkssturm. German militia composed of men who were too young, too old, or physically unfit for regular military service
Waffen SS. Schutzstaffel, the elite military and police organization of the Nazi Party
Wehrmacht. German Armed Forces

Wehrwirtschaftsführer. Leader of the Nazi war economy
ZPI 3. British Military Government–issued Zone Policy Instruction No. 3

Bibliography

Archival Sources

National Archives and Record Administration, College Park, Maryland: World War II Records Division

Record Group 260: Records of the Office of Military Government for Germany (U.S.):
Records of the Adjutant General 1945–1949
Records of the Office of Military Government for Bavaria:
Records of the Historical Branch
Records of the Intelligence Division
Records of the Office of Military Government for Bremen:
Records of the Public Information Office
Records of the Denazification Division
Records of the Public Safety Division
Records of the Bremerhaven Liaison and Security Detachment
Record Group 407: World War II Operations Reports, 1940–1948
29th Infantry Division

U.S. Army Military History Institute, Carlisle, Pennsylvania

Allied Expeditionary Forces, Supreme Headquarters, Office of the Chief of Staff. *Handbook for Military Government in Germany prior to Defeat or Surrender*, 1944.

General Lucius Clay, USA (Ret.). Third Interview by Colonel R. Joe Rogers, 24 January 1973, p. 25, Senior Officers Debriefing Program, U.S. Army Military History Research Collection, Carlisle Barracks, Pennsylvania.

Staatsarchiv der Freien Hansestadt Bremen

Senat und Inneres: Entnazifizierung 3 - B.10.b

Official Publications

Coles, Harry L., and Albert K. Weinberg. *United States Army in World War II. Special Studies. Civil Affairs: Soldiers Become Governors.* Washington, DC: Office of the Chief of Military History, Department of the Army, 1964.

Donnison, F. S. V. *Civil Affairs and Military Government: Central Organization and Planning.* London: H. M. Stationery Office, 1966.

———. *Civil Affairs and Military Government: North-West Europe 1944–1946.* London: H. M. Stationery Office, 1961.

FM 27-5, Basic Field Manual, Military Government. Washington, DC: United States Government Printing Office, 1940.

FM 27-10, Basic Field Manual, Rules of Land Warfare. Washington, DC: United States Government Printing Office, 1940.

Frederiksen, Oliver J. *The American Military Occupation of Germany 1945–1953.* Historical Division, Headquarters, U.S. Army, Europe, 1955.

Germany and Austria in the Post-Surrender Period: Policy Directives for the Allied Commanders in Chief. Handbook. U.S. Army Center of Military History, Fort McNair, DC.

Harris, Charles Reginald Schiller. *Allied Administration of Italy 1943–1945.* London: H. M. Stationery Office, 1957.

Hearings before the Committee on Military Affairs, House of Representatives, Seventy-Eighth Congress, Second Session, part 2, 21 and 25 January 1944. Washington, DC: United States Government Printing Office, 1944.

Howe, George F. *United States Army in World War II. The Mediterranean Theater of Operations. North-West Africa: Seizing the Initiative in the West.* Washington, DC: U.S. Army Center of Military History, 1991 [1957].

Landeszentrale für politische Bildung in Zusammenarbeit mit der Verwaltung der Bremischen Bürgerschaft. *Landesverfassung der Freien Hansestadt Bremen vom 21. Oktober 1947.* Bremen, Germany, 1977.

Lay, Elizabeth S. *The Berlin Airlift, Part I: 21 June–31 December 1948, Part II: 1 January–30 September 1949.* Special Studies Series. Vols. 100, 102. Karlsruhe, Germany: Headquarters, Historical Division, European Command, 1952.

Matloff, Maurice. *The United States Army in World War II. The War Department. Strategic Planning for Coalition Warfare 1943–1944.* Washington, DC: U.S. Army Center of Military History, 1990.

Occupation Forces in Europe Series, 1945–1946. *Planning for the Occupation of Germany.* Frankfurt am Main, Germany: European Command, Office of the Chief Historian, 1947.

Occupation Forces in Europe Series, 1945–1946. *The First Year of the Occupation.* Frankfurt am Main, Germany: European Command, Office of the Chief Historian, 1947.

Occupation Forces in Europe Series, 1945–1946. *Civil Affairs*. Frankfurt am Main, Germany: European Command, Office of the Chief Historian, 1947.

Occupation Forces in Europe Series, 1945–1946. *Troop Basis and the Disposition of Forces*. Frankfurt am Main, Germany: European Command, Office of the Chief Historian, 1947.

Occupation Forces in Europe Series, 1945–1946. *The United States Constabulary*. Frankfurt am Main, Germany: European Command, Office of the Chief Historian, 1947.

Occupation Forces in Europe Series, 1946–1947. *The Second Year of the Occupation*. Frankfurt am Main, Germany: European Command, Office of the Chief Historian, 1947.

Occupation Forces in Europe Series, 1947–1948. *The Evolution of the Occupation Forces in Europe*, by Joseph R. Starr and Francis Chase. Frankfurt am Main, Germany: Historical Division, European Command, 1948.

Occupation Forces in Europe Series, 1950. *Reorganization of Tactical Forces, VE-Day to 1 January 1949*, by Francis S. Chase. Karlsruhe, Germany: Historical Division, European Command, 1950.

Schullze, Erich, ed. *Gesetz zur Befreiung von Nationalsozialismus und Militarismus vom 5: März 1946 mit Ausführungsvorschriften, Formblättern, der Anweisung für die Auswerter der Meldebogen und der Rangliste in mehrfarbiger Wiedergabe*. München, Germany: Bierstein Verlag, 1946.

Senate Committee on Foreign Relations. *Documents on Germany, 1944–1959. Background Documents on Germany, 1944–1959, and a Chronology of Political Developments Affecting Berlin, 1945–1956*. Washington, DC: United States Government Printing Office, 1959.

Starr, Joseph. *U.S. Military Government in Germany: Operations from March to Mid-July 1945*. Karlsruhe, Germany: European Command, Historical Division, 1950.

United States of America, Department of State. *Documents on Germany 1944–1985*. Washington, DC: Department of State Publication 9446, 1961.

———. *Foreign Relations of the United States. The Conference at Quebec 1944*. Washington, DC: United States Government Printing Office, 1972.

———. *Foreign Relations of the United States. Diplomatic Papers. The Conferences at Malta and Yalta 1945*. Washington, DC: United States Government Printing Office, 1955.

———. *Foreign Relations of the United States. Diplomatic Papers. 1945. Volume III: European Advisory Commission; Austria; Germany*. Washington, DC: United States Government Printing Office, 1968.

———. *Foreign Relations of the United States. Diplomatic Papers. 1947. Volume II: Council of Foreign Ministers, Germany and Austria*. 8 vols. Washington, DC: United States Government Printing Office, 1972.

———. *Foreign Relations of the United States. Diplomatic Papers. 1947. Volume III: The British Commonwealth, Europe*. 8 vols. Washington, DC: United States Government Printing Office, 1972.

Memoirs

Churchill, Winston S. *The Second World War. Volume V: Closing the Ring.* Boston: Houghton Mifflin, 1951.

———. *The Second World War. Volume VI: Triumph and Tragedy.* Boston: Houghton Mifflin, 1953.

Clay, Lucius D. *Decision in Germany.* Garden City, NY: Doubleday, 1950.

Eisenhower, Dwight D. *Crusade in Europe.* Garden City, NY: Doubleday, 1949.

Hull, Cordell. *The Memoirs of Cordell Hull. In Two Volumes.* New York: MacMillan, 1948.

Kennan, George F. *Memoirs: 1925–1950.* London: Hutchinson, 1968.

Stimson, Henry L., and McGeorge Bundy. *On Active Service in Peace and War.* New York: Harper, 1948.

Books

Becker, Josef, Theo Stammen, and Peter Waldmann, eds. *Vorgeschichte der Bundesrepublik Deutschland: Zwischen Kapitulation und Grundgesetz.* München, Germany: UTB für Wissenschaft, 1979.

Benz, Wolfgang. *Potsdam 1945: Besatzungsherrschft und Neuaufbau in Vier-Zonen-Deutschland.* München, Germany: Deutscher Taschenbuch Verlag, 1994.

———. *Von der Besatzungsherrschaft zur Bundesrepublik: Stationen einer Staatsgründung 1946–1949.* Frankfurt am Main, Germany: Fischer Taschenbuch Verlag, 1984.

Bower, Tom, *The Pledge Betrayed: America and Britain and the Denazification of Postwar Germany.* Garden City, NY: Doubleday, 1982.

Conquer: The Story of the Ninth Army, 1944–1945. Washington, DC: Infantry Journal Press, 1947.

Drechsel, Wiltrud Ulrike, and Andreas Röpcke, eds. *"Denazification" Zur Entnazifizierung in Bremen.* Bremen, Germany: Edition Temmen, 1992.

Duke, Simon W., and Wolfgang Krieger, eds. *U.S. Military Forces in Europe: The Early Years, 1945–1970.* Boulder, CO: Westview Press, 1993.

Erdmann, Karl Dietrich. *Gebhardt Handbuch der deutschen Geschichte Band 22: Das Ende des Reiches und die Neubildung deutscher Staaten.* München, Germany: Deutscher Taschenbuch Verlag, 1982.

Ewing, Joseph H. *29 Let's Go! A History of the 29th Infantry Division in World War II.* Washington, DC: Infantry Journal Press, 1948.

Foschepoth, Josef, and Rolf Steiniger, eds. *Die britische Deutschland- und Besatzungspolitik 1945–1949.* Paderborn, Germany: Ferdinand Schöningh, 1985.

Friedman, Norman. *The Fifty-Year War: Conflict and Strategy in the Cold War.* Annapolis, MD: Naval Institute Press, 2000.

Friedmann, Wolfgang. *The Allied Military Government of Germany.* London: Stevens and Sons, 1947.

Friedrich, Jörg. *Der Brand: Deutschland im Bombenkrieg 1940–1945.* München, Germany: Propyläen Verlag, 2002.

Fuermann, George M., and F. Edward Cranz. *Ninety-Fifth Infantry Division History 1918–1946.* Nashville, TN: Battery Press, 1988.

Fürstenau, Justus. *Entnazifizierung: Ein Kapitel deutscher Nachkriegsgeschichte.* Neuwied, Germany: Luchterhand, 1969.

Gimbel, John. *The American Occupation of Germany: Politics and the Military, 1945–1949.* Stanford, CA: Stanford University Press, 1968.

Goodrich, Leland M., and Marie J. Carroll, eds. *Documents on American Foreign Relations. Vol. VII: July 1944–June 1945.* Princeton, NJ: Princeton University Press, 1947.

Gulgowski, Paul W. *The American Military Government of the United States Occupied Zones of Post World War II Germany in Relation to Policies Expressed by Its Civilian Governmental Authorities at Home, during the Course of 1944/45 through 1949.* Frankfurt am Main, Germany: Haag + Herchen, 1983.

Herbert, Ulrich. *Best: Biographische Studien über Radikalismus, Weltanschauung und Vernunft, 1903–1989.* Bonn, Germany: J. H. W. Dietz, 1996.

Hesse, Hans. *Konstruktionen der Unschuld: Die Entnazifizierung am Beispiel von Bremen und Bremerhaven 1945–1953.* Bremen, Germany: Selbstverlag des Staatsarchivs Bremen, 2005.

History of the XVI Corps: From Its Activation to the End of the War in Europe. Washington, DC: Infantry Journal Press, 1947.

Holborn, Hajo. *American Military Government: Its Organization and Policies.* Washington, DC: Infantry Journal Press, 1947.

Kaisen, Wilhelm. *Bereitschaft und Zuversicht.* Bremen, Germany: Bremer Schlüssel Verlag Hans Kasten, 1947.

Kimball, Warren F., ed. *Churchill and Roosevelt: The Complete Correspondence.* 3 vols. Princeton, NJ: Princeton University Press, 1984.

———. *Swords of Ploughshares? The Morgenthau Plan for Defeated Nazi Germany, 1943–1946.* Philadelphia: Lippincott, 1976.

Krammer, Arnold. *Nazi Prisoners of War in America.* New York: Stein and Day, 1979.

Lutzebäck, Rolf. *Die Bildungspolitik der Britischen Militärregierung im Spannungsfeld zwischen "education" und "reeducation" in ihrer Besatzungszone, insbesondere in Schleswig-Holstein und Hamburg in den Jahren 1945–1947.* Teil 1. Frankfurt am Main, Germany: P. Lang, 1991.

Meyer-Zollitsch, Almuth. *Nationalsozialismus und Evangelische Kirche in Bremen.* Veröffentlichungen aus dem Staatsarchiv der Freien Hansestadt Bremen, Band 51, 1985.

Niethammer, Lutz. *Entnazifizierung in Bayern: Säuberung und Rehabilitierung unter amerikanischer Besatzung.* Frankfurt am Main, Germany: S. Fischer, 1972.

———, ed. *Walter L. Dorn: Inspektionsreisen durch die U.S.-Zone. Notizen, Denkschriften und Erinnerungen.* Stuttgart, Germany: R. Oldenbourg Verlag, 1973.

Petersen, Edward N. *The American Occupation of Germany: Retreat to Victory.* Detroit, MI: Wayne State University Press, 1978.

Pogue, Forrest. *George C. Marshall: Organizer of Victory 1943–1945.* New York: Viking Press, 1973.

Scharf, Claus, and Hans-Jürgen Schröder, eds. *Die Deutschlandpolitik Grossbritanniens und die Britische Zone 1945–1949.* Wiesbaden, Germany: Veröffentlichungen des Instituts für Europäische Geschichte Mainz, Beiheft 6, 1979.

Schwarz, Hans-Peter. *Vom Reich zur Bundesrepublik: Deutschland im Widerstreit der außenpolitischen Konzeptionen in den Jahren der Besatzungsherrschaft 1945–1949.* Stuttgart, Germany: Klett-Cotta, 1980.

Schwarzwälder, Herbert. *Bremer Geschichte.* Bremen, Germany: Johann Heinrich Döll, 1993.

———. *Das große Bremen-Lexikon.* 2 vols. Bremen, Germany: Edition Temmen, 2002.

———. *Die Machtergreifung der NSDAP in Bremen 1933.* Bremen, Germany: Carl Schünemann Verlag, 1966.

Sharp, Tony. *The Wartime Alliance and the Zonal Division of Germany.* London: Oxford University Press, 1975.

Smith, Jean Edward. *Lucius D. Clay: An American Life.* New York: H. Holt, 1990.

———, ed. *The Papers of Lucius D. Clay: Germany 1945–1949.* 2 vols. Bloomington: Indiana University Press, 1974.

Sommer, Karl-Ludwig. *Wilhelm Kaisen: Eine politische Biographie.* Bonn, Germany: Dietz, 2000.

Turner, Ian, ed. *Reconstruction in Post-War Germany: British Occupation Policy and the Western Zones, 1945–55.* New York: St. Martin's Press, 1989.

Vansittart, Robert. *Black Record: Germans Past and Present.* London: H. Hamilton, 1941.

Wember, Heiner. *Umerziehung im Lager: Internierung und Bestrafung von Nationalsozialisten in der britischen Besatzungszone Deutschlands.* Essen, Germany: Klartext Verlag, 1991.

Wolfe, Robert, ed. *Americans as Proconsuls: United States Military Government in Germany and Japan, 1944–1952.* Carbondale: Southern Illinois University Press, 1984.

Wright, Robert K. *Military Police.* Army Lineage Series. Washington, DC: U.S. Army Center of Military History, 1992.

Ziemke, Earl F. *The U.S. Army in the Occupation of Germany 1944–1946.* Army Historical Series. Washington, DC: United States Army Center of Military History, 2003.

Zink, Harold. *American Military Government in Germany.* New York: Macmillan, 1947.

Articles

"Amerika Haus: US Information Centers in Germany." *Information Bulletin* 148 (November 1948): 19–21 (Office of Military Government for Germany [U.S.], Control Office, Berlin, Germany, APO 742, U.S. Army).

Ellwood, David W. "The Marshall Plan: A Strategy That Worked." *U.S. Department of State EJournal USA* (April 2006): 17–22.

Falkenhagen, Andreas, Christoph W. O. Matthies, and Maik Ziemann. "Die Automobilindustrie im Nationalsozialismus: Drei biographische Beispiele." Referat, Historisches Seminar TU Braunschweig, January 2000, 11, at www.millennum.de/referate/autonazi/ (accessed 10 November 2008).

Kurze, Peter. "115 Jahre Carl F.W. Borgward." *Oldtimer Info* 3 (2005): 4–5.

Margry, Karel. "The Capture of Bremen." *After the Battle* 135 (February 2007): 2–34.

Marshall, Barbara. "The Democratization of Local Politics in the British Zone of Germany: Hanover 1945–47." *Journal of Contemporary History* 21, no. 3 (July 1986): 413–51.

Marshall, George C. "Remarks by the Secretary of State: European Initiative Essential to Economic Recovery." *Department of State Bulletin* 16, no. 415 (15 June 1947): 1159–60.

Müller, Peter. "Die A.G.-'Weser' in Bremen," p. 3, at http://werften.fischtown.de/archiv/agweser1.html (accessed 22 October 2008).

Napoli, Joseph F. "Denazification from an American's Viewpoint." *Annals of the American Academy of Political and Social Science* (July 1949): 115–23.

Plischke, Elmer. "Denazifying the Reich." *Review of Politics* 9, no. 2 (April 1947): 153–73.

Röpke, Andreas. "Entstehung, Status und Verwaltung der amerikanischen Enklave Bremen." *Bremisches Jahrbuch* 66 (1988): 423–52.

Scherer, Michael. "Freie Hansestadt Bremen." *Der Bürger im Staat* 1, no. 2 (1999): 2–4 (Landeszentrale für politische Bildung Baden-Württemberg).

"Sozialistische Mitteilungen: News for German Socialist in England." Nr. 77/78–1945, August/September, p. 22. Newsletter herausgegeben vom Exilvorstand der Sozialdemokratischen Partei Deutschlands (SOPADE) 1939–1948, Ungekürzte Online Ausgabe, Herausgegeben von der Friedrich Ebert Stiftung, at http://library.fes.de/fulltext/sozmit/som-von-aussen.htm (accessed 15 May 2008).

Werften und Stadtgeschichte Bremerhavens. "Franz C. H. Stapelfeldt," p. 1, at http://werften.fischtown.de/archiv/stapelfeldt.html (accessed 22 October 2008).

Ziemke, Earl F. "Civil Affairs at Thirty." *Military Affairs* 36, no. 4 (December 1972): 131–33.

Unpublished Materials

Napoli, Joseph F. Interview by Adams, Bethesda, Maryland, 10 July 1990.

Stewart, Richard W. "The United States Army and Training in Military Government and Civil Affairs." U.S. Army Special Operations Command, Fort Bragg, NC, April 1994.

Trogdon, Gary A. "A Decade of Catching Spies: The United States Army's Counter Intelligence Corps, 1943–1953." PhD diss., University of Nebraska, 2001.

United States Holocaust Memorial Museum. "Non-Jewish Resistance: Overview." Holocaust Encyclopedia, Photography, p. 1, at www.ushmm.org/wlc/media_ph.php?lang=en&ModuleId=10005420&MediaId=1552 (accessed 22 October 2008).

Index

About the Author

Bianka J. Adams is a historian at the Defense Threat Reduction Agency. She received her master's degree in political science from the Christian-Albrechts-University in Kiel, Germany, and her Ph.D. in U.S. diplomatic history from the Catholic University of America in Washington, D.C. Before joining DTRA, she worked as a historian at the U.S. Army Center of Military History, where she focused on researching and writing about the United States Army in Europe, 1945–1952. She is currently serving as the 1st Cavalry Division/Multinational Division Baghdad historian in Iraq.